HUDDLE

HUDDLE

HOW WOMEN UNLOCK THEIR COLLECTIVE POWER

BROOKE BALDWIN

HARPER
BUSINESS

An Imprint of HarperCollins*Publishers*

HarperCollins books may be purchased for educational, business, or sales promotional use. For information, please email the Special Markets Department at SPsales@harpercollins.com.

FIRST EDITION

Designed by Bonni Leon-Berman

Library of Congress Cataloging-in-Publication Data has been applied for.

ISBN 978-0-06-301744-3

21 22 23 24 25   LSC   10 9 8 7 6 5 4 3 2 1

For my Mom—
my original huddle.
How do you hold a moonbeam in your hand?
I love you.

Also for James—
my husband.
Thank you for loving me and Pugsley and for being
one of many good men who support women huddling.

"I am continually moved to discover I have sisters.
I am beginning, just beginning, to find out who I am."

—Gloria Steinem, from her 1972 essay "Sisterhood"

contents

HUDDLE

prologue

A group of women in Selma, Alabama, gather to steel themselves for five days of marching. Their ancestors waged the battle for voting rights many decades prior, and today they will continue the fight. Tear gas and billy clubs await them, but together they summon their strength and courage for the journey.

• • •

One woman at a podium addresses the nation for the very first time as America's first female vice president elect. Although she stands alone on the stage, she reflects on the generations of women who came before her—women who fought, struggled, and paved the way for her success.

• • •

Dozens of women in Silicon Valley enter their salaries on a publicly shared spreadsheet, encouraging their male coworkers to do the same—all in an effort to shine a light on gender-based salary gaps at their tech company. Later, the women team up with other prominent female peers to form an organization that will advocate to diversify their entire industry.

• • •

More than a hundred teenage girls board a flight flown by a female pilot and operated by an all-female crew. They are celebrating Girls in Aviation Day and heading to NASA in Houston, where they will meet female astronauts and begin to dream about their future careers in aviation.

●●●

Two women go surfing off the coast of Encinitas. One is suffering a recent heartbreak, and the other is there to hold her hand.

●●●

What do each of these scenarios have in common? Each is a huddle—a moment that brings women together in any time or place—whether on the front lines of a public protest or in a quiet church basement—to provide each other with support, empowerment, inspiration, and the strength to solve problems or enact meaningful change. "Huddle" is a word associated with masculinity and sports. But what if we flipped it on its head and feminized it? It's a noun. It's a verb. And it's time for us, as women, to own it.

A huddle is a place where women can become energized by the mere fact of their coexistence. A huddle is where we can uplift each other to succeed, thrive, and if I may—get amazing shit done. And even though huddles are productive—they create the conditions for change, progress, and transformation—they aren't always results-oriented. Sometimes they are a space where women can simply bear witness for each other, or quietly sustain each other's very survival. And while there is certainly strength in numbers, there can also be incredible huddle energy between just a few women. Maybe you've felt the undeniable power between two women who make the simple and life-changing decision to lean on each other.

I know women aren't always great to each other. When we compete or trash each other, we miss out on something incredibly valuable. One of the most potent resources we have is each other. I can't say we are each other's *most* powerful resource, because as I write this prologue in 2020, I think most might say the greatest prize for women would be more seats at the table (or maybe to just rebuild the entire table, as many women I interviewed for this book told me). And also, equal pay. Representation. Recognition of the intersecting parts of our identities (our race, class, religion, sexual orientation, age, illness, and disability) that determine our access to power and influence how we move through the world—a world that isn't yet fair or just to all. But beyond those resources, I think women truly are each other's most valuable asset.

And when I started to notice this, I found myself thinking, *I can't be the only woman thinking this, right?*

Let me slow my roll and recognize the dramatic nature of that question. In my twenty years as a journalist and news anchor, I've learned to ask provocative questions; to look for incisive answers at the service of a public who needs to know more. But in reality, there *are* plenty of women talking about huddling right now. I just didn't realize it. So I turned the question on myself:

Why haven't I been huddling more intentionally in my own life?

Who's in my huddle? Do I even have a huddle?!

Do I fully appreciate this incredible legacy of huddling I've been lucky enough to inherit as a woman?

Why am I not devoting every moment of my spare time outside my day job at CNN investigating this incredible phenomenon that is happening all around me?

After being stirred by these questions in 2017, I made a decision to pay closer attention to what women were doing in America. I created a series for CNN Digital called *American Woman*, and then

I launched the journey that became this book. Was this a professional decision? A personal passion? Both? I didn't know exactly. But as a career journalist, I felt compelled to follow my gut and see where that aching question might lead me.

I was born and raised in the South in the 1980s—a time and place where upper-middle-class white girls rarely huddled for anything that didn't involve sequins or tap shoes. From a young age, I always felt my calling in journalism. After graduating from the University of North Carolina at Chapel Hill in 2001, I moved to small-town America, where I worked holidays, weekends, and overnights, often writing, producing, and anchoring my shows while rolling the teleprompter with my foot. And when I clocked out, I rarely had any good girlfriends to hang out with. Several moves to various other cities and a decade or so later, I landed back in my hometown of Atlanta, where at age thirty-one, I became one of the youngest people—male or female—to anchor my own show at CNN.

Since 2008, my career at CNN has taken me all over the world to report on everything from natural disasters to shootings and terror attacks. I've also had the privilege of meeting presidents and interviewing former first ladies, members of Congress, scientists, teachers, nurses, astronauts, actors, activists, rock stars, and ordinary Americans who've found themselves in extraordinary circumstances—such as surviving mass shootings, hurricanes, or COVID-19. And, of course, I spent much of 2015 and 2016 covering the wildest presidential campaign we reporters thought we would ever see in our lifetime—until 2020 rolled around. Since my show airs in the middle of the afternoon when news tends to break, I am often live on camera, experiencing historic moments in real time right along with the rest of the nation. I have lost count of the number of times the teleprompter had gone blank and I began ad-libbing a major breaking news story with just bits and pieces of information coming in from the control room.

I love my job and the opportunity it gives me to connect with other people. I feel privileged to have a front-row seat to history, to engage in difficult dialogue, to celebrate our victories, and to broadcast the moments that shape our collective conversations and memories. I'm especially grateful for this window to the world, this opportunity to *listen and observe*. And during some of the most remarkably "newsworthy" years of my lifetime—these last five years—I've noticed something vitally important was happening with women. But it doesn't surface on the news often enough.

In examining this phenomenon of women huddling, I also began to take stock of my own life—my family, my friends, my community, and my occupation. I realized that as someone who considered it the greatest compliment to be called a "woman's woman," I had ironically picked a career where I was surrounded by men. Like many white-collar jobs in America, journalism is still largely male-dominated. In the hierarchy at my job, I report to several men, and my most accomplished peers are and always have been men. The greatest portion of my show every single day has always been dedicated to covering some of the world's most powerful men. In fact, in the time since I began writing this book, one man, Donald Trump, not only dominated the news, but he also turned the entire news cycle on its head. Most journalists will tell you, regardless of their politics, that their jobs look very different today than they did in 2015. When you add the COVID-19 pandemic, the movement against widespread systemic racial injustice, and the uptick in climate-fueled natural disasters, there isn't a lot of room left for good news these days. People used to stop me in the airport (you know, in the Before Times when we used to fly places) to ask me, "How do you do it? How do you stay sane?"

And even though I always had an answer (that I believe in capital "J" Journalism and seeking the truth), what I really wanted to say was: *I wear a hell of a lot of emotional armor at work, and also, I really have no idea!*

But in reality, the process of writing this book has given me that answer. I have learned that women can be a sustaining force in my life, and that they have contributed to much of my success. I have learned that leaning on female friends, mentors, heroes, and colleagues is how I can get through almost anything. I've learned that groups of women are also changing the face of this country—and long before Americans elected the nation's first female vice president, women have always had a very strong hand in shaping our history. But sometimes these stories don't make the headlines and historians don't always focus on the huddles of women who have helped change the world.

The journey that took me all over the country to write this book sparked some of the most life-changing conversations I've had in my life. Like any good traveler, I took a lot of photos and notes. I had hoped I'd be more an anthropologist than tourist. But by the end, I was even more than just a studied observer, more than just the objective journalist I'd trained to be. I became a part of the story myself. And beyond the physical travels, there were a lot of internal departures and arrivals as well. I learned more than I ever imagined I would.

Embedding myself in so many huddles and bearing witness to the accounts of so many women who were changed by their connections with each other made me a better huddler myself. I sometimes joke with my friends that huddle has become my religion, and that's not far from the truth. Through the process of writing this book I've learned not only how to summon my own huddles at work and in my personal life but I've also tapped into the vulnerability required to let myself lean on others. I've built up the courage and intentionality required to better tend my female friendships, and it has changed my life. I now have a support system that allows me to curse, vent, and ask embarrassing questions. I have women who challenge me, who link arms with me on social justice issues, and talk politics in a safe space. I show up to my huddle deeply vulnerable now, which makes me truer to myself, and thus anything I put out into the world as a journalist.

Toward the end of the writing process for this book, the COVID-19 pandemic swept the globe. It quickly shined a bright light on the systemic racism and socioeconomic disparities that have always existed in this country. I can't imagine how much differently I would have experienced all of this without my newfound belief in female collectives. I watched from my news desk (and my own sickbed when I got COVID) as groups of women organized to feed, nurse, and teach the nation through the pandemic. They also came together to lead and protest the heinous acts of police brutality and widespread injustice all around us. With so many other challenges swirling, they—particularly Black women—still managed to rally for the 2020 election to help increase voter turnout, which reached numbers not seen in a half century. And after the election, women celebrated together all the hard work they had done to help elect the nation's first female vice president. Kamala Harris, a Black and South Asian woman, the daughter of immigrants, said as she addressed them for the very first time as their vice president elect that she stood on their shoulders, that women like them had paved the way for her over several generations.

Even though 2020 will likely always be defined in American history as a year of extraordinary hardship, it might also provide an example of the kind of adversity that is not too daunting for women to overcome when they have each other. As we make our way through the unprecedented challenges our nation faces, I find huddles more relevant than ever. I am inspired by my new awareness that women are positioned to weather difficult times because they are bonded not only through hardship but also through friendship, motherhood, sisterhood, mentorship, sponsorship, self-care and healing rituals, career, education, political change, and so much more.

I want to legitimize the notion that women are each other's greatest allies. That we have each other's backs and then some. But I also know that a gathering of females does not necessarily a huddle make. It's not always harmonious and positive when women come together. For example, there are plenty of instances—both historically and present-day—of white women joining forces to fight for "women's rights" at the expense of Black, Indigenous, and other women of color (BIWOC). As a white woman myself who has grown up with a lot of privilege in this country, writing this book has taught me the ways that we white women have sometimes collectively betrayed or abandoned BIWOC—and still do, to this day. Some of the conversations I had for this book also taught me that women sometimes compete and tear each other down in the workplace or elsewhere. But a true huddle is a place in which women hold space for each other, and lift each other up, regardless of our race, religion, class, or sexual orientation.

I am writing this book because I want to challenge myself to make a very deliberate commitment to huddling, and I hope to inspire other women to do the same. This book is for women who want to join me—all women (cis, trans, and non-binary). This book is for those of you who want to learn how to huddle, and those of you with mothers, grandmothers, and great-grandmothers who have been doing this right for generations. This book is for anyone with a daughter, who wants to pass along this important practice to the next generation. And this book is for men too. Most of you have a wife, daughter, sister, mother, or other women in your life you care about. You too can help create space for women to empower each other. This book is also for those of you who may already have a huddle in your life but just aren't sure how to activate it. I hope you will read these stories and hear the clarion call to find your sisterhood and unlock its collective power. I hope you will discover the same "huddle lens" through which I now see the world. I hope we have something in common, reader, and huddling will change your life too.

one

THE MOTHER OF
ALL HUDDLES

On January 20, 2017, I stepped outside my Washington, D.C., hotel to a drizzly winter morning. The air wasn't nearly cold enough to turn the condensation into snow, so I prepared to spend the day on camera in this chilly, wet mess. I had already encountered a lot of gloom in this city, and not just on that day. Ten years earlier, I lived in D.C., at the age of twenty-seven, in a close friend's basement. I slept on a mattress on the floor with my pug, grateful for this temporary shelter while I figured out how to turn my freelancing job at WTTG/FOX 5 into a full-time gig. It wasn't the most glamorous moment of my life, but for me and my dog, it was home.

And now, the same city where I had spent so much time paying my dues as a reporter was about to be home to the forty-fifth president of the United States: Donald J. Trump. And it was my assignment to cover his inauguration in the presidential motorcade.

It had already been quite a year in my job at CNN. There had been terror attacks in Istanbul, Nice, and Orlando—all of which I was sent to cover. That summer I had traveled to the Middle East, embedding with the U.S. Navy waging the War on Terror. Brexit happened. And back home, there was this presidential campaign coming to an all-out fever pitch.

I'd crisscrossed the country countless times, covering an election defined by surprise and uncertainty. I'd ridden on the back of a Harley-Davidson, interviewing the Bikers for Trump in Ohio. I felt the voltage of so many young people at a Bernie Sanders rally in Iowa. I'd interviewed countless women expressing their hopes and dreams with tears in their eyes as they imagined the possibility of the nation's first female president. Today was the culmination of many things, the last leg of a journey that had delivered a very surreal ending.

There I was with all my various color-coded press credential lanyards dangling around my neck. I came equipped with my rain boots, my new cherry-red down jacket, and the steadiest balance my two legs could muster. I would need it that day, since I was stationed on the back of a moving flatbed truck just feet in front of the new president's limo. I focused on keeping my footing as we bumped along Pennsylvania Avenue flanked by Trump supporters who'd come from far and wide to get a glimpse of the reality-TV-star-turned-president. I watched and narrated as people craned their necks to the sounds of the military brass bands coming closer. It was a lot of pomp and circumstance for a man who just a few months earlier had been heard on an old tape boasting about grabbing women "by the pussy." He had enraged millions of women—including many from his own party—by bragging about his sexual conquests and frequently using demeaning language toward women. As a woman and a journalist, I too was troubled by his record with women. Nonetheless, upward of 52 percent of our nation's white women still voted for him. It was a frustrating reality for so many.

I told myself to stop thinking about that and focus on the task at hand. I planted my feet as if I were on the world's saddest surfboard, white-knuckled that mic, and did my very best to perform my job. The rain spat intermittently. Clashes broke out among the protesters. Several people tasted pepper spray that day and a limo was set on fire. By nightfall, two hundred had been arrested.

•••

The next morning, a new day had dawned in D.C. Despite the cloudy cold, the sun was shining through. A faint drumbeat cut through the damp air. The day before I had been surrounded by men in black suits; today, I found myself in a sea of women in colorful T-shirts. They raised homemade signs above their heads as they sang, danced, cried, laughed, and cheered. It was as if I was living in the "bizarro-world" version of the previous day. The red MAGA hats were now pink pussyhats, and everything—the sounds, the colors, the clothing, the mood—felt like the opposite of Inauguration Day. I was experiencing more than just a little emotional whiplash.

But I had to pull myself together. I was on the clock again for CNN and busy speaking to women who had come from all corners of the country to be together at the Women's March. It was an event like no other in recent history. Although it would receive a lot of fair criticism in the months and years to follow (which I touch on later in this book), the stated purpose of the march was to "harness the political power of diverse women and their communities to create transformative social change." The march organizers had been deliberate in trying to create an intersectional movement, collaborating with women from all walks of life, representing various ages, races, religions, nationalities, and sexual orientations.

I tried to take it all in as I stood there among the enormous crowd that ballooned to half a million. I interviewed dozens of women that day, including celebrities, politicians, and what I like to call ordinary-extraordinary women from all over the country who had traveled hundreds or thousands of miles to be there. Attendance exceeded everyone's expectations. It was, without a doubt, one massive huddle.

On the stage speaking to this sea of women was Tamika Mallory, a Black woman and one of the march founders. She addressed the portion of the crowd who were new to marching and protesting, reminding them that this was not a concert, parade, or party. "This is a resistance," she said—and one that required their focused and enduring solidarity. She anticipated what might have drawn many women to D.C. that day and offered a wise warning: "Some of you came to protest *one man*. But I didn't come for that," she proclaimed. I took her point. Trump might have activated and angered a whole new group of (mostly white) women—who were likely not as accustomed as BIWOC to experiencing regular assaults on their humanity—but he shouldn't have been the sole reason for our being there that day. Now was the time to tap into a deep well of unity we may not have known we possessed. Women were facing many threats to our rights, our safety, our well-being, and our dignity, and we would need each other to dig our way out of this. Mallory explained that now was the time to take care of each other and to stand up for the most marginalized among us.

Although many women were there to represent specific causes—the climate crisis, immigration reform, Islamophobia, racism, sexism, and so much more—the widespread demand for change that day was no less palpable than the overwhelming spirit of togetherness. Change and resistance were certainly in the air, but unity was the fomenter for that change. That sense of unity—the sheer joy and force of it surging among us and binding us together—was what felt new and different. All around me, women were energized by each other, feeling the kind of motivation and possibility that is only realized in the presence of others.

When then senator Kamala Harris took the mic, she proclaimed, "There is nothing more powerful than a group of determined sisters." Janet Mock told the crowd she was there to speak up for her fellow trans women who were plagued by intolerance and violence in America. "I am my sister's keeper," she said. Angela Davis, the political activist and scholar, called for "an inclusive and intersectional feminism," and Gloria Steinem, who had commented that the energy at the gathering was "like none [she] had ever seen in [her] long life," reminded everyone to stay linked to one another, to learn one another's names, and make plans together for tomorrow. "God might be in the details," she said, "but the goddess is in connections."

So many American women have their own specific memories of this day, whether they were in D.C. or in any of the other cities around the world where millions of women gathered to be together for the largest single-day protest in American history. Some women followed along on Twitter. Some considered it a joyful day and others bonded over their rage. Some—including the more seasoned activists and BIWOC—were rightly skeptical about whether or not this moment would turn into a movement. As for me, I stood there deeply compelled and surprised by the simple fact that so many women had purchased plane tickets, split tanks of gas, or rented buses just to be here in person, *together*.

As a journalist I knew immediately I had to dig deeper. But as a woman, I felt so much more. I'd never been surrounded by so many other women—not in my entire life. *This* was the energy and potential I had never fully tapped into. *This* was my purpose. *These* were my people.

And yet, at the same time, in this vast sea of women, I was

standing on the sidelines. All day long, I watched groups of women dressed alike, holding hands and sharing snacks. I witnessed clusters of women representing various political, social, and religious groups embracing each other; I saw sisters and friends of all ages crying and comforting one another or waiting in those godawful long porta-potty lines to pee. Standing there clutching my microphone, I wondered who I would have attended the march with had I not been the journalist assigned to cover it. Would I have attended at all? I had lots of great female friends, a few who were absolute touchstones throughout my adult life, but did I have a crew of girls I would have made plans to march with, the way all these women had? Did I belong to any organizations that brought women together like this? Would I have been likely to board a bus of strangers to make the trek here just so I could experience the unity of this huddle? I wasn't sure, but I knew something had been sparked in me.

I knew I needed to bring women into sharper focus—in both my career *and* my personal life, to do my very best to unlock this collective power in my own life. It was like a religious moment. I wanted to figure out why being in the midst of half a million women inspired me like that. Was I the only one who felt gobsmacked by all this? I wondered if this sense of unity and empowerment could be felt anytime women gather and why it had required a massive historic protest for me to take notice. Had I been missing out on an amazing resource all these years? I knew I had to find out.

•••

Meanwhile, somewhere across the mall, a forty-nine-year-old white woman named Chrissy Houlahan was having a similar religious experience. And spoiler alert: in case her name isn't familiar to you, Houlahan went on to become a U.S. congresswoman two short years later, but at the time of the Women's March, she was a woman from Pennsylvania who had never run for office of any kind.

"I'm not a spiritual person," she clarified for me later, "but it was a very powerful day." After spending hours in lockstep with the crowd, she and her group of friends and family decided to break loose and head over to the Washington Monument. "Walking against the crowd was even more rewarding," she said. "Instead of being one of the masses, you actually got to see this massive thing you were a part of." A Navy veteran and mother of three, Houlahan exudes a quiet strength with a flame of intensity behind her eyes. She has the air of a kind schoolteacher who could also beat you in a footrace. She didn't strike me as someone easily swept up by emotion. But the sight of the huddle was no less moving for her than it was for me.

Crowds and protests weren't something she typically sought out. And yet this self-proclaimed "private introvert" with only a few close female friends managed to fill a rented bus with fifty-one women and two men (one of them being her husband) to drive from West Chester, Pennsylvania, to D.C. She hadn't imagined she'd organize such a large group for the trip, but when her mother offered to pay for the bus if she could fill it, Houlahan accepted the offer. One Facebook post and a very small word-of-mouth campaign later and Houlahan had a waiting list for her fifty-three seats. People who didn't get a spot on the bus still wanted to help decorate signs the day before the trip.

"I don't know what I was thinking," she said with a laugh. "I invited all these people I didn't even know to my house. We decorated signs and I made chili."

Houlahan isn't prone to false humility. When she tells you she's shy, it doesn't sound like one of those quaint confessions politicians make to humanize themselves to you. You believe her. When she tells you that she and her daughter had spent time knocking on doors for Hillary Clinton's campaign in 2016, you understand it was a stretch outside her comfort zone. Maybe the experience of talking to strangers warmed her up for the chili party and the rowdy bus ride that were in her near future. Or maybe a little shyness wasn't going to get in the way, because there was a lot motivating her.

"The day after Trump won the election was a hard day for many of us, but my daughter and father were devastated," she said. Houlahan's daughter—a member of the LGBTQ community—felt even more unwelcome in her own country while Houlahan's father—a Holocaust survivor who came to America as a young boy with nothing but his parents—was terrified for fellow refugees. A career Navy man, he had felt grateful for all the opportunities this country had afforded him and yet very distraught that refugees in the future wouldn't be treated the same.

Houlahan felt more than a little compelled to pay a visit to the nation's capital when she heard about the Women's March. She had real concerns about the state of her country. She was also a fighter and a passionate defender of her values—something she'd built up over years as a Navy veteran, a mother, a businesswoman, a nonprofit director, and an educator. Her upbringing in a military family probably had something to do with it too. Her impulse for service and action emerged several times in our conversations.

So the day after the chili-fest/sign-making party, Houlahan and her new friends boarded a bus stocked with Dunkin' Donuts coffee and pastries ("because we're from Pennsylvania . . .") and proceeded to have the time of their lives. This was the part Houlahan hadn't expected: the joyous atmosphere she would encounter even before the bus arrived at the capital. "It was really heartening to see all the buses on the way there. They were coming from every direction on the 95 corridor, with women banging their windows and cheering for one another." There was also the consummate ladies-bonding-while-waiting-to-pee experience. At every rest stop and restaurant, the lines for the bathrooms were out the door. "Women took over the men's restrooms that day," she said with a laugh.

Once they arrived, Houlahan, like so many other attendees, spent hours at the march crammed between other women. Her children had flown from California and New York to be there with her, and they were all reassured by the variety of messages they saw plastered on signs around them. "Whether it was LGBTQ, or people with disabilities, the planet, women's health, education, or science, everyone had a reason they were standing there." Like me, Houlahan was struck not only by the diversity of platforms represented but also the unifying surge of positivity and energy that permeated everything. That powerful sense of togetherness continued on the bus ride home.

Sharing KFC and wine as they bumped along the highway, the women passed around a microphone to share their reasons for attending. A little PA system projected their stories through the dark bus. Houlahan learned that the women's individual motivations for attending were as diverse as the messages on the signs they'd seen at the march. She marveled at the fact that they could all come together over such a variety of causes, that women's unity is a power in and of itself.

She voiced what I came to realize over the course of writing this book—that one of our superpowers as women is our ability to find agency in each other's company. When we put our heads together and *use our voices in one another's presence*, we become more potent. Houlahan told me that she had arrived at a "crucible moment" on that bus ride and that her decision to explore running for public office was a direct result of the inspiration she took from other women that day at the march. And even though she'd never so much as served as a city councilwoman, she had her sights set on the U.S. Congress in the upcoming 2018 midterms. She had less than two years to pull it off, and she knew enough about politics to understand she would need a sizable community of support.

"I didn't have a vast network of women, or even men, to tap into," she told me. But she *had* just met a lot of women on a bus. Turns out, there were several busloads of women in her area who were attending post-march huddles (a brilliant suggestion made by the Women's March organizers themselves) to keep the spark of change alive after their day in D.C. Houlahan started attending several of these huddle meetups.

"I would just go have coffee or wine with these other busloads at their huddles and introduce myself as someone forming an explor- atory committee to run for U.S. Congress." It was a pretty rapid evolution: she rode a bus one day with a bunch of ladies she'd never met, and within days, a seed was planted to run for U.S. Congress. Not that she didn't take a careful self-inventory before making the decision. But to put this ambition into context, at the time Houla- han decided to run, there were no women serving *any* of the Penn- sylvania districts in the U.S. House of Representatives, and there had never in history been a female senator from the state. Even at the state and local levels, Pennsylvania ranked very low in terms of female representation. A woman had never been elected governor, and only 19 percent of the state legislature were female. One study, the Gender Parity Index, even ranked Houlahan's home state as forty-ninth in the nation for gender parity in elected office. Only Mississippi ranked lower than Pennsylvania that year.

At the post-march huddles, Houlahan met several women who

had decided to run for public office as well. Many of them ended up campaigning for local and municipal elections in Pennsylvania in 2017, which created a perfect spontaneous training ground for Houlahan, who would run for Congress a year later. "I learned how to be a candidate by helping them. I learned how to knock on doors, how to network. And then when I ran, they became my support network." She marvels at the fact that a massive collective of women was available to her, right in her backyard, and she didn't even know they existed until she boarded that bus. This struck me as so similar to the way I felt that day at the march, realizing I was surrounded by an amazing resource I had never intentionally explored.

Enveloped by the power of women, Houlahan and many of her friends made resounding changes across their state. In Houlahan's county alone, female Democrats were elected as treasurer, controller, clerk of courts, and coroner—a first in the county's three hundred years. And then one year later, in 2018, Houlahan became the first woman to represent her county in Congress in its 230-year history.

Houlahan's rise seems pretty extraordinary—and quick. Just two years after she took a leap of faith and made chili for dozens of strangers, she was sworn in as a U.S. congresswoman. And yet, her success is not unlike that of many women who were part of the 2018 "pink wave" (not the color I would use to describe this force of nature!)—when a record-breaking 127 women were elected to the U.S. House of Representatives. This trend continued through the 2020 elections as well, when women won yet another historic number of seats—134 in all—in the 117th Congress. Perhaps not all these women had a backyard huddle like the one Houlahan described, but many were supported by groups like EMILY's List, Emerge, VIEW PAC, and E-PAC—female-led organizations that work to get more women in office by surrounding them with re-sources and mentoring them in the fundraising and campaign pro-cesses. Houlahan herself sought the help of some of these groups, alongside her original network in Chester County. In the end, these tactics worked for her and many women in both 2018 and 2020. (Houlahan held on to her seat in her second run as well.)

After the 2018 midterms, people in my profession were quick to opine that the success of the wave of women elected to Congress was due to some sort of nationwide female anger about Trump that somehow took on magical properties. But from where I'm sit-ting, women's anger alone doesn't usually win elections. If it did, we'd have won plenty more in the last century. Not to mention, the last time I checked, women were roundly penalized for expressing emotion, particularly in an election setting. (We all remember the ways Hillary Clinton was scrutinized anytime her face broke on the campaign trail.) Pure emotion rarely gets you anywhere with-out strategy, hard work, and vast networks of support—the latter of which caught my attention. In other words, it seems to me that women have been winning more races because they are working more collectively. The 2020 elections showed us that women's wins in the 2018 election weren't an anomaly—and they weren't fueled purely by anti-Trump rage either. If that were the case, Re-publican women wouldn't have won so many seats in 2020 as well.

There is no doubt that huddling is part of the reason women have gained momentum in politics, and this energy started esca-lating around the time of Houlahan's first run. If you consider the timeline, it's impossible to ignore the monolithic sweep of it:

- **IN JANUARY 2017, THE WOMEN'S MARCH** became the largest single-day protest on American soil—and it was organized and attended by 99 percent women, drawing an estimated five hundred thousand people in D.C. and between four and seven million people nationwide.

- **IN OCTOBER 2017, THE #METOO MOVEMENT** assembled the voices of women from all walks of life—from A-list celebrities to college girls on Facebook—to publicly rally and share their stories of sexual assault online—to force the world to pay attention to the severity of a problem (affecting 81 percent of American women and 43 percent of American men) that had been swept under the rug for years. In the first year alone, the #MeToo hashtag appeared in more than nineteen million tweets.

- **IN JANUARY 2018, THE TIME'S UP INITIATIVE** launched a collaboration of more than three hundred of the most well-known and powerful women in entertainment, creating a bold public plan to combat sexual assault, harassment, and inequality in every workplace for every female employee, whether they were Hollywood actresses, Fortune 500 CEOs, or hotel maids. By the one-year mark, the Time's Up fundraising effort had raised $22 million—more than any other GoFundMe in history.

- **IN NOVEMBER 2018, A HISTORIC NUMBER OF WOMEN RAN FOR PUBLIC OFFICE**—more than had ever run in the history of the United States—by a landslide. (A total of 183 ran for the House, besting the previous record of 52; 15 ran for the Senate, besting the previous record of 7; 12 ran for governor, besting the previous record of 4; and 2,380 ran for the state legislatures, besting the previous record of 985.) The result was that for the first time in history, women made up a quarter of the House and the Senate. And that's not to mention all the local elections women won in cities and small towns across the country.

There have been plenty of other books written about these movements, and they don't need me to qualify them here. But what interests me most is what they all had in common: they were all massive female huddles. These were broad, inclusive movements that created space—or at least attempted to create space—for the participation of women from all backgrounds. And their emergence was so abrupt in the scope of things. It was as if women hadn't consulted with one another in a great number of years and suddenly they had a moment to chat and a massive dam broke. Instantly, a stream of urgent conversations ensued, and women were finally talking more openly and publicly about rampant sexual assault and violence, egregious workplace inequalities, pervasive sexism, and the widespread lack of female representation in the halls of American power. And beyond these conversations, there was also a new unspoken mandate of *intentionality*, urging us to lean on one another for support in the face of all these social ills. It was an incredible sequence of events that changed the way women moved through the world.

It turns out I wasn't the only one who felt like I was witnessing something seismic and *new* at the Women's March. According to Kristin Goss, an author and political science professor at Duke University, women *really were* suddenly finding each other again after spending roughly three decades in relative isolation from one another. Goss's book *The Paradox of Gender Equality* explores how before the 1980s, women of all races were consistently and collectively leading the charge on US policy issues as diverse as international relations, environmental protection, crime and justice, democratic governance, poverty, housing, civil rights, and education. By measuring various political activities, including the number of times groups of women testified before Congress, Goss determined that nineteenth- and twentieth-century women's organizations played an important role in far more social and policy change than we often give them credit for. In fact, I was surprised to hear that the vitality of women's collective action peaked not in the 1960s or '70s, as you might imagine, but at midcentury. Goss explained that June Cleaver and Betty Crocker were hopping their white picket fences, joining mass membership organizations like the League of Women Voters, and locking arms to demand change from local, state, and federal lawmakers.

But, according to Goss, much of this well-documented activity—particularly among white women—took a steep and sudden nosedive right around about the time I was born in 1979. Meaning, this three-decade huddle hiatus she spoke of spanned what was basically *most of my life*. The reasons for the pause in huddling surprised me.

"During the '80s and '90s, women finally had formal legal equality," Goss explained. And white women especially were able to take advantage of this. "Women were attending college at rates greater than men," she continued. "They were attending law school at rates greater than men. They were populating the professions," she explained. Yet, at the same time, according to Goss's data, the rate at which women's groups testified before Congress suddenly declined dramatically, and large female civic and political organizations were fading—now feeling old-fashioned or outdated. Not to mention, the unprecedented numbers of women entering the workforce meant less time for coordinated volunteering and community activism outside their nine-to-five jobs and family duties.

Meanwhile, for Black women, Indigenous women, and other women of color who weren't afforded as much access to this new "formal legal equality," there was a whole other set of challenges. Their perspectives had already been excluded or ignored by many factions of the feminist movement, not to mention some of the male-led movements for racial equality in the previous decades. Black women in particular were being directly criminalized and dehumanized during this era, disproportionately incarcerated, and unfairly depicted as "welfare queens," even though a significant number of them were single-handedly raising families and working full-time jobs without spousal support. As one Black woman, T. Morgan Dixon (whom you'll meet later in this book), so aptly put it: "While there is a glass ceiling for mostly white middle-class women, we were still not even let into the door. So we never had that lean-in mentality." Later I'll discuss in more detail the ways that Black women in America seemed to better maintain their huddle through the 1980s, '90s, and 2000s, when white women were often more disconnected from one another.

Now fast forward to 2017, when Goss explained we were beginning to see "a rebirth, a new women's movement that is more intersectional—though not enough—and more conscious of women's complexity." This resurgence of huddling has been fueled by our urgent need to settle what she called a lot of "unfinished business" that affected a broad swath of women regardless of race or class, including "violence against women, domestic violence with firearms, and sexual assault and pervasive sexual harassment in the workplace, not to mention the problem of political representation." She reminded me that no matter how far we've come, "It's still crazy that in the twenty-first century, after decades and decades of women being highly educated, employed in all the pipeline professions, and highly engaged in politics, we still only make up—at best—about 20 to 25 percent of our country's elected officials, whether you're talking about the city, state, or federal levels of government."

I thought of Congresswoman Chrissy Houlahan deciding to run for Congress because she wanted to fight for the rights of her gay daughter and refugees like her Holocaust survivor father. I remembered the story she told me about her service in the Navy in the 1980s, where she had but a few female colleagues to speak of; how she had to retire early from the armed services essentially because she could not find affordable childcare on base. Not only was her pay insufficient to fund childcare off-base, but her employer (the US government) didn't provide enough supportive maternal benefits. Houlahan—and many of her female colleagues in the 2018 freshman class of the U.S. House of Representatives—certainly had a lot of unfinished business to attend to.

And even though Trump's election in 2016 might have initially prompted some women to attend the Women's March or spark an idea to get more involved in politics, I reject the notion that our resurgence of huddling was merely a defensive action or a response to one person. In the process of writing this book, I've learned that huddling is something in our DNA, so to speak, as women. Huddling is a practice and survival mechanism honed over generations. There may have been a drought of official female collective action for a few decades—particularly among white women—but we hadn't lost the thread of our collective power entirely. In other words, even though Trump might have angered a lot of women in 2016 (and, well, every year since), he's not responsible for the kind of huddling that was happening across political, social, class, and age lines. And just as Tamika Mallory said that day at the Women's March, huddling is never about *one man*. Women are finding our way back to each other—we will always find our way back to each other—because *female huddling is a part of our legacy*. Like Houlahan after her fateful bus ride to D.C., I left the Women's March hungry to connect with more women who were working together to make change or simply connecting with each other in quiet yet powerful ways. I wanted to learn more from the women out there in America who had a better practice of linking arms with each other, who had attended more marches and protests with each other, who had managed to keep each other close through all manner of class and racial struggle, who had formed entire movements that were powered by their bonds with each other. I wanted to compare notes with other women like me who had found ways to support each other in the workplace during so many years of lean-in-or-die. I wanted to listen to women whose lives were different from mine—or maybe more similar than I realized—to find out what these strong huddlers could teach me. I'd always believed in women and admired the strength and leadership of women wherever I encountered it. But this was different. I was summoning some intentionality around this.

I wanted to huddle.

And I wanted to show other women in this country how they can do it too.

The journalist in me wanted to find out not only *why* these huddles were suddenly happening everywhere I looked, but also how huddles work, what makes them effective, and what they can accomplish. But most of all, I wanted to learn what happens when women harness the power of each other.

So I hit the road to find out.

two

THE HUDDLE WASN'T INVENTED BY WOMEN IN PUSSYHATS

I was in the back seat of a Lyft cruising slowly through a stately, sunny neighborhood called River Oaks in Houston, Texas. The streets were lined with wrought-iron gates that encase giant multimillion-dollar homes. These were the houses that old money built—or at least as old as money can get in this part of the country. The azaleas were in bloom, popping pink on the thick manicured hedges that lined the streets, and giant Texas flags beckoned and waved over many a doorway. As we rolled through the shade of live oak trees, the driver blasted Beyoncé ("Come on ladies, now let's get in formation!") because, of course, this is *her* town.

This was my first time in Houston—minus a family wedding I'd attended a few years back. I travel so often for business and pleasure, but I'd never had a reason to spend much time here before. I was surprised by the city's diversity, which I confirmed with a quick Google search. Harris County, which encompasses most of Houston, has no racial majority. Forty-three percent of its 4.7 million people are Hispanic (white or other), 28 percent are white (non-Hispanic), 18 percent are African American (non-Hispanic), and 7 percent are Asian (non-Hispanic). It's not all white cowboys and astronauts as the movies would have you believe.

After "Formation" ended, I asked the driver if he was here during Hurricane Harvey in 2017, and he turned down his SiriusXM station to tell me how his great-grandparents had crossed the border from Mexico in the late 1800s, and his family has been here ever since. He helped me understand the ripple effects of the hurricane and gave me a primer on the entire city. By the end of the car ride, I probably could have passed an elementary school–level test on Texas state history. And between stories of Sam Houston and the Texas Revolution, he kept interjecting with details about these majestic homes we were passing; which ones were three feet underwater during Harvey, which were recently purchased by an international oil baron or megachurch pastor, and which were bought or sold for $10 million plus.

After we passed the Buffalo Bayou ("you could hop a canoe and paddle yourself all the way to Cuba from here"), he pulled into a restaurant called Ouisie's Table, where I would be enjoying an "upscale" Southern brunch. The six women I would be dining with had recently been elected as judges there in Harris County during the 2018 midterm elections. Two years after Hillary Clinton lost her bid to become the nation's first female president, women (such as Chrissy Houlahan) signed up in record numbers across the country to run for public office. According to EMILY's List, a political action committee that helps Democratic women run for public office, more than forty-two thousand women contacted them after Clinton's 2016 loss to express interest in running. And that's just the Democrats. This number was a massive jump by any standard, given that prior to Clinton's loss, fewer than a thousand women had expressed interest in running.

These women I was about to meet at Ouisie's Table were, in some ways, not unusual. They were part of a larger trend nationwide. And because I don't typically keep close tabs on county-level judge seats in a state where I don't live or vote, I doubt I would have heard of this huddle of judges had their group campaign photo not gone viral.

I saw the photo for the first time on the day after the 2018 midterm elections, and one of my line producers sent the image to me and my team at work. For several months that year, I'd been chasing stories of women running for office, and she knew I'd want to see it. She was right. As an aside, something to know about me is that on a typical morning at CNN as we prep for my show, I read no fewer than five bazillion headlines and news articles. Just on my commute to work alone, I digest more news on my phone than can be considered healthy for my eyeballs or humane for my soul. Beyoncé might "slay all day," as the song goes, but as for me? I scroll all day. That doesn't have the same ring to it, but it's the truth. I wade through so much information on the regular that—I admit—I can sometimes be jaded. But this headline? This photo? It stopped me in my tracks. I dropped everything and just stared at it. Pinched the screen, zoomed in on all those faces. Nineteen women. Nineteen *Black* women. All in the same county, and they had all *just won their races.*

I immediately texted the photo out to several friends and female colleagues: "LOOK at this!!!"

In the photo, which no doubt you can still easily find on the internet today since it trended on Twitter and Reddit and appeared on dozens of news sites, all nineteen women are dressed in black, donning white pearls, and standing at a judge's bench in a wood-paneled Houston courtroom. With the red, white, and blue of the Texas and American flags behind them, it is a stunning image. Their proud smiles and stark poses make them look almost royal. But also kinda fun. At first glance, you might mistake it for a poster of a blockbuster movie about some badass group of women, or maybe an ironic remake of a *Last Supper* painting, but not something that is actually *real*. Because, sadly, an image like this is still pretty rare in America—not because there aren't plenty of Black women who have shaped history together, but because our culture hasn't celebrated them enough. The history books aren't filled with many photos like this. As a journalist, I hadn't often seen a widely distributed photo of this many Black women in one place, standing in positions of power, giving off so much heat and light. It just had that weight to it. No wonder it went viral.

The caption varied depending on which outlet was running it, but most listed the name the women had used to call themselves ("Black Girl Magic") and read something like this:

> BLACK GIRL MAGIC: Nineteen black women make history in Harris County, Texas, after winning their judge seats yesterday.

I wanted to know how so many first-time Black women running as judges on the Democratic ticket were elected in a county where Republicans had held most of the seats for years. I wanted to know more about these women, how they came together, and what they had to do to win these seats. The photo provided some indication that they might have beaten the odds by joining forces. In campaigning together—which all started with this strategic photo—they'd inspired voters to show up and elect judges who demographically better represent the county they serve. And I was guessing that was something of a feat; voters don't typically show up to the ballot box excited to vote for a specific judge. (Do you remember the name of the last judge you voted for? I'll admit it. I don't.) This was exactly the kind of huddle I wanted to interview for my show.

But immediately I knew I couldn't.

One of the most frustrating things about my job is the fact that airtime is finite. You could give me all day on TV and I'd still never get as many minutes with guests as I'd like. And so often, I can't cover all the stories I'm drawn to because of the sheer volume of news that commands what space I do have. When I saw the viral photo of the judges, I immediately knew we wouldn't be able to interview them on my show because we were already bursting at the seams with national news stories that week. The nation had just elected a parade of female firsts to the U.S. House of Representatives: the first Muslim and Native American women; the first African American and Latina women, from Massachusetts and Texas, respectively; the first two women from Iowa; the youngest congresswoman ever elected in US history; and Arizona and Tennessee had elected their first women to the Senate as well. We were also covering the president's firing of Attorney General Jeff Sessions and the governor races in Florida and Georgia that remained too close to call for several days. With all of this (and much more) going on, my interviewing a bunch of judges who won on the county level in Texas just wasn't going to make the cut. CNN .com wrote an entire article on the judges, but I didn't get to bring them on my show.

So, four months later, when I found myself in Houston, opening the big red doors to Ouisie's to meet the judges at last, I felt a little sense of anticipation. This magnetic pull I'd been feeling since November would finally be satisfied. Not to mention, this was my first huddle interview!

The comfortable blend of high-end and down-home was just about perfect in that restaurant—something I appreciate as a Southern woman. The place was loud and loose, but also proper enough you could bring your granny there after church. On one side of us sat a table of prim women sporting floral Sunday dresses and super fresh blowouts, pretty Bellinis in hand. On the other side was a table of jolly men in their sixties eating glistening plates of ham omelets and chicken and waffles, laughing uproariously between deep slugs of coffee. And then there was our group, including one extremely enthusiastic gal who'd flown in just for this moment (me) and six of the nineteen members of Harris County's Black Girl Magic judge huddle—Germaine Tanner, Linda Marie Dunson, Angela Graves-Harrington, Latosha Lewis Payne, Shannon Baldwin, and Sandra Peake—all looking sharp but entirely relaxed in one another's company, holding court at a round table in the center of the room. I felt something akin to starstruck, seeing these women in the flesh after studying their viral photo so many times.

As we devoured our shrimp and grits and several of Ouisie's dainty-but-no-joke cheddar and scallion biscuits, the judges told me about their backgrounds. "I've known for a long time that I wanted to be a family judge," said Germaine Tanner of the 311th Family Court. "But we've never had a Black woman elected as a family judge in Harris County. Ever."

"Never, okay?" she clarified, and paused for a moment to let this sink in. She told me she had been a practicing attorney for fifteen years, and was initially inspired to concentrate on family law by her experiences helping incarcerated fathers maintain relationships with their children. Motivated also by the aforementioned lack of Black female representation on the bench, she had lent her leadership to Annie's List, a group similar to EMILY's List that recruits, trains, and supports Texas women in their bids to run for public office.

Tanner's years of experience are fairly representative of the other women at the table, as well as the rest of the huddle not present that day. Most had a decade or more of legal experience as practicing attorneys, despite the claims of "unqualified" from their detractors during the campaign. In fact, the *Houston Chronicle* quoted Judge Dedra Davis as saying the group represented more than 220 years of experience in total. It's pretty telling that these professional and highly qualified women had been driven to tally up numerical proof of their collective—and considerable—expertise. But voters in this county weren't used to seeing Black women ask for their votes, much less witness them win elections and visibly inhabit positions of power.

"Very few of us have appeared [as attorneys] in front of female judges," Judge for the 55th Civil Court Latosha Lewis Payne told me. She had just joined us, having rushed over directly from a meet for her daughter's track team, which she somehow found the time to coach. As a former college conference champion in the 400-meter hurdles at Tulane, it's yet another job she was extraordinarily qualified for. "I've practiced law for eighteen years," Payne said, "and I can count on one hand, probably on just my pinky, how many times I've appeared in front of a judge who is Black, but a judge who is a Black woman . . . ?" Her voice trailed off, emphasizing the odds they've beaten.

Their sheer determination and belief in one another might be the most striking thing about this huddle. Throughout the nearly three hours I spent with them (I ate a lot of biscuits, y'all), the message was repeated over and over that the secret sauce for them is *believing in themselves.* And believing, they said, starts with representation. Representation means seeing role models who look like you and represent what you can become. It's the ingredient that activates possibility. It's the commonsense idea that tells us that little girls are far more likely to become doctors one day if they grow up under the care of a female pediatrician. It's that catchy yet tried-and-true belief that *you have to see it to be it*. Representation especially matters to these women who grew up seeing so little of themselves inhabiting the aspirational roles they now occupy.

Perhaps this lack of representation is the reason Black Girl Magic—the movement, not the viral photo of these judges in Houston—began in the first place. Initially emerging in 2013 as a hashtag on Twitter by CaShawn Thompson (@thepbg on Twitter), Black Girl Magic became a much beloved phrase used by celebrities, regular women, little girls, and even First Lady Michelle Obama to "uplift and praise the accomplishments, beauty and other amazing qualities of Black women," according to Thompson's website. It has become a battle cry, a motto, and a catchy reminder that the excellence of Black women is alive and well in a culture where it has been unfairly overlooked. In a 2015 interview with the *Los Angeles Times*, Thompson explained exactly what *magic* has to do with it: "Sometimes our accomplishments might seem to come out of thin air, because a lot of times, the only people supporting us are other Black women." In other words, so many Black women—and their perspectives, their pain, their joys, and their successes—go unseen in America.

Don't these judges know it. Cut to Houston, Texas, in March 2018, where the nineteen women were at the first Democratic Party event just after winning their primaries. Many of them were meeting each other for the first time, and they had certainly never organized themselves as a group before this day. Dozens of mostly white male judicial candidates were also in attendance, and everyone was celebrating their status as the official Democratic nominees for the midterms that fall. Meanwhile, all the Black women in the room were slowly turning their heads, looking around the space and seeing a lot more representation than they'd expected. "We just started counting and said, *wait a minute, this is amazing,"* said Judge Angela Graves-Harrington of the 246th Family Court, recalling her surprise to see so many Black women there that day. "It was a sisterhood immediately."

Thus was born an instant—if seemingly accidental—huddle that day, and the Houston 19, aka Black Girl Magic (two of the nicknames they began calling themselves) began organizing a collective campaign strategy. It hadn't been a plan to gather a bunch of Black women to all enter the primaries at the same time. This wasn't a premeditated huddle. It just happened. But now they'd found themselves in the company of each other, having won their primaries, and it was time to get serious. It was time to focus on winning the election—something *no one* thought they could do. But they believed in themselves and wanted others to see their worth. So they collectively proceeded as if winning were the only option.

They formed a private Facebook group, started a group text, and met at someone's house to quickly formulate a plan. They swiftly predicted it would be a powerful campaign tool for voters to simply *see them all in one place,* and decided to petition the Democratic Party to allow them to campaign together. Their premise was that this would galvanize not only the Black vote, but the *Democratic vote across the board* in Harris County. And beyond shooting a campaign photo together, they would actively pound the pavement together, showing up for community events as a group, shaking hands, answering questions, and generally inspiring the public with their huddle.

It was unconventional and against typical party protocol for judicial candidates to campaign in this manner. But the group was savvy enough to recognize that an unsexy judicial race in a midterm election (where voter turnout is traditionally very low)—in a red county, for that matter—could use a little infusion of #BlackGirlMagic. Not to mention, increasing voter turnout could help all the Democrats on the ticket.

Nonetheless, the Democratic Party promptly shot down their idea.

"We were sitting at a table across from them, and they were basically amazed that we were even opening our mouths to suggest such a thing," Graves-Harrington recalled.

With nary a Democrat elected to any countywide position since 1994 in Harris County, the party leadership was hedging its bets. They'd been cautious since well before the primaries. The judges told me that some of the nineteen had even been discouraged by their own party from running in the primaries in the first place. They were told they'd get waxed. Even worse, some who'd signed up to run unopposed in the primaries were given the ultimate gut punch when their own party rounded up "more viable" opponents to run against them at the last minute.

"We were considered a guaranteed loss," said Judge Linda Marie Dunson, of the 309th Family Court, who spoke softly but with a commanding intensity that cut through the happy racket of plates and spoons clinking all around us.

"Not only were they saying we weren't going to win," said Tanner, "they were also saying that we could cause a *backlash* if voters saw too many Black women running for spots that aren't traditionally theirs."

Judge Shannon Baldwin, who presides over the 4th Criminal Court, cut to the chase: "The message from the party was that we were possibly going to scare the current voter base, particularly the white voters, who we can't afford to lose. So they were basically telling us to sit down and keep a low profile." Baldwin, who had recently been elected by her peers to serve as the administrative judge over all the county courthouses (an achievement her friend Tanner proudly calls "superstar level"), also became the first openly LGBTQ African American judge in Harris County, and only the second in the entire state of Texas. "I don't fault them entirely for where they were coming from," she said, acknowledging the party's penchant for acting cautiously based on very realistic data and voting trends. But it still must have stung to feel this initial lack of support from their party, especially because Black women have long been considered the backbone of the Democratic Party nationwide—serving as a solid voting bloc time and time again. The judges' solution to this lack of confidence from their own party? "We came together and just *believed* that this could be different," Baldwin said.

Believing in themselves was the foundation of this huddle, something they'd learned reflexively over what I imagine was years and years of pushing back against other people's low expectations of them.

But low expectations be damned, they fermented their plan to take a photo, determined to convince the party to pay for it later. They'd need the party's authorization to campaign with it as well, but first they focused on the optics.

THE PHOTOSHOOT
AND THE PLATFORM

"There was a serious debate on what to wear in the photo," said Dunson.

"She's talking about me," laughed Baldwin. "They wanted me to wear a dress, and I said in order to take a good picture, I needed to be comfortable." Suddenly the debate came alive again.

"I wanted us to wear all different colors. Let's show brightness, right?" Tanner's smile beamed even brighter than her sunny yellow dress.

"This was a serious conversation," Baldwin deadpanned. "I kept explaining that no matter what they said, I was *not* wearing a dress."

The table exploded in laughter, and I could feel the heated intensity of these type-A, overachieving litigators melt into the kind of loving teasing that only happens between true friends. At some point, the group settled on wearing all black—pantsuits permissible—and white pearls. This color palette felt judicial, powerful, and professional.

They wrangled nineteen schedules—a feat in and of itself—for a quick photoshoot in a courtroom, wherein one woman who shall remain nameless had to come straight from a flight and literally jump in the corner of the photo at the very last minute—right before the photographer almost gave up on them.

"What's beautiful about that picture is that everybody was doing their own thing," Tanner reflected. "No one posed us."

"And it felt big in the moment too," recalled Graves-Harrington. They remember the photoshoot as a jubilant hour during which they played their hometown fave Beyoncé as background music so they could sing and dance between takes and keep the vibe happy. By this point, the Democratic Party had agreed to pay for the photo, which would be used to create campaign promotional materials and a billboard.

"I promise you, we are *alllll* hair and makeup women," Baldwin assured me, recalling the poor guy from the Democratic Party who had to incorporate nineteen different opinions about which shot he should select as the final one for printing.

Our laughter at this point drew some curious glances from neighboring tables. In a very loud room, we'd become the loudest.

And then it got quiet again when Tanner explained the moment they all saw the final photo for the first time.

"I got chills. I think we all did. It was really moving."

With the photo printed on fliers and billboards, they were able to take Black Girl Magic on the road to fire up voter interest as "the new faces of justice" (the text that ran across the top of the photo). And the same party that had once suggested they water down the slogan to be "She's Got Magic" (meaning: take the *Black* out of it) was now polling the county and finding that these candidates garnered a largely positive reaction with voters. But the judges were already confident that the county was ready for change, and they believed in their abilities to be the agents of that change. What they didn't quite believe, however, was just how explosive the photo would become.

It inspired people of all races and professions—flight attendants, janitors, lawyers, and teachers—to run up to hug them in public with tears in their eyes, thanking them for representing women and people of color in Harris County. Mothers would come up to tell them they'd printed the photo and hung it on their walls to inspire their daughters. "We'd show up—ten or fifteen of us—and people would have questions for us about the role of judges." This might have been the most "magical" feat of all—that the photo became a teaching tool and they were able to open conversations about legal matters that most voters ignore—even at their own peril. The ordinances, laws, and positions of individual judges themselves can have a profound impact on voters' daily lives and welfare. Tanner recalled, "There's *never* been that sort of attention or interest in what we do."

Unfortunately, there were also the blatantly racist responses—the worst being that Black Girl Magic actually meant "black magic" or "voodoo." And potentially more insidious (read: more rampant and inexplicably socially acceptable) were the accusations that the nineteen were *against* diversity, an echo of the oft-used and very flawed notion that when people of color support each other en masse they are somehow practicing "reverse racism." The photo uncovered a very discouraging phenomenon: the same voters who are used to seeing large groups of white men run government, corporate boards, or just about any other organization in America, could look at an image of a group of Black women (who were running for just nineteen of fifty-nine judicial seats total) and have a reaction that basically amounted to: "Well, *that* doesn't look very diverse. I'll pass on them, because *I'm* for diversity."

A segment of people from the Black community—men mostly— also voiced a negative reaction to the photo. "The stereotype about Black women is that we are mean, and that we are harsher on Black men than anyone else," explained Baldwin, and this group of men was afraid "partially because they thought we might feel we have something to prove once we got ourselves elected to these positions." While so many Black men in Harris County had indeed been harshly penalized for decades, directing this accusation at the Houston 19 felt painfully ironic. Not only are successful Black women often saddled with this unfair stereotype, but the group's unified platform was specifically one of *restoring compassion* to the bench in a county where people of color and the poor were disproportionately penalized by the justice system. "There hasn't been compassion here [in Harris County]. Across the board. Judges haven't been fair," said Graves-Harrington, the sadness in her voice no less urgent than her sense of justice.

According to a 2018 report in the *Houston Chronicle*, Graves-Harrington's statement is not unfounded. Two sitting white, male, Republican judges in Harris County had become notorious for penalizing children and were responsible for more than one-fifth of all children sent to juvenile prisons in the entire state of Texas. And a whopping 96 percent of all kids sent to state lockup from Harris County juvenile courts were children of color. Additionally, the number of kids from Harris County who were sent to youth prisons had more than doubled since 2014. This was a grave crisis to the Houston 19, most of whom had spent the last decade in courtrooms as practicing attorneys, seeing firsthand the way judges can dramatically change the course of a young person's life. They were on a mission to balance corrections with compassion, for the sake of real families in Harris County they saw needlessly damaged by the system.

With their photo and campaign platform well established, their huddle became a great source of comfort, strategy, and stamina. Moral support was never too far away thanks to their private Facebook group and active group text threads. "We'd have our list of events posted and someone would text, 'I'm too tired. I'm not going to that event,'" Baldwin recalled. "And then ten more of us would inevitably comment back and say, 'Oh, yes you are.'"

"We went everywhere. And because there were so many of us, we were able to fan out," explained Judge Sandra Peake of the 257th Family District Court. They formed subcommittees to reach certain blocs of voters—such as the group that organized visits to Black churches every single Sunday between the primaries and Election Day. Large groups—sometimes a dozen, sometimes all nineteen of them—would visit up to four churches per Sunday to meet the voters. Pastors would march them onstage in a line, the Black Girl Magic photo projected on a screen behind them.

"As we took our places onstage, there would sometimes be an

audible gasp," recalled Tanner. Standing before members of the Houston Black community, they saw there were many elders in the congregation. And although some of them had themselves been participants in the civil rights movement in their youth (and they had all lived to see a Black president), they were still taken aback by the mere sight of so many empowered Black women. And even in the Black churches where family, friends, and their clients of several decades sat, there was still an uphill battle to get the community to believe they could really win. But they could feel energy shifting and they had confidence their plan could work.

They not only kept each other motivated, they also supported one another in the way you don't often see male candidates do. Since many of the nineteen had young children, and because campaigning is a second-shift job, kids were often brought to campaign events to help their mothers fight the good fight. "When we started campaigning in the primaries, my foster daughter was only two months old," said Baldwin. "By the time she could crawl, she would just choose which auntie she wanted to crawl over to. There was her Aunt Sandra, her Aunt Germaine . . ." She beamed, gesturing to said aunties to her left and right at the table.

Dunson, who as a child watched her divorced mother join forces with her divorced aunt to raise their collective twelve children together, confirmed the group's it-takes-a-village stance: "Shannon wasn't the only one with a two-month-old baby. We *all* had a two-month-old baby," she said with a laugh.

Taking kids to knock on doors or to attend rallies and parades makes sense when you consider the role judges play in the lives of families in the community. Whether through matters of divorce, custody arrangements, conflicts with Child Protective Services, or situations where parents or juveniles have to be penalized, judges have an incalculable effect on shaping the health and well-being of families—for better or for worse. And they don't just administer punishments; they also use their position on the bench to educate and direct people toward much needed social services and resources. Even more profound is the inspirational role they can play in conversations they have at the bench with people who find themselves at the mercy of the justice system. It's easy to forget that judges aren't just punishers—they can actually raise the bar for many people simply by vocally setting higher expectations for them. Instead of giving up on them as so many in society already have, judges can use their position to express their confidence and belief in people who are struggling. And this can have real impact on their long-term success or failure.

"I firmly believe that the voters needed to see that we were family people as well," said Baldwin, "and that we truly cared." By this point in our conversation, plates cleared, everyone still sipping on their sweet tea or coffee, it had become clear to me that for these women, becoming a judge was about more than reaching the pinnacle of a legal career or donning a prestigious robe. Being a judge is *a calling* for these women, a way of activating their personal care and concern for real families in crisis who are part of a society that is deeply imperiled by injustice.

THE HUDDLE MOVES TO THE COURTHOUSE

When Election Day came, they gathered to watch the election results come in. Tanner told me the mood at Chapman & Kirby in East Downtown was incredible as their "huge leads" were obvious early on. When the races were called and their wins were official, Tanner said the screams were deafening. "My knees literally got weak," she recalled. "We made history several ways over—Harris County flipped every single judicial seat, which hadn't happened in twenty-five years." The Black Girl Magic campaign had been an enormous success.

With their victories secured, their group photo (which had already been a big hit locally) went viral nationwide, and many locals were stunned that the nineteen had actually won their races. It began to feel to the judges as if the entire county's eyes were on them—whether it was the young women who looked up to them or the disgruntled voters who hoped for their failure. They felt pressure to shine in all these glaring spotlights. There was no room for error.

Meanwhile, some of the outgoing judges who'd just lost their seats to the nineteen were refusing to help transition their courts over to the new judges, sometimes downright sabotaging them or resetting problematic trials so they'd be automatically passed on to the women. But the experience of being held to a higher standard wasn't something unfamiliar to these women; in fact, they'd had years of practice coping with this. They assured me they didn't have time to be angry about it. Instead they just dealt with it practically. And that meant leveraging their huddle.

Several were given offices in the same courthouse, so they immediately began taking advantage of the fact that they were within arm's reach of each other. "It's a whole new sisterhood now," Baldwin told me, describing a positively hive-like environment where they are in and out of each other's offices and courtrooms whenever assistance is needed. Their years of experience were put to good use, and when any one of them had a specific question, they weren't afraid to lean on each other for advice. A knowledge base that is nineteen women deep is a superpower that should never be wasted.

"If I've got an SOS situation, I just pick up the phone or walk across the hall," said Peake.

Graves-Harrington agreed: "I can always pick up the phone and call Shannon and say, *Hey, I'm reading the rules of evidence this way. How are you interpreting them?*"

Sometimes they quite literally swoop into one another's court-rooms mid-trial to assist. "I just text from the bench: *Come now,*" Dunson said bluntly.

"Wait," I stopped her. "You mean, while you're sitting up there on the bench, with people in your courtroom, you just text an-other judge for help?"

She repeated herself in that did-I-stutter manner while mimick-ing typing into an invisible cell phone: "Come. Now."

Everyone burst into laughter again and Graves-Harrington put it into perspective: "We provide each other a safe space. Our male predecessors didn't know everything either. But the difference is they were *allowed* to make mistakes and ask questions. If we ask questions of the wrong person, we're perceived as being unknowl-edgeable or unqualified." *There they go again,* I thought, *fighting un-fair perceptions in a manner so unflappable.*

I was also touched by their humility. What if we were all able to admit so easily that our value isn't diminished by the degree of advice we receive from our trusted peers? Why don't more women talk about this? Why hadn't I found more strength and comfort in leaning on other women in the workplace? And how many op-portunities had I missed over the years by letting this amazing re-source go untapped?

When I asked them if huddling came easily to them—or where they'd learned it in the first place, Graves-Harrington replied: "We've been *raised* to be our sister's keepers." When I asked how a person is "raised to huddle," they seemed a little baffled, like I was suddenly speaking another language. It seemed like huddling was so deeply ingrained in their lives, it was hard to step outside of themselves to explain it. But they gave it a shot and walked me through the strong roles their mothers, grandmothers, and aunts played in their upbringing, as well as the unbelievably strong friendships they enjoy. Peake told a funny story about the way the network of Houston's Black women's hair salons showed up big-time for them during the campaign, and I lost count of the number of times the judges referenced the two Black sororities represented at the table (Delta Sigma Theta and Alpha Kappa Alpha). It was not just the lasting friendships and mentorships they gained from their membership they wanted to tell me about, but also the continuing protective network the sororities had provided through their entire adult lives—both professionally and socially.

In Paula Giddings's book about the history of Delta Sigma Theta, *In Search of Sisterhood*, she shows the ways that "the largest black women's organization in the United States" has always aimed to prepare its members to become "agents of change" whether during the suffrage movement, the civil rights movement, or the formidable challenges of social justice in the current day. A Black woman herself and alumna of the sorority, Giddings remarked on her time spent researching the organization to write the book: "Black women may be among their freest, their happiest, and in some ways, their most fulfilled when they are together in their organizations." Stunning words that caught my attention because Giddings published them in 1988, a time that was a huddle drought for many middle-class white women in America.

The Black historian Kimberly Springer has written about the major formal Black feminist organizations in America (the Third World Women's Alliance, Black Women Organized for Political Action, National Black Feminist Organization, National Alliance of Black Feminists, and Combahee River Collective) that were all defunct by the 1980s, much like the formal women's organizations that scholar Kristin Goss described as having declined by the 1980s. And yet, even after the decline of these formal organizations, the social network for Black women remained strong in many ways, according to Springer. In her book *Living for the Revolution* Springer notes the founding of the Black Women's Health Imperative in the 1980s. She also recalled the Clarence Thomas Supreme Court confirmation hearings as being "so activating" to many Black women she knew. She detailed in her book the moment in 1991 when a group called African American Women in Defense of Ourselves "raised $50,000 in a matter of weeks to place full-page newspaper ads in national and local African American newspapers protesting Anita Hill's treatment before the U.S. Congress."

There was also, of course, the Million Woman March in Philadelphia in 1997—when an estimated five hundred thousand Black women came together to march, pray, listen, speak, and bond—with the common goal of rebuilding Black communities and families. So right in the middle of what was considered a huddle drought for the majority of white women—and a full twenty years before the Women's March in D.C.—Black women gathered to empower each other in numbers that rivaled the 2017 march I attended. Huddling among Black women had been going on for a very long time—well before white women donned pussyhats. What's more, the Black women who organized the Million Woman March didn't rely on any large civil rights movements or celebrities to attract attendance to their gathering. They didn't even have the organizing power of the internet at that point. It was instead a grassroots effort that succeeded thanks to a preexisting network of Black women's organizations who leveraged Black-run media, dispersed fliers, and relied on word-of-mouth efforts. Although some Black feminists criticized the hetero-centered politics of the Million Woman March and others still were skeptical of its projected outcomes, it remains, at the very least, a solid testament to the strength of Black women's community and connection during a time when so many other American women were adrift from one another.

The judges confirmed the notion that Black women never really stopped huddling. And all of this underscored for me that although I'd been raised in the same era as some of these judges just a few states over in Georgia, I grew up in a different country, with a different experience of female community. It seemed that while many white American women were *neglecting* the huddle during the 1980s, '90s, and early 2000s, many communities of Black women were still robustly showing up for one another. Springer told me that even though many formal organizations had faded during this so-called huddle drought, Black women were still gathering informally to support one another. "It was just what we did and how we are," she recalled. She told me about the huddle she had formed with some of her peers in graduate school at Emory University during the '90s—again, not as any sort of formal organization, but just a group of women who read each other's work, reserved tables for nine at Red Lobster, and went to see movies together. The huddle also provided them a place where they felt safe to share with each other academic feedback that was free from the "racialized sexism" they experienced at Emory. "We not only validated each other's ideas, but also challenged them, and we knew everyone was coming from a place of love and critique, as opposed to a place of bias," she recalled.

The judges explained that the bonds between Black women were not so easily broken by a temporary huddle drought, partially because they had been built over a great deal of time. Baldwin explained it like this: slavery created a context in which Black women relied on each other exclusively to survive. ("At one point in history, we were all we had," said Tanner.) Post-slavery, they continued doing everything—from running households to civil rights movements—with their sisters by their side. T. Morgan Dixon (a Black woman you'll meet later in the book) reminded me that Black women's talent for huddling actually preceded enslavement: "[huddling] was our strength culturally for generations prior to slavery," she said. Springer concurred with this, telling me, "Black women have been huddling for generations. We have done so not only out of necessity, but also just out of a genuine love, affection, and respect for one another." In looking at the time period of the huddle drought, Dixon also mentioned the ways Black women were nourishing and maintaining strong social ties through everything from the Black Women's Health Imperative to The Links organization, to the Womanist movement, and even social activities like drill team. The judges' ability to summon their huddle so quickly, to unite and ignite a sister network to help them get elected, was just another case in point.

This very first group of women I was fortunate to be interviewing wasn't an "instant or accidental" huddle after all, as I'd hastily assumed earlier in our conversation. Rather, this huddle was seeded by lifetimes of women, securing and strengthening bonds over generations through struggle, hardship, patience, and joy.

BALANCING COMPASSION WITH CORRECTION

I asked the judges if together they'd been able to effect the change they'd hoped for when they were running for office. Although they were only a few months into the job, they supplied me with example after example of the ways they were "cleaning up the courts" and ridding them of some of the bad practices they'd witnessed in the past. They'd seen offenders' constitutional rights violated, for example, when judges would order drug testing for people who had never been accused of using drugs; they'd seen fathers' parental rights being taken away in proceedings they weren't even present for; they'd seen low-income children repeatedly assigned to the same few county attorneys due to what the *Texas Tribune* reported as alleged "cronyism between private attorneys and powerful judges." Lewis Payne told me about personally tracking down an African American man who was not being summoned in the proper channels because he was hard to find, due to the fact that he had been displaced multiple times by Hurricane Harvey. He would have lost his right to an attorney had Lewis Payne and her clerk not personally put the time in to locate him. Baldwin and the other criminal and civil court judges had been very busy creating new rules for a revised bond system that would ensure poor people wouldn't stay in jail while awaiting trial solely because they couldn't afford bond. Baldwin told me her new system was now being held up as a model program for other cities across the country.

The family courts were in the midst of a transformation as well. "So many children and parents have suffered because of the system," Graves-Harrington told me. "The parents would often just give up hope and stop showing up for court dates altogether," she said. "But now they appreciate our compassion. They are showing up."

"The atmosphere is entirely different. It's palpable," Tanner said.

Like many other institutions in our country, this one had been plagued with systemic racism. Outdated policies, structural inefficiencies, and unfair judges can result in permanent harm to the people who most need help—and this becomes a repeated inevitability until crucial agents of change, like these nineteen judges, step in and dedicate their time and attention to fixing the flaws. Through their examples and stories, these judges were making a real difference—largely through their willingness to view their jobs in a whole new light, to truly *see* and *honor* the humanity of the people they served.

Graves-Harrington told me about an interaction in one of her cases that stuck with me long after. One day during a trial, when Child Protective Services provided Judge Graves-Harrington with routine information about administering psychotropic drugs to a child in their custody, she noticed the child's mother across the courtroom. The mother—already distraught by the separation from her child—was now visibly in anguish to be learning about the psychotropic drugs for the very first time. Graves-Harrington halted the proceedings. "I said, *let's stop,*" she recalled. And looking at the mother, she said, "I can see your face, and I want to know your thoughts. Even though your child is not currently in your custody, you are still his mother and you still have the right to know what's going on in your child's life."

After the trial, the child's attorney approached Graves-Harrington to thank her for what was deemed extraordinary behavior. "I know the mother is not my client," the attorney said, "but you talked to her like she was a person. I appreciate that."

This small moment, where Graves-Harrington paused to speak to this mother woman-to-woman—to look at her face and recognize her pain—seems emblematic of the spirit of this powerful huddle of judges. Working together, finding common ground, and lending your compassion to another woman might be one of the most important things a huddle can accomplish. Election won, history made, sure—but there is also immense power and potential in a simple act of solidarity such as this one.

•••

When we stood up around our table to say goodbye—after two hours of what felt like church in the very best way—the judges surprised me with a gift. It was an enlarged version of their viral campaign photo—the one I'd zoomed in on so often on my iPhone screen. Along the top it read "The New Faces of Justice" and it was framed and signed on the back by each one of them. I thanked them and we exchanged hugs and selfies before going our separate ways. When I flew back to New York later that evening, I thought about the Monday ahead of me at CNN. I'd be knee-deep in covering the Mueller investigation, discussing the possibility that our president had committed an "obstruction of justice." It felt good to have started this project in my free time, to begin telling stories about what women were capable of when they worked together. And it felt surprisingly comforting to make a plan for where I'd display the photo as soon as I got back to my office. It would go on the shelf just above my computer—right at eye level, where I could see it every day. Seeing these women as they had seen themselves—as a huddle worth believing in—encouraged me to believe more in myself too. I couldn't wait to continue this journey I'd begun to make women's collective power more visible.

three

GIRLS GETTING LOUD IN BOY-FREE ZONES

s there anyone on Earth more confident than a four-year-old girl playing make-believe? I can still feel the intoxicating confidence of spinning around and around on the playground, believing I would transform into Wonder Woman. I was a brunette (no, I'm not a natural blonde) just like my idol, and I figured if I spread out my arms and twirled long enough, I'd reappear in those shiny gold cuffs and star-spangled briefs. I was a tall and sturdy preschooler in Atlanta, Georgia, and I felt I had a lot more in common with Lynda Carter—she who captured bad guys with her golden lasso and piercing blue eyes—than I did with my Montessori teacher—she who corralled children in her fuzzy pastel sweaters and whispery-sweet voice. She once busted me for inciting a group of five other kids to duck under the school's wooden fence and cross the busy street on a very important mission to collect acorns.

My entire childhood, up through my teen years, is filled with stories of bold little Brooke, doing backflips off the diving board at age four, stunning all the other families at the pool into silence. I was big-boned and assertive, never too shy to take up space or speak my mind. In third grade, I was voted in as a student council leader, which granted me the distinct privilege of taste-testing new foods in the lunchroom after hours. (I recall trying a new fig-based dessert and saying to myself, I am on the inside now!!) My big booming voice often worked to my advantage, even landing me the role of George Washington when our fourth-grade class visited some Colonial site where we were asked to reenact history. I remember sitting at the head of a table, nostrils slightly flaring and head tilting upward just so, bearing the weight of my invisible powdered wig. The following year at our elementary school's talent show, I had the moxie to break with tradition. Instead of performing in tandem with three or four other heavily sequined gals from tap class to a Debbie Gibson or Paula Abdul song, I worked with my teacher to choreograph my own breakout solo dance, with Louis Armstrong as my soundtrack. It didn't win me the popularity contest, but it was a ballsy move just the same.

I was rarely deterred by things like gender restrictions or talent requirements. If I wanted something, I simply worked hard for it and believed I was worth the effort. Case in point was my fairly respectable gymnastics career, which began at the age of three and ended around twelve, when I'd already reached a height of five feet seven—which was near giant status in gymnastics. I was so tall that it took a little extra "umph" to fling my body around the parallel bars, and the beam became mighty narrow from my Amazonian perch. And I wasn't a spindly five seven. I was muscular, powerful, and persistent—all of which were necessary for a sport that required you to tumble, stretch, spin, and tuck over and over and over again—no matter how many ankles you sprained or limbs you bruised. One day when I was eleven, a tiny teammate of mine couldn't take her eyes off the pit stains on my leotard. I remember her snide expression and her perfect bun as she asked the coach, "Why does Brooke sweat so much?" My face went white, and I suddenly felt self-conscious about something that had never occurred to me as shameful before. As I looked down at my ripped hands, covered in chalk and dried blood, my coach came to the rescue: "Because she works twice as hard as you," she said, without missing a beat.

That moment stands out to me to this day. I already knew I wouldn't be the next Mary Lou Retton, but that coach sustained my confidence. She confirmed my sense that sweat was a sign of strength, that trying hard—even if you weren't the best—really counted for something.

And try hard I did. Maybe it was the adventurous journalist already budding in me, but I went out for every sport and participated in nearly every extracurricular I could. I was lucky to have very encouraging parents, and I was also privileged enough to have parents who could financially swing all this. In addition to gymnastics, I danced (ballet, tap, and jazz!), played soccer and softball, and threw the shot put. I attended Space Camp, took art lessons, joined the swim team, and tried out for several school plays. Even though my singing voice can shatter glass, I somehow talked my way into singing Handel's *Messiah* one Christmas with my high school choir. I took guitar lessons and ran for student council way more times than is normal. I dedicated hours of my life over four years on the cheerleading squad (served as captain for one year) and enrolled in all the upper-level AP math, Spanish, English, and history classes at my high school. I didn't excel in all of these pursuits (I wrote out math jokes on my AP calculus exam, hoping whoever was grading it would chuckle and show me a little mercy), but damn if I didn't stretch myself as far as I could.

If you had asked me at any point in my childhood or teen years, I would have almost always described myself as confident. It wasn't until I entered the career stage of my life that my confidence began to falter. It isn't lost on me that my entrance into a very male-dominated field might have played a role in this. And even though I grew up in that huddle drought of the 1980s, '90s, and 2000s that

Kristin Goss described, I was often surrounded by a group of girls or leading a pack of them myself. After spending time with the supportive circle of judges in Houston that day, I realized that being surrounded by other females in childhood who both challenged and supported me might have had something to do with my inexplicable confidence in the early years of my life, which begged the question: *Is there a connection between huddling and self-assurance for girls?*

Plenty of women were several steps ahead of me in asking this question. When I began looking around, I found many all-girls organizations that had formed in the last handful of years. There are now dozens of huddles designed for girls who want to do things like build an app, play in a rock band, design a robot, run for public office, or climb a mountain. Groups like Girls Who Code, Black Girls Code, Girls on the Run, Girls Rock, Girls in Politics Initiative, Girlstart, and Inspiring Girls Expeditions are gathering young girls across the country with the express notion that they need to try male-dominated pursuits in boy-free zones—not only because we need more women in these fields, but also because *trying hard things within the safety of a huddle builds the confidence and grit girls need.* What I would go on to find out by looking at a number of all-girls organizations is that hardiness in girls has a direct correlation to huddle-ness. And across America, girls were huddling just as much as women—and the ramifications of this made me very hopeful for our future.

A SISTERHOOD OF STORYTELLING

In Santa Monica, California, a group of teenage filmmakers were huddling in yet another male-dominated industry at the AT&T

Hello Sunshine Filmmaker Lab for Girls. If you're a sixteen-year-old filmmaker, you might look to someone like Ava DuVernay, Patty Jenkins, or Reese Witherspoon to be your role model. However, you would not, by any stretch of the imagination, expect to get direct hands-on mentoring from any of these powerhouses. But every summer, a handful of teenage girls get exactly that from Reese Witherspoon and her partners at AT&T and Fresh Films. The Filmmaker Lab brings twenty sixteen- to nineteen-year-old girls to Los Angeles to create, produce, and shoot a half-hour documentary film during an eight-day crash course in all things filmmaking—with an emphasis on the technical elements required to learn the ropes. Participants are given access to all the sound, camera, and lighting equipment, taken on tours of film sets and production facilities, and also given the chance—as part of the documentary they are making—to interview a handful of successful women who work in Hollywood.

On a sunny Friday, the girls were gathered at a makeshift film set in the offices of Hello Sunshine, Witherspoon's media company. The room was positively buzzing with energy as the two dozen girls and their instructors prepared for their final shoot of the week: an interview with Reese Witherspoon herself. In one corner, a girl with a red flower in her hair held a boom mic, while an interviewer in ripped jeans and a black choker practiced her questions. In another corner, a girl was preparing a slate, while others looked into camera lenses, adjusted their headphones, and checked their clipboards. Everyone was wearing the Filmmaker Lab's uniform T-shirts, distinguishing themselves with their individual pops of blue lipstick or brightly colored Vans. They looked like regular teenage girls, except they just happened to be hefting around massive film cameras and expensive sound equipment.

One of the instructors hollered that Witherspoon would be

arriving on set in two minutes and a collective *Eeeeeeeeee* vibrated the entire room. This was followed by a final shuffling of papers and physical scrambling into place until utter silence befell the room a few seconds before Witherspoon entered. Her presence melted the frozen, wide-eyed girls. With her bright yellow sandals and the marigold sweater draped around her shoulders, Witherspoon was not unlike liquid sunshine, warming every molecule in the room. The first thing out of her mouth was a big juicy Southern "Hiiiii, y'all!!!!"

Everyone clapped, giggled, and cheered—and within a few beats, the girls got down to business. After a week of interviewing other top female directors, production designers, studio executives, writers, editors, and costume designers, the girls knew what they were doing. For the next hour and a half, they rotated through the various jobs on set in a highly organized manner so that each girl got the chance to work the various equipment for the sound, lighting, and cameras.

Instructor Amy Calderone-Blommer, from the partnering organization Fresh Films, provided a summary of the week leading up to this moment. "We trained them on all the camera, audio, and lighting basics super fast. We threw them in and taught them more than they could typically learn in a whole semester," she said. The program was designed, she explained, for high stakes. "For a majority of these girls who have never even touched any of this equipment, there is a real intimidation factor. So we provide a safe environment to break through that barrier."

"I was scared I was going to drop and break the super heavy camera when we went on location shoots," one of the participants, Emily Clegg, a sixteen-year-old from Fontana, California, remarked. Juliana Regueiro, a freshman in college from Miami who was the first to interview Witherspoon that day, expressed her disbelief at the entire situation: "I can't believe they trust me to do this stuff. I'm just . . . a girl." Her implication was not that her gender made her untrustworthy, but rather that she hadn't yet racked up the kind of credentials that would typically score someone this kind of high-stakes opportunity.

Regueiro alternated out of the interviewer's chair to allow another teen a go, and Witherspoon was asked to cold read a voice-over script the girls would be editing into the documentary. For instructional purposes, Witherspoon seemed to treat the task like any other actual assignment she'd be given on a film set. She looked over the paragraph briefly and asked the teenager for some direction: "Do you want me to read this with excitement? Surprise? Or maybe a more serious tone?" She didn't patronize the girl or push too hard. She merely spoke to her like one professional to another. The girl who had just rotated into the director position looked nervous to provide instructions to one of the most powerful women in Hollywood, but she answered the question firmly. A few seconds later when the girl/director had to yell "cut" and interrupt Witherspoon midsentence in order to correct her pronunciation of a tricky word, the tension suddenly became too much for her. She turned away to fan her face, trying not to cry while the entire room (including about thirty of her peers and teachers, plus one megawatt movie star) all looked directly at her.

Having worked in live television for twenty years (and being chastised by a few male producers and colleagues—even being threatened once: "Do. Not. Cry. On. The. Air!"), I admire the way the instructors handled this situation. The girl was clearly upset by all the eyeballs on her—not to mention she had Elle freaking Woods staring back at her. (Kindly of course, but it was still likely intimidating.) But no one swooped in and removed her from the room or attempted to "fix" the awkward moment. They simply afforded her space, without donning the kid gloves too quickly. She had been put in a challenging situation, and they believed she could handle it. Their high expectations were a vote of confidence. And there was power in the space they gave her to feel her feelings, pick herself up, and get back to work. After a moment, Calderone-Blommer calmly placed a hand on the girl's back and whispered a brief word of encouragement. She didn't get too personal or try to get in her face; she merely stood next to her, offering her silent strength, as if confidence could only be recovered by merely respecting the difficulty of this moment. The girl took a breath and collected herself, and everyone moved on.

This trial-by-fire-while-in-the-company-of-friends element of the Filmmaker Lab reminded me of the same prescription so many other huddles used to jump-start girls' confidence and success. There was an emphasis placed on finding aspirational role models, but even more was placed on *learning to trust yourself* to do daunting things—with the help of a supportive huddle of course.

Many of the girls confirmed that they felt an instant bond with one another upon arriving at the Filmmaker Lab, not only because they had already been talking to each other online for a few weeks thanks to a group text chain the instructors had set up, but also because there was an instantaneous feeling of solidarity in the work they were doing. Because the group was collaborating on the same final project, yet constantly rotating roles on set, it felt natural to assist one another. "Instead of trying to constantly critique each other"—something Regueiro said happens a lot in her mostly male film classes at college—"we helped build up each other's skills."

Throughout the course of the interview and post-interview chat with the girls, Witherspoon shared how vitally important her Hollywood huddle had been for her. She told them how she had found the courage to help form Time's Up—the movement to fight harassment, assault, and discrimination at work for women ("When Shonda Rhimes believes in you, it makes you feel confident"); and how huddling has been instrumental to some of her success ("there's a great sisterhood in this industry"). She recounted her biggest career risk to date ("starting my own company and investing my own money in it") and reminded the group why she formed the Filmmaker Lab in the first place. "I have no idea where you guys will go with the information you've learned here and the friendships you've made," she said earnestly. "But I hope this experience gives you a sense of belonging, because you deserve it." She began tearing up as she continued: "You stuck your neck out to be here and that is the first thing you have to do." Bravery, she implied, was half the battle.

Later, she mentioned why this bravery mattered. This industry, she explained, was greatly lacking stories like theirs. The majority of the girls were BIPOC, and they were all aspiring storytellers. Scratch that. They weren't *aspiring* storytellers. They were already *active* storytellers. Regueiro said she was rewriting a Zach Braff movie from a female perspective. Clegg explained she had just finished a play with a foster girl as the main character. Another teenager, named Sadie Staker—who went back home to Marion, Iowa, to work in her family's cornfield after leaving Santa Monica—talked about loving to write female superhero stories. They could all appreciate the fact that the high-pressure film sets and intimidating tech equipment they'd been struggling with all week were worth the challenge. These tools would help them craft the transformative stories they were destined to tell.

Calderone-Blommer, the instructor, had gotten her start as a sportscaster around the same time I started my career trucking around small towns chasing stories. She painted a picture of herself running along the sidelines of football fields with a forty-pound tripod on one shoulder and a thirty-five-pound Betacam on the other. "I see this equipment as power for these girls," she said, "because without a camera and without sound, they can't reach us with their voices." Her point was poignantly made in a room filled with teenage girls who want to be part of an industry that rarely represents them favorably on screen. According to a 2020 report by the Media, Diversity, & Social Change Initiative, of the top one hundred films in 2019 only seventeen depicted a young female lead or co-lead from an underrepresented racial/ethnic group.

Kelsey Conley, another Fresh Films instructor, provided a critical reminder of why this statistic matters: "Media shapes the way these girls develop, how they grow, and how they think about themselves. Bringing more of them into the media production industry allows *them* to shape that media." Calderone-Blommer agreed: "If you have a bunch of men behind the camera, that's the perspective from which every story will be told."

After the shoot wrapped, Witherspoon circulated among the girls for more than an hour, giving hugs, asking for selfies, and listening intently to learn more about each one of them. The message was loud and clear as she looked in the eyes of each girl: *Your story matters, and this huddle is going to help you tell it.*

BEYOND TEAM SPORTS

Clearly, the girls-only landscape in America today looks a lot different than it did when I was a kid. I don't recall any all-girls film-making experiences in the 1990s, not to mention any big-hearted Hollywood powerhouse women who were so directly putting cameras in the hands of girls to help them tell their own stories. In fact, beyond Girl Scouts, cheerleading, and dance classes, most women my age simply didn't have many all-girls activities available to them back then—particularly if they wanted a pursuit that wasn't gendered as traditionally "girly." Team sports, however, did offer some outlet for huddling, and the breadth of options was in the process of expanding during my childhood, thanks in part to the passage of Title IX in 1972 and its more earnest (yet still imperfect) enforcement later in the 1990s and 2000s. Because of this historic measure, teenage girls today participate in high school sports at a rate "greater than ten times what it was when Title IX was passed," and the trickle-down effect to elementary-aged girls' leagues these days is surely apparent to anyone who's ever driven by a soccer field on a Saturday morning.

Not surprisingly, the benefits of girls playing sports have been proven by studies. A 2014 report by EY Women Athletes Business Network and espnW found that a whopping 97 percent of C-suite women have played a sport at some point in their life, with 52 percent of them having played at the university level. Few would deny that when a girl plays a team sport, she is likely to develop leadership skills and confidence that she can draw on for the rest of her life.

Yet, despite these encouraging numbers, I've reported enough stories about young female athletes to know that sports aren't the be-all and end-all huddle for American girls. The USA Gymnastics sex abuse scandal, in which national team doctor Larry Nassar abused hundreds of girls and young women, was shocking not just because a large sports organization could inadvertently harbor horrific, long-term criminals like Nassar, but also because they can foster a culture of silence and obedience among their most disciplined and stellar athletes. These young teenage teammates who might have found comfort and solidarity with one another over their shared torment were instead isolated and remained quiet for years about their individual suffering.

The story of middle-distance running prodigy Mary Cain comes to mind as well. After Cain (who was known as the fastest teenage girl in America) was physically and emotionally traumatized by "the world's most famous track coach," Alberto Salazar, at the elite Nike Oregon Project facility, she developed RED-S syndrome—the result of a humiliating and grueling weight-loss program enforced by Salazar. Cain stopped menstruating for three years and ultimately broke five bones and experienced a mental downward spiral. She began cutting herself and feeling suicidal. Needless to say, her running performance suffered, and she left the program, telling the *New York Times* in late 2019 she was "caught in a system designed by and for men which destroys the bodies of young girls."

Though these are more extreme examples of women being harmed by their participation in sports, the underlying point is that intense athletic training alone does not instill confidence and leadership skills in the participant. But when female coaching and an intentional sisterhood ethos are specifically paired with the physical drills of the game, a team can become a protective and supportive huddle. At least that's what Theresa Miller explained as the mission of Girls on the Run, a female-led nonprofit she helps lead as chief engagement officer. Serving more than two hundred thousand girls a year in all fifty states, the program's goal is to "inspire girls to be joyful, healthy, and confident." Twice a week for ten weeks, girls between the ages of eight and thirteen get together to set personal goals, make friends, and ultimately complete a 5K. More than one hundred thousand volunteers (mostly women and older teenage girls) help administer the program, which teaches participants above all else the importance of *confidence and connection*—at a time in their lives when both of these things tend to plummet. The 97 percent female coaching staff is carefully trained with an evidence-based curriculum to get girls sprinting around a track—but the running is actually just a vehicle for something more important.

"We have stories of Girls on the Run participants who moved on to become cross country or track stars in their high schools. But that's not our goal," Miller said. Instead, the vision is to focus on self-awareness, friendship, and community, while conveying critical life skills such as realizing their personal potential, managing emotions, and making intentional decisions. "Our goal is to build positive inclusive environments for girls," Miller said. Some of the interactive lessons taught throughout the program are designed to help girls explore the characteristics of good friendships and ask themselves what qualities they personally can bring to a friendship. "Too often, girls and women can feel like we're supposed to be in competition with each other," Miller said, which is why the program encourages collaboration and friendship above all else. Girls who are on the cusp of entering their preteen and teen years need all the peer fortification they can get. Girls on the Run helps normalize leaning on female friends to a demographic that is too often presented with the Mean Girl stereotype in media.

The organization's website makes a bold claim: "Evidence shows Girls on the Run makes a stronger impact than both organized sports and physical education." Miller explained that although many girls do gather confidence and teamwork skills from their experiences in team sports, these skills are not intentionally baked into the coaching methodology, as they are in Girls on the Run. She backed this claim by sharing the results of an independent study, in which the organization was able to verify that 85 percent of girls in the program improved in the "five Cs": confidence, caring, competence, character, and connection. Because girls are statistically short on confidence (compared to boys in the same age group), this kind of "confidence curriculum" is a vital companion to a running program, not to mention what Miller said best: "When you feel really good about your own potential, you can more easily connect with others and appreciate their potential too." Gaining confidence can actually make a girl a better huddler—the kind who in turn helps boost the confidence of other girls around her.

This idea made me infinitely grateful for the oddly superhero-like confidence I often felt in childhood. Perhaps my self-assurance made it easier for me to bond with other girls, which in turn likely further increased my confidence. It's a feedback loop that makes sense to me when I look at the patterns throughout my life. The peaks and crashes in my confidence often correlate with the strength or weakness of my huddle.

THE CONFIDENCE THAT COMES FROM DOING HARD THINGS

Tammy Proctor grew up in the 1970s and '80s in Kansas City, Missouri, with brothers. But when she was old enough to attend Girl Scout camp in the summer, she found the absence of boys there to be surprisingly "wild and exciting." She recalled that camp activities were led by a staff of young women in their late teens and early twenties who wore braids in their hair and had names like Flower. It was inspiring for an eleven-year-old Proctor to witness their "excessively cool" version of female leadership. Perhaps most memorable for Proctor was the opportunity for the first time in her life to team up with other girls her age to play practical jokes. "The kind that wouldn't have happened had boys been around," Proctor recalled, "such as sending the girdle of an older and more, shall we say, robust troop leader up the flagpole." The owner of the ample corset took it well and everyone got a lot of laughs while it flapped in the breeze at flag drill the next morning. I'm imagining it was a liberating and bonding experience to defile a highly restrictive female undergarment together.

Back at school in the fall after camp, the young Proctor was truly changed by the outdoor adventures, physical challenges, and raucous pranks she enjoyed with her fellow Scouts. When her gym class segregated the boys and girls for what were deemed gender-appropriate activities—the boys were taken to run track while the girls had to stay inside and do gymnastics—Proctor promptly resisted. "I knew from camp and Girl Scouting that there was no reason I shouldn't be able to run track like the boys." Proctor ultimately won her argument and went on to run track and cross country in high school. She also grew up to become a historian who traced the history and impact of Girl Scouts in America—perhaps the oldest and largest girl huddle in our nation's history. She was quick to point out that many of America's most successful women (everyone from Sally Ride and Mae Jemison to Hillary Clinton and Michelle Obama) were once Girl Scouts. "There is a significant correlation, especially among female political leaders, which signifies if nothing else that Girl Scouts helps create a level of confidence that allows girls to embrace opportunities later in life," Proctor explained.

Although it might sometimes be dismissed as a domestic organization for little girls who sell cookies and sew cute badges onto their polite uniforms (*Troop Beverly Hills*, anyone?!), that's just one facet of this organization's long history—and perhaps indicative of the way girls-only organizations have historically been marginalized in our culture. The Girl Scouts founders intentionally designed their organization to be for girls only not because they were focusing on cookies and crafts, but because they believed "the single-sex environment allows girls to blossom in a way that they wouldn't otherwise," Proctor explained. "When they're not in the shadow of men or boys, they aren't afraid to speak, weather the outdoors, build fires, pitch tents . . ." or ultimately foster a deeper form of independence and confidence that might inspire them to ascend into leadership roles. The logic in getting girls into the outdoors is that if we constantly "protect" them from rugged and untidy settings, we are also denying them access to the confidence that comes from doing hard things.

More than one hundred years later, women are again building all-girl huddles based on the same premise. Reshma Saujani, the founder of Girls Who Code, explained in her TED Talk that girls are "taught to smile pretty, play it safe, get all As. Boys on the other hand are taught to play rough, swing high, crawl to the top of the monkey bars and then just jump off headfirst." Saujani diagnosed the error we're making in raising our girls to be perfect and our boys to be brave.

Her answer to this quandary was to teach girls a skill that specifically involves frequent failure. Coding, she found, was well suited for this, because it requires an inordinate amount of trial and error that could help habituate girls to mistake-making and risk-taking. Coding requires repetition, experimentation, and even collaboration—all things that are outside the comfort zone of many of today's girls, she explained. Saujani decided the all-girl environment was a necessary component: "We have to begin to undo the socialization of perfection, but we've got to combine it with building a sisterhood that lets girls know that they are not alone. When we teach girls to be brave and we have a supportive network cheering them on, they will build incredible things."

Katty Kay and Claire Shipman, authors of the books *The Confidence Code* and *The Confidence Code for Girls*, outline a similar recipe: "Girls desperately need more risk in their diets, and a bit of failure too." They explain that the process of *taking action*—and faltering along the way—is at the heart of becoming self-assured. This introduces a paradox that flies in the face of parenting trends in the last few decades that have tended to be heavy on encouragement, praise, and achievement, and lighter on letting kids get messy and embrace a growth mindset. Thoughts of my mother and my gymnastics coach come to mind here; they must have both known that my sweaty, oversized efforts were not going to ever lead to an actual mastery of the sport. But they probably also knew that my continued effort and constant failure, my repeated crash landings and bounce backs, and even my profuse perspiration—so embarrassingly noted by my perfect teammate—were actually more valuable than any projected outcome of becoming a bona fide athlete. Had I been prone to overthink my chances of becoming a professional gymnast, I might just have doubted my way out of that very valuable experience. Kay and Shipman explore the ways women and girls tend to ruminate more, often overthinking their way out of daunting tasks. But "confidence hinges on action," as they say, so there is inherent value in working toward a difficult goal, and letting them see you sweat along the way, even if you never end up succeeding. The action matters most.

This prescription to get out of our heads and take action is paired with a suggestion by Kay and Shipman to find friends to be your safety net throughout the process. In their handbook for girls, they explain to their young readers: "Friendships are pretty much the best place for testing and nurturing your confidence skills," while noting that "girls who have even one good friend don't produce as much stress hormone."

PERFECTION 2.0

When I met Karlie Kloss in her Manhattan office one rainy day to talk about her coding camp for girls called Kode with Klossy, it occurred to me that Kloss's childhood could be a prototype for the kind of ideal girlhood described by Saujani, Kay, and Shipman. Even though she might look perfect (which is actually in her job description, since she's a supermodel), Kloss is an excellent example of someone who isn't afraid to sacrifice some poise in order to try something difficult. Maybe because she grew up in a house with four girls—all very close in age—she never really thought of herself as inferior to boys. Like her father, she genuinely loved math and science, but she also took ballet, played softball and soccer, and was a member of the swim team. "I was always tall and athletic and could sometimes outpace the boys. I was the star wide receiver during recess football games in the sixth grade," she said with a laugh, sipping her iced coffee through a paper straw in a very large mason jar she'd brought in from home. As she delicately repositioned her six-foot-two body in the smallish chair, it was hard to imagine her going head to head with boys on a football field, particularly at that nearly adolescent age when showing your masculine side can have serious social repercussions.

Not long after the football phase of her life, she was discovered in a mall in St. Louis at the age of thirteen and began her modeling career. By fifteen she was traveling 60 percent of the time, attending her regular school the other 40 percent, and managing to stay on the honor roll along the way. She loved the close female friends and mentors she found in the modeling world, and her capacity for taking on challenges never waned. "I love trying new intimidating things. I ran a marathon for that reason," she told me.

At another point in the conversation she offhandedly shared she'd been recently trying to learn more about quantum physics, and coding held much of the same appeal when she initially decided to pursue it in her early twenties. "It was previously seen as this unattainable skill that only guys in hoodies in Silicon Valley knew how to do . . . but with me, if it's a boys' club, I want to be in it and I want to disrupt it."

Unfazed by intimidating barriers and gender conventions? Check. Unlikely to ruminate before diving in headfirst to something hard? Check. A true lifelong girl's girl? Check. It seemed like Kloss had already cracked the confidence code in her short twenty-seven-year lifetime. Next, coding became something she was eager to share with teenage girls; thus Kode with Klossy was born in 2015. Every summer, the camp brings thirteen- to eighteen-year-old girls together for a challenging semester's worth of learning stuffed into an action-packed two weeks. Girls can choose to attend a web development camp (where they learn to use HTML, CSS, and JavaScript) or a mobile app development camp (where they learn to use programing languages like Swift).

Regardless of how confident Kloss may have been as a teenage girl, she recognized that most teenage girls might be more likely to push themselves harder if the environment were an all-female one. "I think a lot of the girls in our program have experienced that feeling in a classroom full of boys when you're afraid to raise your hand and look stupid. I wanted to eliminate that dynamic," she explained. "And with all females, there's a lot of huddling that happens, because it's an intense program." Many applicants show up on their first day having never tried coding in their lives, knowing no one else in the room. By the end of the two weeks, they have collaborated closely and bonded with a few new friends to build an entire app or website.

At the Demo Day for the mobile app camp, some of the girls mentioned that not only had they never coded before, they didn't even have computer science classes offered at their schools. Just before their app demos were set to begin, they provided a lot of rapturous details about how fun camp had been. They were gathered in a brand-new conference room inside one of the sparkling new skyscrapers in Hudson Yards. After finishing lunch on the balcony with their parents, enjoying the view of lower Manhattan, the families filed in. Parents sat in the back with their iPhones out, ready to film, like it was graduation day, and the girls took their places in the front rows, nervously scanning the room. One of them whispered to her friend, "I'm actually kind of excited!" An African American woman stepped up to the podium to kick things off, introducing herself to the parents as one of the camp instructors. There was one male teacher—an affable white man who pulled a major dad move by sharing a video of the girls "dancing their jitters away" to Dance Dance Revolution during an icebreaking activity at camp. The girls collectively groaned and then two college-aged instructor's assistants (who were also Kode with Klossy alums) called up the first team of app developers to demo their creation for the audience.

Throughout the next few hours, the girls in teams of three stepped up to present a broad range of app designs—including a budgeting tool, a time management app for teens, a book recommendation program, and a system to help ESL parents navigate the infrastructure of their kids' schools. When some of the groups reached the podium, they delivered elaborate introductions where they announced the name of their app in unison. One girl in braces who introduced herself as being "only" thirteen years old was part of a team that designed an app to help connect students with disabilities. Another group introduced themselves one by one as a "proud Nigerian" and a "proud Latina" before detailing their app, designed to encourage teenagers to become more politically engaged. "You know how older generations like to blame you for problems they caused . . . like pollution?" said Esther Olojede, the fifteen-year-old girl who declared herself a "proud Nigerian." All the girls laughed while Olojede continued: "Well, our app, the Youth Vote, gives you inspiration to talk to adults and make decisions for yourself," she explained.

Later Olojede's partner, eighteen-year-old Destiny Ortiz, said her inspiration for creating the app was watching all her friends in the Bronx give up on engaging in politics after they were shocked by the outcome of the 2016 election. Most of the girls in the room were BIPOC, and many of them brought up the issue of inclusion and representation in their presentations. There was great camaraderie among all of them—not unlike the bonds I remember forming with summer camp friends after playing relentlessly long and terrifying rounds of Capture the Flag. But these girls weren't just roasting s'mores and singing *Kumbaya* around a fire. They were writing code and solving technical quandaries, not to mention their discussions were peppered with flashes of that Gen Z social-entrepreneurial hope and inspiration that made a Gen Xer like me feel like everything is going to be okay when they grow up and take the reins.

What struck me as even more valuable than the creative and political muscles these girls were flexing was the intentional acknowledgment of their collective failures. Each group was assigned to talk about the speedbumps they'd encountered throughout their app development, and it was clear these stumbling blocks served as bonding mechanisms as well as confidence builders. There was lots of grimacing and hair-pulling for dramatic effect as the girls recalled bugs and snags they couldn't overcome. "We were trying to run this so many times," explained Olojede of a final moment launching her app, "and it kept failing and failing. So when it finally worked, we were praising things that don't even exist, like every alien in the sky," she exclaimed. All the girls laughed in recognition. Another girl voiced what seemed like a universally learned truth: "We learned that if plan A doesn't work out, you better have a plan B, *and* a plan C. But there's always a way." They were also assigned to discuss what they'd like to add to their products in future versions, a requirement that seemed to underscore the iterative process of coding. The message seemed loud and clear: there is no shame in not delivering a perfect 1.0. There's always a 2.0, and a 3.0, and a 4.0.

A couple months later I learned that Ortiz and another Kode with Klossy scholar, Kyara Torres-Olivares, were spreading the love in their own communities. Ortiz started a Girls Who Code chapter at her high school in the Bronx because she wanted to help more BIPOC like herself gain exposure to coding in a comfortable, welcoming environment. "When you relate to each other, it's easier to work together and help each other solve challenges," she said. "I was drawn to Kode with Klossy because the all-girl environment made me feel more safe and comfortable." Ortiz also convinced one of her teachers to petition for a computer science class, something the school now has for the first time. Torres-Olivares, who is a first-generation Mexican American and the younger sister of Valeria, a Kode with Klossy alumnus and assistant instructor, told me about the club she and her sister founded, Code Equal, in Princeton, New Jersey, where they live. Together they run yearlong computer science classes (some of them bilingual) out of the public library for fourth to eighth graders who they believe deserve to learn code and to see representations of Latinas in tech. Using funds they won from a hackathon, the girls were working to turn Code

Equal into a formal nonprofit and expand their reach. "We wish we would have started younger, and we're really grateful for our experiences at Kode with Klossy, so we want to bring that into our own community," Torres-Olivares explained.

While one might consider programs like Code Equal as the clearest testament to the success of Kode with Klossy, the founder told me she defines the program's success instead by how much confidence it builds in the participants. Kloss's greatest hope for the program is that the graduates recognize their "infinite potential to build or be whatever it is they dream of." Working at Google or entering a STEM field matters far less to Kloss than the outcome that each girl walks away with confidence, new friendships, and the passion to pursue her goals.

•••

Until I took a deep dive into these girl huddles, I'd never considered the ways our bravery is constructed in childhood—and just how responsible some of my childhood female friends are for my own self-assurance. One of my most unlikely teenage huddles was my shot put and discus team.

We were a ragtag group of larger-than-average girls in an era when it wasn't so cool to have Michelle Obama arms. I was a cheerleader, mind you, who had no idea what a shot put was, but I was "discovered" by Mr. Neu in my Old Testament Bible class when my friend Jacquelyn lovingly (and painfully) punched me in the arm. "JQ" was a dirty blonde with some heft to her, always wearing corduroy pants, flannels, and Birkenstocks. Apparently, Mr. Neu saw some potential in our gruffness, and we were plucked from our regular lives and placed in the sweaty (read: mostly dudes) section of the gym where we were instructed to spot each other at the bench press. At first, I was mortified to let the cute baseball players see me in the weight room, but I secretly loved the Guns N' Roses blasting on the speakers and the way it felt to see myself getting stronger. Mia, the other member of our "throwers" huddle, was African American, a year older than me, and far more poised than I ever was. I looked up to her and followed any advice she offered.

I'd grown up hearing tales about my mom and her cheerleading days at Coral Gables High in Miami. I remember a photo of my dad years ago playing pick-up soccer. But let's just say that neither of my parents took me aside and said, "Brooke, you know what would really make us proud? If you bulked up and hurled an 8.8-pound rust-stinky metal ball during track season." During cheer season, my mother attended every football game, and helped me stay up late making glittery posters and trays of brownies for the football players. She didn't show quite the same enthusiasm for my shot put career. Who could blame her? I don't think anyone considered themselves a spectator of our sport.

But this was a huddle that was not fueled by any sort of external recognition. Unlike cheerleading, we weren't doing this for anyone but ourselves. Together, JQ, Mia, and I became stronger, lifting together and making space for ourselves in that weight room. We became obsessed with "hitting 30," which meant throwing the shot put beyond the 30-foot line—a milestone distance that earned you a spot at State. My coach Frank Keifer started calling me a "happy warrior" because I was so enthusiastic about achieving this goal. I even embraced "the grunt"—the loud, guttural, unladylike noise you make when you release the ball from the crook of your neck with as much force as possible. Thinking back now, it feels like a vital lesson for any girl to learn—that in order to improve the intensity of your effort, you must be willing to release a high-intensity roar for all to hear.

Mia, JQ, and I really cheered each other on—I'd never felt so supported—and we eventually all managed to hit 30 together. But even more important was the confidence and volume I figured out how to harness when I shamelessly grunted my way through that incredibly effective maneuver. I got loud and I fucking loved it.

four

FROM SCARCITY TO ABUNDANCE IN A MAN'S WORLD

The voice. My whole life, I've had it. It was a gift given to me by either God or my Granddaddy Fulton, a Presbyterian minister who had a tone so astonishing and authoritative that when he opened his mouth, the whole room went quiet. I remember being a little girl and listening to him preach in his church, or hearing his voice echo through our house when my mom would play tapes of his sermons. And much like my granddaddy, I had a voice that commanded attention. Even as a young girl, the volume, resonance, and depth of my vocals always stood out. I recently listened to an old cassette tape in which I interviewed a few of my fifth-grade girlfriends, asking the searing question of the time: *Would you rather marry Tom Cruise or Patrick Swayze?* Even though I was discussing the eye candy in *Top Gun* and *Dirty Dancing*, the gravitas in my ten-year-old voice suggested otherwise.

In college, some of my female classmates took courses to help them better control the diction and pitch of their speaking voices, but I was lucky to be genetically blessed with a voice so well suited for journalism. Everything else about the profession appealed to me as well: the fast pace, the front-row seat to history, the pressure of live television, the writing and storytelling, the travel, and the people. Being from Atlanta, I had been aware of the CNN head-quarters there my whole life, and my dream was to one day work there—or maybe the *Today* show. In my sophomore year of college, when my application to intern at CNN was denied, I immediately called the guy—named Willie—in charge and did some fast talking, ultimately convincing him my resume was worth another look.

Confidence had never been a problem for me—at least up to that point in my life. I wasn't afraid to be persuasive when I really wanted something, and thanks to my chat with Willie that day, I got to work for a whole summer on a (now-defunct) CNN show called *Travel Now*. The experience confirmed all my instincts: this was the path for me. During lunch breaks, I'd sneak into the big newsroom and press my face up against the glass wall of the set so I could watch the "big time" CNN anchors deliver the news live. There were more than a few accomplished women working around me, including the head of the unit, several travel correspondents, and the associate producer with whom I worked very closely every day. I felt fortunate to be joining an industry that appeared to place female journalists in the spotlight. As a little girl, I never imagined any sort of gender disparity existed within the profession. Between Jane Pauley, Diane Sawyer, Barbara Walters, Maria Shriver, and Katie Couric, I had been lucky to see a lot of representations of successful newswomen in my childhood. Not to mention, I grew up in the time of Oprah (Let's be real, I am actually still growing up in the time of Oprah). So I never hurt for female role models. This perhaps gave me a false sense of security about the male-dominated world I was entering when I transitioned from college to my first job.

When I graduated from the University of North Carolina at Chapel Hill in 2001, I said goodbye to my sorority sisters and watched them move to big cities, where I imagined they would live out a thrilling *Sex and the City* existence. Meanwhile, I worked local news jobs in smaller towns in Virginia and West Virginia, where the nearest Starbucks might be an hour away and most of my new friends were the dudes I worked with. I hung out with Luke, a tough-as-nails, blue-eyed reporter who had a lot of law enforcement sources, and I wanted to learn how he nurtured them. My second-best friend was Lonnie, a retired soap star turned weatherman who regaled me with outrageous stories from his past life in Hollywood. I spent most of my workdays mere inches from an older male photographer in the live truck. We'd drive around covering floods, drug busts, murders, coal mine explosions, and snowstorms and then sit in that truck for hours reviewing the footage, writing the story, and editing the final piece—all in some random parking lot. I was barely drinking age and I was constantly shooting the shit with older men, some of whom would comment on other women's anatomy or ask me too many questions about my sex life. Plenty of these photographers were also generous enough to take me under their wing and teach me how to write to their video, how to shoot compelling standups, and how to fight for my pitch in an editorial meeting. But I also had to put up with a certain amount of awkward sexual banter that I wanted no part of. This was nothing like my college journalism classes, where my female huddle had been strong.

Sometimes, I'd become friends with women at work, but soon enough one of us would get promoted and move on to the next TV station in another state. In one job in my mid-twenties, my shift was from 3:30 a.m. to 1:00 p.m. each day, so even if I'd had girlfriends, it wasn't like I could meet them after work for drinks and commiseration. One year over the holidays, I was so lonely, my mom sent my brother Ryan to me for Christmas. The three of us (me, Ryan, and my pug) bought dinner from the 7-Eleven and spent the night making White Russians and laughing about our childhood. Even when I moved in with my first serious boyfriend, a nurse named Bart, there was still something missing without a group of girlfriends to anchor me. Bart was lovely and selfless, moving from city to city with me because of my career, but our paths weren't exactly aligned. I remember being the ripe old age of twenty-four when he told me his definition of happiness was to get married, have kids, and live on a cul-de-sac. I think my exact response was, "Well, I want to work for CNN." And that was the beginning of the end of us. (All these years later, Bart is kind enough to stay in touch with me despite how indelicate my younger self was with him in what feels like a lifetime ago.)

Even worse than the loneliness or the lack of female colleagues were the times when my male colleagues would underestimate my abilities. Egos are always on display in this business—even at the local news level. Male coanchors with more tenure and clout would sometimes speak over me at meetings. When we were live on air and it was my turn to read from the teleprompter, they'd kick me under the anchor desk. Maybe they thought I was too stupid to understand the concept of the red light signal I was given, or perhaps they liked feeling as if they were directing all my cues. I tried not to let them rattle my composure, but it didn't take long to realize that some of the men I had looked up to were my equals, even if they didn't see it that way (and even if they didn't have to fool with hair and makeup nearly as long as I did).

It's no wonder I would sometimes find myself in a competition with a female colleague I hadn't even signed up for. We were all in a cutthroat environment where the men edged us out and there were very few prized positions for women—or at least that's the way we perceived it at the time. We had to be ambitious and focused on landing those few spots available to us, but the path to ascending was never very clear. Although I wasn't aware of the concept at the time, the "scarcity mentality" pervaded every aspect of those jobs. Contrary to what I'd thought as a little girl watching Jane, Diane, Maria, Katie, Barbara, and Oprah, few doors seemed to swing open to women in this profession. The culture wasn't exactly hospitable to women either. Sometimes I was made to feel (by condescending men) that I was more of a mouthpiece than a journalist, even though I had earned every ounce of my success the same way they did. Other women likely felt the same way—and somehow this pitted us against each other. Enter the flawed logic of the scarcity mentality: if you want success, you must sharpen your elbows, push other women out of the way, and hoard whatever you can get for yourself—female solidarity be damned. This approach could lead otherwise kind and generous women to become jealous and hostile toward each other. I now can recognize that this scarcity mentality is one more example of how white women in white-collar jobs were only perpetuating the problem. Instead of collaborating with each other to skirt the systems created and run by men, we tried to beat the men at their own game. The problem with this strategy is that it caused us to compete with each other and leave women of color behind. Instead of fighting for one another, and for those women who were even more marginalized than us, we fell prey to the logic of a very flawed system.

One of my first experiences with the destructive scarcity dynamic was during my first job in Virginia when I'd scored an assignment to be the beat reporter for Albemarle County, which was the biggest county in our TV market. Translation: this was a BFD. Taking on this role meant that anything that happened in the massive area surrounding Charlottesville—crimes, court cases, property disputes, waterskiing squirrels—would be my responsibility. I eagerly took my first lunch with the head of Albemarle County, only to be called into my boss's office the very next day and informed that I wouldn't be taking over this beat after all. My bosses had decided to give it to another female colleague, who I'll call Amanda. The rumor was that Amanda had gone behind my back to our bosses and convinced them the spot should be hers since she'd had her eye on it and had six months more tenure than I did. I was blindsided and furious. Why hadn't she come to me first? We could have worked something out—maybe split the beat as partners or rotated on and off.

I can't think of a time in my entire career when I intentionally railroaded another woman like that, but I can also understand why Amanda did what she did. She was a talented young woman who deserved a good spot, and her method was right out of the Scarcity Playbook. Not that I sanction that kind of behavior, but it was an understandable response to the environment in which we were both struggling to be seen and heard.

I was seeking a dynamic that was quite the opposite of scarcity. I was looking for fellow women with an abundance mentality. An abundance mindset rejects the notion that there are only so many seats at the table for women in a male-dominated industry. Instead of elbowing your coworkers out of the way, you open your arms, maybe even actually huddle with one another. You pull up as many folding chairs as you need or build a bigger table. You create more resources and options for the benefit of everyone in the huddle. When I entered the workplace, abundance mentality wasn't exactly circulating among women. There weren't even that many women in the industry to begin with.

Today, in an era when women are leaning on each other more intentionally and frequently, Madeleine Albright's famous quote ("There's a special place in hell for women who don't support other women") comes to mind. But in those days, ladies who huddle were outliers, and when I found them, they became my lifeboats. I felt so privileged when Beth Duffy, Linda Thomas, and Stephanie Cornwell—anchors who had more than a decade of experience— would periodically allow my twenty-two-year-old self to tag along and drink wine with them while I was in my first TV job in Charlottesville. I admired them deeply, and they offered incredible advice: how to handle newsroom egos and perverts; how to pitch yourself to the boss as a fill-in anchor; why it matters to have a confident boyfriend who isn't threatened by female ambition; and even how old is too old to start trying to have babies. Stephanie took me under her wing and helped nurture my loud-and-proud aspirations. This was a pivotal relationship for me, showing me that mentorship and community among women in the workplace are possible and powerful.

As it turns out, this practice was actually beneficial to us professionally. The *Harvard Business Review* published a study confirming that women benefit uniquely from leaning on each other at work. According to the 2019 study, "In order to achieve the executive positions with the highest levels of authority and pay," extremely qualified women must also have "an inner circle of close female contacts." Because we face several "cultural and political hurdles" in the workplace (e.g., we aren't admitted entrance to the boys' club), our fellow female contacts and "work wives" often serve as crucial resources to us. We can provide each other with critical inside information that elevates our job searches, interview opportunities, and salary negotiations. One of my proud moments in recent years was telling a female colleague my salary—a simple action I could take to arm her with information as she entered into pay negotiations with her boss. Later, I discussed the decision on my show, telling my viewers that even though it can feel taboo or uncomfortable to talk about money, revealing our "worth" can be revolutionary. I wanted women watching my show that day to know how easily we women can become a powerful resource to each other—simply by being real with each other.

Women with the abundance mentality don't just huddle, they also intentionally seed each other's success through a concept known as sponsorship. According to another study, by Catalyst, a global nonprofit dedicated to women in the workplace, when women use their influence to catapult other women to success, this sponsorship can have an incredible impact on closing the advancement gap that persists between women and men on the job. Although many of us grew up seeking the counsel of mentors, the Catalyst study says mentorship isn't enough: "Sponsors go beyond the traditional social, emotional, and personal growth development provided by many mentors." Instead, "sponsorship is focused on advancement and predicated on power." The priority of a sponsorship is for a woman in a leadership position to help fast-track other women to join her at the top, where power is more readily replicated and dispersed. A sponsor can change the dynamics of a workplace by "advocating for, protecting, and fighting for the career advancement" of women lower down the ladder.

Stacey Abrams personifies this concept. Long before she became known as perhaps the nation's leading voice on voting rights; years before she became the first African American woman gubernatorial nominee in the nation; and well before she made history as the first woman to lead either party in the Georgia House of Representatives, she was a twenty-nine-year-old tax attorney and entrepreneur who was appointed deputy city attorney for my hometown, Atlanta. As someone who grew up "genteel poor" (as she says her mother called it) in Gulfport, Mississippi, Abrams says the deputy city attorney job was her first real access to power.

And what did she do with this power? She immediately began to share it.

When she recognized that the group of talented secretaries she relied on daily were ineligible for raises because their job title didn't technically allow them to move up a pay grade, Abrams got creative. "They were mostly Black women who had worked there for fifteen years. They knew the law and could tell me the legislative history of any bill, but they couldn't afford to go to law school to earn the paralegal title the city required to promote them," Abrams told me. So she promptly petitioned the city to create a paralegal training program that would elevate the women's education, titles, *and* salaries. Even though her newfound power was still relatively fragile, Abrams did not hesitate to lift while she climbed.

It is not surprising that later in her career, when she had a national platform and the name-recognition to raise significant funding for her decade-long effort to strengthen the Democratic Party and end voter suppression in Georgia, she continued to share her power. "While women often huddle for collective communal power, we rarely have the collective financial resources to accelerate that communal power, to strengthen it, to turn it into the fierce engines that we need," she said. So in the years leading up to the 2020 election, when Abrams led her landmark efforts to register voters and flip the state of Georgia, she gave away a quarter of the funds she had raised for her own organizations to other groups across the state that were also largely run by women and doing similar work. Abrams told me she wanted to make sure she didn't "hoard" her access and power because then, she said, "you become just as problematic as those who were against you."

Another woman who refused to hoard her power, the renowned producer and director Ava DuVernay, told me a similar story on the New Orleans set of her award-winning TV series *Queen Sugar*.

DuVernay had thrown down her ladder so gloriously that "sponsorship" feels too weak a word. For all twenty-six episodes of the first two seasons of her series, DuVernay chose to hire only female directors—a majority of whom were women of color. Moreover, most of these directors were from the indie-film world and DuVernay was entrusting them with their first shot at the more commercial and lucrative TV scene. In the time since we spoke, DuVernay has shot two more seasons of *Queen Sugar*, and has continued to exclusively hire female directors—something only a few other shows on television can boast.

When I asked DuVernay why she chose to use her show as a mechanism for empowering other women when she could have kept the spotlight for herself, she answered with a story about attending a birthday party for a white male friend in the industry. In this room full of her professional peers, DuVernay was the only Black person and the only female. "I don't want to be at the party by myself!" she answered with a laugh. Instead of seeing the one female seat of power as her own exclusive prize, DuVernay saw it as a lonely throne. "How does this ever change if I don't open the door for my friends?" she asked. "Let's bring them into the party too!"

DuVernay was excited to tell me that she had already made headway in opening the gates to women in her profession, having helped circulate an entire new class of female directors into the television industry. Some of the women she'd hired for *Queen Sugar* had already gone on to direct episodes of other top television shows such as *American Crime Story, Greenleaf, Dear White People, Transparent, Scandal,* and *Grey's Anatomy.* Her decision to sponsor these women had already paid off. She reminded me that because *Queen Sugar* is produced by OWN, Oprah had been responsible for giving her the green light to hire these less experienced directors in the first place. It was an unconventional choice that may not have gotten approval at other networks, but because a woman like Oprah threw down her ladder to DuVernay, many other women benefited. And today, those *Queen Sugar* directors are infusing television with more female perspectives that touch the lives of many viewers. It is said that power can corrupt, but in the right hands, it seems that it can also cascade quite beautifully.

Although a high-level sponsorship is certainly the clearest path to elevation for a woman in just about any field, my career is proof that success doesn't necessarily require a sponsor as omnipotent as Oprah. Sometimes a coworker with a little seniority or an encouraging, levelheaded member of your huddle can empower you in very meaningful ways too. When I graduated from local news, I was still wandering through the scarcity desert. So intent on pursuing my dream to work for CNN, I moved back in with my parents in Atlanta and worked as a freelancer to get my foot in the door. I became scrappier and lonelier than ever. Other aspiring female anchors could be particularly competitive, but fortunately I was the beneficiary of some sponsorships that propelled my career forward in powerful ways. Mary Lynn Ryan, a Southeast bureau chief, opened up her Rolodex, gave me names of all the Atlanta-based executive producers, and coached me on how to sit in front of them and ask to be on their shows. She noticed the pathetic little Post-it note I'd devised as a makeshift nameplate for myself outside the freelancer office I was squatting in at the time and had her assistant replace it with a legitimate name plaque. This was abundance mentality in action—a gesture that inspired confidence and gratitude in me, making me want to work harder and make her proud, and one day pay it forward to another young woman.

And then there was Patricia DiCarlo, who was (and still is) like a big sister to me. (She was even there when I got my wedding dress!) She had left the Oprah Winfrey show and became Wolf Blitzer's *Situation Room* executive producer in Washington, D.C., and stuck her neck out to help me get my first story and live shot on Wolf's show. I was terrified but ready, and she knew it. I can still remember her words seconds before I went live on air, smiling triumphantly as she said, "Love you, Brooke—don't fuck it up!" She knew I responded well to that kind of pressure, and she was right. That one successful live shot on Wolf's show created a domino effect in my career, leading to many other opportunities on other shows.

Thanks to a combination of hustling and huddling, I began to make a name for myself as a valuable freelancer at CNN. All I wanted was a full-fledged correspondent job, but in the meantime, I became like a Swiss Army knife to the network. One day I could be thrown into a story about gun laws changing in Georgia, and the next day I'd anchor international news at 2 a.m. And yet, I still felt as though I was standing on shaky ground. I was thirty-one and wondering if CNN was ever going to offer me a full-time position. I remember an older female anchor I'll call Leanne taking the time to encourage me and lift my spirits. She'd take me out for beers, teach me to navigate the bosses, and root for me when I'd fill in for her on her show. Around the same time, in what would become my final months as a freelancer, CNN anchor Rick Sanchez and his executive producer Angie Massie took a liking to me. Their show (called *Rick's List*) was a big hit at the time, and I had served as a correspondent in the studio a few times a week. But then Rick and Angie asked "Little Brookie" (as Rick sometimes called me on the air) to become a special correspondent and appear on the air with them every day. It was a dream. After nearly two years of freelancing, I finally felt like I had steady work. I was finally able to afford to move out of my parents' place. Even better, I was work-

ing with a well-known anchor (Rick) and a female executive producer (Angie), both of whom really believed in me.

Like many big names on cable news at the time (in 2010), Rick
was a polarizing guy, but he loved his job and was good to his staff.
What did he see in me? Maybe someone who wasn't threatening to
him. Maybe a talented underdog he could help. A few months into
this gig, the show's set got a slick upgrade, with fancy lights and
lots of modern glass. Angie and Rick took the show's format up a
notch, in particular by integrating Twitter in its nascent stages, but
also in the way they shot the show. They added a lot of movement
and began filming me *as* I was walking onto set, creating a more
dynamic visual. And though it might sound funny now, it was
unique to a news show at the time. Of course, the fact that I was
young and wore a lot of heels and skirts probably didn't hurt either.
I wasn't thrilled to read creepy compliments about my legs on message boards or find weird tribute videos about my appearance on
YouTube, but I rationalized that the unwanted attention was just
something I had to endure in exchange for this prime spot on a hit
show. At that point in my career, I was just so damn grateful to
work five days a week that I didn't let it bother me. To be honest,
they could have said, "Brooke, we're getting ropes installed in the
ceiling and were going to spin you in upside down" and I probably would have replied, "Great, how high do we want the ropes?!"
CNN had been my greatest aspiration since I was a child. This
show was finally my home.

And then, just as I was beginning to adapt to all this, Rick got in
a very public argument with *Daily Show* anchor Jon Stewart, and
while appearing on a live radio show, Rick made some anti-Semitic
comments and bashed CNN. I was devastated that these kinds of
remarks were made by a man whose help and support I had accepted. To his credit, Rick apologized publicly several times over,

including on *Good Morning America* and to the Anti-Defamation League, saying, "I deeply, sincerely and unequivocally apologize for the hurt that I have caused." But CNN fired him, and we all had to adapt. In the weeks that followed, I was asked to keep his seat warm, and some of the writers and producers in the newsroom were saying to me, "Brooke, try to see this as an opportunity." However, I suspected the CNN bosses thought of me as a temporary stopgap until they could find a more seasoned anchor for those two plum afternoon hours. I confirmed this to be true years later when a CNN executive (who is no longer with the company) ran into me at an event and slapped me on the back the way men sometimes do when they are about to put their foot in their mouth and said, "Well, Brooke, didn't think you had it in ya! I told them you weren't ready for Rick's spot! But look at you now!"

Filling in for Rick was the biggest challenge of my career at the time. And instead of having a supportive network of friends to turn to in that moment, I faced the reality that several coworkers were angling for my job and weren't at all happy it had been given to me. "Leanne," the more seasoned CNN anchor who had previously taken me under her wing, suddenly stopped talking to me. It was crushing. I felt so much pressure to prove I deserved my job, all while trying to maintain the focus required to actually pull it off. It was a pivotal moment in my career—a test of my strength and grit. But I didn't climb that mountain all by myself. I was fortunate that one woman was there to give me the foothold I needed to rise to the challenge.

Angie, the executive producer, was my rock. She had just had her whole world shaken to the core when she'd lost Rick, her working partner. Everything was in flux with the program she had helped create—it couldn't have been easy for her—but she still made it very clear to me that she *wanted* me to succeed. She implemented the sudden and dramatic change to her show with her rare mix of strength, smarts, depth, softness, and feels. In a time when she could have left me to fend for myself, she instead worked to recalibrate that entire program to actually play to my strengths. She nurtured my voice and *gave me a platform to use it.* This was the biggest turning point in my career, and I owe so much to her for the way she helped me through those early moments. Together, Angie and I created something special. Not only did I not fuck it up, but I kept Rick's ratings right where he left them, and within a few months, CNN made the job mine permanently. I became one of the youngest people—male or female—to ever anchor a show on CNN.

Reflecting back on the first decade of my now twenty-year career, I wonder how my trajectory might have been different had I graduated from college in 2021 instead of 2001. Women entering the workforce today—particularly BIWOC and economically disadvantaged women—still don't have it easy, of course, but if you are reading this as a recent college graduate and you're looking for some reason to be optimistic, hear this: women today—especially those in male-dominated industries—are collectively stepping up to the plate for each other more and more. Hard work and talent matters just as much as it ever did, but I see more and more women huddling with other talented and determined women, in recognition of the fact that a rising tide really does lift all boats. I've seen enough of the "every woman for herself" mentality in my career that I now bend over backward to offer advice and support to younger women. I take calls from talented correspondents who want to learn how to become anchors; I let people sit near me on the desk during breaking news; I mentor younger journalists in local news, watching their reels, giving them feedback. I see many other women in my industry doing the same thing. Not to mention, we all support each other in moments when subtle and not-so-subtle sexism and racism in the workplace need to be called out. We are feeling more emboldened to lean on each other. If there's one thing I've learned from the Stephanies, Patricias, and Angies in my life it's this: fuck sharp elbows. Women are pulling up more chairs at our ever-expanding table and learning that abundance begets abundance.

BRINGING MORE COOKS INTO THE KITCHEN

Anytime I consider the difficult aspects of working in a male-dominated environment, I think about Chef Dominique Crenn—or any woman who works in the swashbuckling, macho culture of the culinary industry. I'm not saying all male chefs are jerks—Anthony Bourdain once took me under his wing and gave me wonderful career advice—and I've savored the genius creations of so many wonderful male chefs, but there's no denying, the food industry has been less than empowering for women.

Chef Crenn of San Francisco's Atelier Crenn is the only woman in America to receive a third Michelin star, but it hasn't been an easy road. She bears several battle wounds to prove it. As we sat in the richly furnished lobby of the Lower East Side hotel where she was staying, having tea by a cozy fireplace, she pulled back the cuff of her denim jacket, revealing tattoos on her forearm and a scar on her hand. In this room full of velvet high-backed chairs and dark mahogany wood, Chef Crenn provided a stunning visual contradiction, looking more punk rock than high tea from her perch on the antique sofa. Dressed in black and denim, she wore high tops on her feet and a scarf/beanie combo on her head—her signature dark coif having recently been affected by chemotherapy treatments for her breast cancer. She emanated strength and feminine intensity as she ran her finger over the scar, telling me in her thick French accent about the restaurant job where she stood shucking oysters at the bar, chatting with guests. When she sliced a deep gash into her hand and began to openly bleed, the head chef's terse response was, "Don't be a pussy. Pour some tequila on it and get back to work." There was another time at another restaurant involving hot oil and a sizable burn. That chef's response: "Put some butter on it and get back to work."

When she went on to detail the abusive behavior (physical, mental, and sexual) rampant in much of the food industry, these hot oil and oyster blade gore scenes seemed mild. But if you've seen any cooking shows or visited the kitchens of any of the world's beloved restaurants, you know her stories are not unusual. Ironically, the art of feeding other humans often happens in adrenaline-filled, ego-ridden chambers of manliness. A lot of yelling and humiliation tends to go on. It seems incongruous that the act of nourishing and delighting people's senses has traditionally involved so much male rage, but ask any female chef and she'll confirm this for you. As you might imagine, there's not a lot of female sponsorship going on in this industry.

But Crenn has created her own version of sponsorship and abundance mentality at Atelier Crenn, not only by maintaining a female majority staff—in both the back and front of the house—but also by fostering what she calls a "togetherness" culture. She has intentionally rejected the "every man for himself" vibe you find in most restaurant cultures and even rearranged her kitchen based on this concept. Staff are still divided into stations based on their specific role in the food preparation process, but the production is not as heavily siloed as it would be in a typical kitchen. "If someone spills or burns something at their station, we help each other out," she told me, recalling the ways many lower-level staff elsewhere are expected to stay quiet, keep their heads down, and fend for themselves. The togetherness culture normalizes the simple practices of greeting each other upon entering the kitchen and bidding farewell before leaving. It discourages angry yelling—all things that might seem like they should be a given, but are exceedingly rare in the restaurant business.

Outside the walls of her own kitchen, however, Crenn has raised her voice, but only in the name of helping other women in the industry. Crenn is concerned with the fact that it is statistically easier to become a female (cisgender, heterosexual, white) CEO in America than a head chef—which is particularly worrisome because more than half the culinary school graduates in America are women. She told me that less than 7 percent of prominent U.S. restaurants are female owned. While there might be myriad reasons for this disparity, Crenn has done her best to call out the culinary culture as partially responsible for not allowing women to thrive. When she won the highly influential San Pellegrino Award for World's Best Female Chef in 2016, she questioned the logic of segregating awards by gender, and one year later, she publicly demanded San Pellegrino improve their female representation when the list of jurors for the prestigious World's Best Young Chefs included not a single woman.

As she continues to be one of the most celebrated chefs in the world, she has also used her clout to make room for other up-and-coming female chefs, treating them as stars instead of would-be competitors. In 2018, she created a huddle by launching her first of two Women of Food events to feature trailblazing female cooks who are categorically ignored in the industry. "I got sick and tired of every editor of every food magazine telling me there aren't enough women in the industry for them to feature," she said. Instead of calling out the media further, she simply made it easy for them to do their jobs by inviting them to join her and a bevy of female chefs to dine at her world-renowned restaurant. The sold-out events included brilliant and creative collaborations, which showcased the groups' talents and ultimately amplified their names in the press.

Like DuVernay selecting talented indie filmmakers to direct episodes of her television series, Crenn wanted to share the spotlight she's enjoyed almost singularly as a woman in her industry. Perhaps she too didn't enjoy being at the party alone. And like DuVernay, she had unconventional notions about the gatekeeping that goes on in selective male-majority fields like her own. "When I hire someone at my restaurant," she said thoughtfully, "I don't care about their resume. I want to know who they are and what they think about themselves, humanity, and the planet." She smiled in the way that adventurous rebels smile while they're in the process of upending a system. Powerful women, she explained, should push back against the tyranny of prerequisites that often prevent them from ascending in male-dominated industries. This is not to say that she favors unskilled or unqualified women, but rather that she seeks to shine a light on those with potential who have been denied access from the traditional credentialing mechanisms that have helped men get through the door for decades.

I had a similar conversation about this gatekeeper-busting with Leanne Pittsford, founder of Lesbians Who Tech, who told me, "We have to shift the paradigm from who's the most 'qualified' person for the job [on paper] to think about what *traits* are going to be most connected to the *success* of the job." Pittsford works in another one of the most male-dominated fields in America—the tech industry, where only 2.4 percent of companies elect a woman to their top position. In response to this (and because she was seeking some lesbian community herself), Pittsford founded Lesbians Who Tech, an organization for LGBTQ women as well as nonbinary and trans individuals who want to improve their representation and community within the tech industry. "We are not going to live our best version of the world unless women, people of color, and LGBTQ people have more power," she told me. Shifting our traditional notions of prerequisites might be one key to changing things for the better. She gave the example of assembling a corporate board, where the prerequisite for joining is often previous membership on another corporate board. "If we only considered candidates who had former board experience, our list would almost always be white, straight cis men, with maybe one gay man out of a thousand." But by shepherding people with demonstrated potential vs. exact prerequisites, she explained, she can create a board that better represents the balance of power we all want to create in the world. "It's not about who has *had* the most power *in the past*. It's about who is the most creative, the most intelligent, the most driven, and the most collaborative *right now*," she explained.

While it might seem unconventional to cast a wider net in the hiring process, to reconsider the dominating premise of a resume, to take a chance on rising talent, it also feels like yet another component of the abundance mentality. Another way powerful women can sponsor and uplift their junior counterparts. Crenn and Pittsford also seemed to be identifying the bonus that comes with abundance mentality: when you welcome in people with a wider range of skills and perspectives, it ultimately boosts your organization's creativity and problem-solving prowess. I thought about that moment in college when I'd taken a chance on myself and urged Willie at CNN to reconsider my resume for that fateful internship. It got my foot in the door, but it was a messy move—not at all sanctioned by anyone above me. How inspiring, on the other hand, to see so many female trailblazers now taking steps to formalize this notion—to unbolt the locks on those heavy doors and let more women inside.

A CONGRESS OF WOMEN

After talking to women in the restaurant industry, the film industry, and the tech industry, I knew my tour of male-dominated professions wouldn't be complete without a visit to Capitol Hill. It was early April—the spring after the 2018 midterm elections when that new and unprecedentedly large crop of women had been elected. The weather was unseasonably warm that week, and my Lyft driver made small talk about the fact that it was the peak time to see cherry blossoms. Since I'd been working in a studio all day, I hadn't managed to see any of those pink buds yet, and now it was already too dark. I looked out the window to see the surreal scene that is the National Mall at night. Instead of feeling like you're at the epicenter of American politics, you feel like you're on an abandoned movie set. No one's around, you're surrounded by several stark neoclassical structures, and everything is alarmingly well lit.

I had arranged to meet with a group of newly elected congresswomen: Elaine Luria, Abigail Spanberger, Chrissy Houlahan, Elissa Slotkin, and Mikie Sherrill. They were far outnumbered by the men in Congress, but this huddle had years of practice being the minority gender because they'd all had former careers in the military or CIA. Their schedules that week were so tight that we'd had to resort to meeting at 9:30 p.m. in one of their offices after they'd spent a full day in session. I was nervous and excited about this interview. I've always revered members of the armed forces as if they are superheroes. One of my closest friends from childhood, Rashad (otherwise known now as Commander Bobby Jones), is a commander in the U.S. Navy and has served on various ships including guided-missile cruisers in the Middle East. I've seen close up the sacrifice, the loyalty to country, and the enduring strength of mind and body that is required of him and his fellow servicemen and women. I was particularly in awe of the courage and fortitude it must take to be a female in national security or the armed forces—both of which are male dominated.

The car pulled up to the entrance, and I climbed the stairs under massive white columns bathed in white light. Once inside, I passed through the metal detectors in the stately building, where I was met by a young staffer who led me back to a cozy office. The five congresswomen were all settled around a coffee table, scooping ice cream into little paper cups, laughing and talking over one another. My nerves melted away immediately.

Congresswoman Slotkin opened a bottle of red wine and everyone dipped into their ice cream as they chatted about who had been recruited to the congressional women's softball team that would meet the next morning for practice at 7 a.m. "I don't have that on my calendar!" said Spanberger, whose effusive nature didn't instantly scream CIA operative. "I think they must have seen me throw that first pitch at the Little League game and were like, 'We don't want her,'" she said with a laugh.

"Well, I got caught in the elevator with some of the team and they were really putting the pressure on," said Sherrill, a former Navy helicopter pilot and federal prosecutor with a New Jersey no-nonsense air about her.

"Debbie Wasserman Schultz is hard-core!" said Houlahan, the former Air Force officer from Pennsylvania whom I introduced earlier as the woman who decided to run for Congress after attending the Women's March.

If these women had been plagued by the scarcity mentality all their lives, you wouldn't know it now. Their group dynamic made me think of sisters who tease each other a lot, or maybe athletes on the same team who know how to cut loose and have fun when the game is over. They were dressed like picture-perfect politicians having come from a long day in session, but they were lighthearted with each other, down to earth, even dropping some f-bombs into the conversation.

I got the sense that there was a lot of mutual relief and exhaling going on when they were in one another's presence. They'd all spent their lives traveling for work—whether that was a military deployment, a CIA mission, or now the grueling commuting situation required of members of Congress. Ranging in age from forty to fifty-two, three of them—Luria, Spanberger, and Sherrill—are mothers of young children, while Houlahan and Slotkin have grown children and stepchildren. I'd heard talk of Spanberger's three young daughters hanging around her office during spring break and of Girl Scout cookies being sold around the building. In the Venn diagram that represents the various quadrants of their lives, they all share a unique overlap not many of us can boast: mother, veteran, *and* congresswoman. I'm guessing that they hadn't always had opportunities to huddle like this in the past, so when they did find a group of like-minded, accomplished women, they wasted no time on formalities.

I kicked off the conversation by asking about their time huddling in their respective military and CIA careers. There was a brief awkward silence, then Luria broke it to me gently: "To be completely honest, I don't think women in the military bond very well." Luria should know, given she was the first female American sailor to spend her entire twenty-year military career on combat ships. Her kindly delivered truth bomb deflated the room, and then everyone busted out laughing. There were a lot of jokes following about how the military isn't exactly full of group hugs and nourishing female mentorships.

"I came into the CIA right at the tail end of the generation where senior women automatically hated every other female who served around her," said Slotkin, who hails from Michigan and decided to serve her country after experiencing 9/11 as a graduate student in New York. She has since served three tours in Iraq. "When I was a baby CIA analyst, serving on war zone accounts, anytime I walked into the room, there was always one senior woman and she always hated me."

"Yeah," Spanberger chimed in, "and not only does she hate you, but she's going to tell you all the reasons why your marriage will fail. I had women I thought were mentors tell me that if I wanted to have kids, I should probably become a report officer instead."

"I always preferred being the most senior woman in the command, because otherwise it was such a pain," recalled Sherrill on the difficulty of navigating this tricky dynamic. Coming from a woman who is literally trained to find her way out of a submerged helicopter while blindfolded, it was a meaningful statement.

Houlahan, who was the oldest of the group at fifty-two, concurred that her years in the Air Force were also bereft of female support from above. She remembered seeing her husband working his way up the ladder in the corporate world and envying the formal mentorship structure he enjoyed. "That never existed in my life—not in any of the sectors I worked in," she explained.

Slotkin was quick to qualify her statement about senior CIA women by explaining that the incoming generation is much different. "In my lifetime, I've watched that generation of women who hated each other retire, and now there are more females in national security leadership roles, and therefore a more positive environment for all." Like women in so many other industries who made it to "the top" in the huddle drought years, the colleagues Slotkin described were likely made to feel like outliers for achieving their high ranks, which in turn may have made them prone to being overly protective of their prized seats at the table. The scarcity mentality doesn't originate from some innate catfighting penchant among women; it is instead symptomatic of male-dominated environments in which white women in particular take the bait to compete for very slim pickings. It's hard to use your seniority to sponsor another woman when you're busy fighting for crumbs yourself.

And yet despite a lack of mentorship or sponsorship experiences, everyone in the group—or any veterans I've met for that matter—credited the military for perfecting their ability to work as a team. So despite the scarcity mentality they'd endured, they were also perhaps better huddlers than many of their civilian counterparts. That level of teamwork is required in Congress but can sometimes feel like a bit of a lost art in this era of political renegades and establishment egos. In one of her campaign ads, Luria showed herself at work aboard a ship, saying, "When *this* is your office, your only option is to work together . . . Congress could learn a thing or two at sea." It's an unusual message to run on, particularly for a first-time candidate trying to credential herself to voters. America is more accustomed to politicians touting their accomplishments, but it's unusual for them to boast about their ability to be one among many.

Along these same lines, Slotkin explained the not-so-subtle culture shock she experienced in transitioning from the Pentagon to Congress. Although both jobs are oriented around service to her country, only one of them has involved daily meetings where colleagues constantly pontificate about their own qualifications and contacts. "At the Pentagon, I literally can't remember a single time when someone talked about themselves and how great they were. It would be grounds for being excused from the mission. But it happens at almost every meeting I attend in Congress," she said dryly. This ability to keep the team central to all operations may have been responsible for their wide appeal to voters. "In a time when so many issues are instantly politicized and when people of different political persuasions have trouble talking to one another, I think our mission-first focus was very welcomed," Slotkin reflected. "People needed to hear that someone will put country before party."

Knowing about their past experiences, it made sense that a huddle of former military and CIA women would be supremely mission-focused in a way that a deeply divided country found refreshing. (Voters showed their love again in 2020, when all five kept their seats in the election.) It also did not come as a shock that after many years in environments without female huddles, they worked together to create this environment where the abundance mentality reigns supreme. And they didn't even have to generate it all themselves. They told me about how Representative Lois Frankel welcomed them to Congress "as if the cavalry had arrived." (Luria was quick to remind me, "It's not really a cavalry yet! We only make up 23 percent!") But nonetheless they reported for duty along with the rest of the freshman congresswomen excited about the notion that there would be strength in numbers. They were constantly championing each other's work and thinking through important legislative decisions together. As a matter of survival, they allowed themselves to vent properly and regularly via a highly active text chain they called "the Badasses." Their camaraderie and practical support of one another was clearly part and parcel of their daily success—and not unlike many other huddles I'd been learning about. There was no whiff of competition, but rather a clear mandate for cooperation and support. They had each other's backs and were having a lot of fun along the way.

Much like the Houston judges, the congresswomen had quickly realized during their campaigns in 2018 that their cohesion as a group would inspire more donors and voters than if they went at it individually. Despite their party leaders frowning on this idea, they knew there was something special happening anytime they'd appear side by side at fundraising events for Serve America—a PAC that supports service-oriented candidates. They'd line up onstage—eight women in a row (including the three other service candidates who were part of their huddle but ultimately lost their elections, Amy McGrath, MJ Hegar, and Gina Ortiz Jones), and people would listen. Houlahan would tell the story about her Holocaust survivor father feeling unwelcome in America after Trump's win, and Slotkin would recount her recent experience of losing her mother to stage four cancer after a preexisting condition made it impossible for her to keep her health insurance. They all shared stories that were uniquely their own—grounded in extraordinary service to their country—but that were also universal enough to connect with voters. Their connection with each other translated to a connection with the female audiences they addressed.

"Some of our male colleagues—who we love—would go chapter and verse on what they've accomplished. But we would tell the emotional stories of why we were running. Our backgrounds were important, but the stories took center stage," explained Slotkin.

The power in this, Spanberger explained, was "profoundly noticeable when there's a line of eight women standing onstage."

"We struck a nerve," Sherrill explained. "Women liked us and they were completely activated by us."

Reflecting on this, Luria posed this question to the group: "Did you guys think this was the first time in your career when being a woman was such an asset?"

It was a stunning question, and I immediately wondered if I'd ever felt being a woman was an asset in my own career.

"First time ever." Spanberger broke the silence, with others nodding in agreement.

With staffers checking their watches and a security guard coming in to do a head count, we wrapped up our conversation. I didn't want to take up too much more of their time, so we took the last few sips of wine from our paper cups and said our goodbyes.

As I walked back out into the night air, gazing out on the National Mall, I thought about all the speeches, protests, and shouting matches that have taken place there. Oratory has always greased the wheels of our democracy. It's how we pass laws, testify about our values, and win over hearts and minds. I scanned the horizon, looking for cherry blossoms and thinking about the so-called pink wave. I couldn't help noticing that nothing around here was really pink enough just yet. *Men have been doing a lot of talking around here,* I thought, and it felt good to hear some women speaking for a change.

A SILVER LINING IS A TERRIBLE THING TO WASTE

On the sofa in my CNN office, I have a white pillow with fuzzy pom-pom edges. Emblazoned in the center are gold sequin letters that spell out *BSD*. To anyone who walks in my office, it's a curious acronym, but surprisingly few people ask what it means. One of my favorite coworkers, chief political correspondent and overall badass Dana Bash, gave me this pillow and told me *BSD* stands for "big swinging dicks." It's a sly and hilarious reminder that we're always there to comfort and uplift each other—even when the men who like to flex their egos and drown out our voices become a little too crushing or loud.

Twenty years into my career, I've landed a role working in the epicenter of media in New York, but it wouldn't be half as fulfilling if I weren't surrounded by such talented and inspiring women. And I never would have made it this far without the incredible huddle I have at CNN. This includes women who have been there for me in my personal life (such as CNN's then documentary chief, Jen Hyde, meeting me in my office and peppering me with excited questions after I told her about meeting my future husband at the age of thirty-six in New York City); and women I massively admire (such as Dana, who recently received a lot of emoji-rich texts from me while she was killing onstage as a moderator in a presidential debate); and women I trust to listen to and advise me (such as CNN special correspondent Jamie Gangel, who has served as a sounding board for me during some of the most intense moments of my career).

I'm not kidding myself about the fact that the scarcity mentality can still rear its ugly head. But I feel lucky to be a part of a huddle with female colleagues at CNN and even other networks within the industry where women often reach across company lines to support each other. I think of myself as pretty seasoned at my job, but I still rely on my work huddle to make me smarter, kinder, more compassionate, and, yes, more aware of all the slings and arrows I still have to dodge on a regular basis. In mid-September 2018, Hurricane Florence was brewing, and all the networks were fanning reporters along the Carolina coastline. Each hour, meteorologists led our shows, telling people to take precautions or evacuate. That same week at CNN was coincidentally "Make You Matter" week, in which our parent company showed its appreciation and investment in us by hosting workshops and guest speakers to promote our professional development. The very day Hurricane Florence was about to make landfall, I was a guest speaker at a featured event, "Breakfast with Brooke Baldwin." My friend and fellow CNN huddler Alisyn Camerota, who hosts our morning show, had been tapped to interview me in front of a room of about one hundred mostly female employees. What no one in that room knew was that later that afternoon, I would *not* be hosting my own show. The first mega-hurricane of the year would be churning toward the Carolinas and our three prime-time anchors (who all happen to be male) would be hosting my show *for* me, from various locations along the beach. I would instead spend the afternoon alone in my office, angry that I was not given the opportunity to cover this national emergency on my own show.

So there I sat at this Make You Matter breakfast not feeling like I mattered as much as I would have liked. I swallowed my disappointment and fielded all kinds of questions about my career and what it's like to be a woman in a still male-dominated profession. I answered all the questions truthfully, smiling through some of the tougher subjects, pretending I wasn't annoyed that I had just been bumped by the boys. I wanted to blurt out: *Being a woman in this profession isn't always fair! Even twenty years in! You work hard! You're kind! You earn your stripes! And you still don't get to do it all!* But I held my fire.

After the Q&A was over, I went straight to Alisyn's office, and we huddled. She's got about ten years experience on me and a lot of wisdom, as well as three kids and a very full life. At this point in her successful career, she has an incredibly cool presence of mind in heated moments. I threw myself on the couch in her office and we talked candidly about our jobs, our salaries, and our desire for a sense of fulfillment from our careers. At the end of our twenty-minute conversation, I left her office with more hope and enough gumption to ask for what I wanted.

That afternoon as the TVs around the studio flashed a three-box split screen of those three guys reporting live from the hurricane zone, I marched the fifteen paces across the newsroom and into my boss's office. To be fair, he always hears me out, and this day was no different. I laid it out plain and simple: "I want to be there. Why did you send the boys?"

"Because they were banging down my door and being a pain in my ass."

"I am more than happy to be a pain in your ass," I said, not missing a beat.

He smirked and replied, "I appreciate you coming in here. Duly noted. Next time."

And true to his word, three weeks later, my boss sauntered into my office and casually asked if I had packed my bags yet. I looked at him quizzically. "There's another big hurricane coming," he said, "and you're leaving tonight."

I was grateful he'd truly listened to my requests and even more appreciative that Alisyn had reminded me to ask in the first place. Not to mention, I'd finally reached a point in my career where it was a no-brainer to seek refuge in a work huddle when I was feeling slighted and insecure about my position. How fortunate I was to have this resource right in front of me, all around me—actually baked into my job. There were plenty of women within reach who had wisdom I could learn from.

What followed was an incredibly powerful experience that remains one of the most important of my career. While Hurricane Michael was a difficult assignment, I rode out the category 4 storm in Destin, Florida, and along with my amazing crew, was able to talk my way into a helicopter with very short notice and obtain the first aerial images of ground zero in Mexico Beach, Florida. It was a devastating scene. An entire town was leveled, with trees, homes, restaurants, boats, insulation, and metal littered everywhere. Once on the ground in Mexico Beach, where there was utterly no cell service or electricity, we found a local man named John willing to offer his storm-battered truck engine to power our BGAN (satellite uplink) computer, enabling us to provide the first live images of the aftermath from any network—for hours. John's truck, in fact, powered the entire two hours of my show that day, in which I ad-libbed for two hours, talking with hurricane survivors and helping them call their loved ones via our patchy satellite phone.

Later that year, CNN submitted my reporting for a Peabody Award. I've never forgotten how powerful Alisyn's small act of encouragement was for me. The memories of all the past loneliness and unspoken competition with other women in my early career days make it all the sweeter to know that the abundance mentality has truly become more of a default for me. Not only am I surrounded by helpful women, I am also more willing to accept their assistance. I didn't think twice before I plopped onto Alisyn's couch that day—and it happens all the time among women in my office. It has become almost a reflex that *this is just the way women get things done.*

For me, this is one of the ironic benefits of working in a male-dominated field. It has given me the opportunity to hone my huddle skills, to become more perceptive about how I can help other women and become less guarded about my own vulnerabilities in the workplace. That alone is a tremendous gift. Losing the fear of asking other women for help has changed my entire approach to ambition and friendship. I might not be able to change the forces at play in our culture that have resulted in gender disparities and lopsided power balances in the workplace, but I *am* able to locate my best allies for weathering this storm. I've learned firsthand how fulfilling it is to root for a female colleague; to openly and honestly express my deepest frustrations about my career; and to share the secrets of my own success with someone who is struggling to find her way. More than just comfort, there is *power* in female coworkers talking to each other. Even if it's still a man's world we're working in, the huddle is the silver lining.

five

PASSING THE MIC

I know it might sound a little too on the nose for a journalist to get excited about using her microphone for good—but after realizing how instrumental other women had been in my life, I reached a point where I wanted to share my platform and "pass the mic." The best way I knew how—besides being a good huddler at work—was to amplify the stories of other women. I've got one hell of a megaphone, and I knew I could share the messages and experiences of other women out there. I wanted to help cast them in the light they deserved, and to make visible their struggles, talents, fear, and joy.

The way I see it, the act of amplifying can take many forms. It can mean complimenting another woman or giving a much-needed shout-out to a coworker whose accomplishments haven't been adequately credited. It can mean simply recognizing all the complexities in a woman's lived experiences and seeing her for the nuanced human she is, or it can mean celebrating the role women have played in our history. Amplifying a woman can also mean just showing up for her, rooting for her, and allowing her to be her real unvarnished self.

I see amplifying as a natural outcome of huddling. Once women get good at leaning on each other in a huddle, they gain the strength to form more intentional habits of uplifting others. Amplifying women often results in their empowerment, in boosting their self-esteem, or providing them much deserved recognition, but perhaps even more transformative is the way it can free a woman to *be authentic*. To amplify a woman is to invite her to simply live and breathe as her true self in a culture that has often denied her this privilege.

I am still learning what I have to offer, still evaluating how I can best help and *receive help*, but one thing that was a no-brainer for me pretty immediately was that I knew I needed to seek out more women's stories and use my mic to amplify women's voices. I knew it wouldn't be easy to get a TV series about women off the ground in 2017. Trump had just taken office and the news cycle was in overdrive. There was so much to cover on TV every minute of every day. Historically speaking, it was, and still is, an unprecedented era (volume- and speed-wise) in journalism. I knew there wasn't going to be a lot of extra room for me to share more uplifting stories about women on my regular news show (as sad as that may sound), but I felt urgency around materializing this project, so I went to my boss and asked anyway. I got the *no* I was expecting, so I quickly moved on to plan B, to pitch to CNN Digital, which produces online content for the network. I got the green light there, and my digital series *American Woman* was born.

I spent all my free time that spring and summer of 2017 spotlighting trailblazing women who have broken barriers in their respective fields and who were helping other women do the same. In season one, I interviewed accomplished women including Diane von Furstenberg, Ashley Graham, Sheryl Crow, Issa Rae, and Ava DuVernay. They were all well-known people whose work was already being amplified, but I learned from their backstories and I knew they would inspire audiences. When I interviewed Ava DuVernay on the set of her critically acclaimed TV show *Queen Sugar*, she mentioned something about her approach that inspired me: "Amplifying the magnificence of Black people is a big part of my work," she said. There was something about the intentionality of her statement—and also the joyful commitment in her voice—that motivated me to think more about amplifying. I began to think about working with more women on my crew and making it a priority to interview more "ordinary extraordinary" women.

For the second season of *American Woman*, I worked with an all-female crew (plus one man), many of whom were in early phases of their careers. I decided to let them in on my entire process, involving them in the conception, writing, editing, traveling, and shooting far more than most veteran anchors typically would. It was the summer before the 2018 midterm elections, so we decided to dedicate the season to spotlighting women across the country who were running for public office. Many of these women were entering local and state elections and were not widely known public figures. Our entire team was moved by how these American women were making themselves vulnerable to a new challenge and sacrificing so many hours and dollars, all to do better by their country.

Many of the younger women on my *American Woman* crew were experiencing career firsts that summer, and I drew energy and fresh perspectives from their excitement. I too was experiencing a career first—to be working so vulnerably on a passion project that I had fought so hard for. I was entering new territory, making a very deliberate choice to focus my career on women, and it felt great to be doing it with this specific team.

That summer, we interviewed Paulette Jordan in Idaho, who was running to become the country's first Native American governor. We profiled Gina Ortiz Jones in Austin, Texas, where she was running to become the first lesbian Filipina American in Congress (and as an Air Force veteran, she was also campaigning with the five congresswomen I ended up meeting in chapter 4). We criss-crossed the country in ninety-degree heat, on shoots so sweltering the battery packs sometimes melted. In Birmingham, Alabama, we interviewed seventy-nine-year-old Marian Haslem, an African American woman who grew up in the time before the Voting Rights Act of 1965 when a Black woman like her had to pass a literacy test and pay a poll tax in order to cast a ballot. She showed me her actual poll tax receipt from 1964—a delicate piece of paper that reminded me of the importance of telling and retelling the stories of women's struggles in the past. "I don't want my great-grandchildren to think this was a movie," Haslem told me. "This really happened," she said, speaking about the forces of segregation and disenfranchisement that had shaped her life experiences. With the Supreme Court having gutted the Voting Rights Act in 2013 and voter suppression persisting in the modern day, Haslem knew her message continued to be critical. She told her story on CNN not just to amplify her own personal pain, but also to magnify the brighter future she was trying to pave for her children and grandchildren.

We also spoke with Cara McClure, who was one of seventy-plus Black women in Alabama who had decided to run for office that year. Many of these women were running for the very first time. McClure was campaigning to become a public service commissioner in Birmingham out of the desire to represent poor and marginalized communities who often struggle to access basic utilities. McClure's own experience with housing insecurity made her a passionate advocate for others like her. She was unashamed of her past struggles and spoke openly of the fact that a GoFundMe campaign was the only reason she was able to scrape together the $1,900 necessary to file an application to run. She shared her story bravely, knowing it would amplify the struggles of so many others like her. I remember the strength of her statement as she looked into the camera, as I asked all my interviewees to do, and asserted that what made her an American Woman is her ability to be "unapologetically authentic."

When the season had wrapped, it was Marian Haslem's and Cara McClure's stories that helped me understand the power of amplifying. When I shined a light on them, they used that spotlight to amplify the struggles of their communities. They were brave enough to be unabashedly authentic, to share their personal and painful struggles, which underscored for everyone watching that *women's lived experiences and truths matter.* When women signal boost the messages of other women, powerful things unfold and huddles are created. Amplifying women's stories accomplishes so much more than just plastering more female faces on TV screens or magazines; it actually creates the conditions in which authenticity and empowerment are possible.

CHANGING THE GAME

When I met Lindsay Colas, I wasn't expecting to talk to her about authenticity. She's a sports agent who represents some of the badass professional athletes I ended up talking to for this book, so I was connecting with her hoping to line up some of her star clients for interviews. I don't know about you, but when I think of sports agents, I'll admit to the firmly planted (and completely unfair) stereotype in my head of a white frat boy in an expensive suit (a la Tom Cruise in *Jerry Maguire*) who likes to kick walls and yell a lot about money. Colas, on the other hand, is a Japanese American woman who could probably teach a college-level course on feminism. Yet another sports cliché I can't knock is the notion that agents are always trying to get their unruly clients to behave. But Colas, I learned, has built a reputation on empowering her female clients to do just the opposite—she fully encourages them to "misbehave" and disrupt the status quo in the process.

Colas represents some very well-known names in women's sports—women including WNBA sensations Sue Bird, Breanna Stewart, and Maya Moore; Olympic swimmer Simone Manuel; and Olympic fencer Ibtihaj Muhammad. Colas's clients are all athletes known for excelling at more than just their game, and Colas's unique approach to working with them is to amplify more than just their physical prowess and merch-selling capabilities. "I don't want my clients to segment their business self from their political self or their personal self. I want them to make an impact by bringing their whole selves." Authenticity, she explained, is more than "just a buzzword . . . it really just means bringing your whole self."

When I asked Colas how she empowers a sports phenom—someone who already has the talent to propel them to the top of their profession—she told me how she elevates these superhuman women by helping them focus on what happens outside the game. She encourages them to investigate their values and determine how they want to leverage their high profiles to make an impact on the world.

Two weeks into her working relationship with Breanna Stewart, Colas counseled Stewart through the difficult decision to go public with her story of childhood sexual abuse, making her the first athlete to add her voice to the #MeToo movement. Stewart's harrowing story was published in the *Players Tribune*, showing solidarity with countless other women and assuring other victims of abuse that they were not alone. Within a year of going public with her story, Stewart had won the world championship with the

Seattle Storm, and also been named MVP of the world championship and the league.

"Lindsay is the amazing woman behind all the amazing women,"
Ibtihaj Muhammad, the Olympic fencer, told me. When Muhammad was an "unknown Black fencer," as she put it, who had just
qualified for the Olympics, she was scrambling to find representation. "I needed an agent who would be on board with me being vocal about issues of social justice," she said. This was during the time
when Trump was campaigning for the presidency and floating the
idea of a Muslim ban, and Muhammad—who was about to become
the first Muslim American woman to wear hijab while competing
for the United States in the Olympics—knew she'd want to use
her Olympic platform to defend her faith. In the four years since
Muhammad met Colas, she has medaled at the Olympics, penned
an open letter to Trump asking him to reconsider his campaign
against Islam, written a memoir and a critically adored children's
book about a little girl wearing hijab, and had a Barbie designed in
her likeness. Having a doll based on her isn't about earning more
money or recognition for Muhammad. Colas and I discussed the
powerful effect the Barbie could have on Muslim girls who might
be afraid to play sports because of their religious commitment to
wearing hijab. For these girls, Muhammad had proved she could
don a uniform and a hijab at the same time—without compromis-
ing her values or the ability to rack up the medals.

Colas also represents Paralympian track and field athlete Scout
Bassett, who lost her leg in a chemical fire as a baby in China. As
a seven-year-old, she was adopted from a Chinese orphanage by
an American family and grew up to become the fastest woman
of her classification to ever run the 100-meter dash for the United
States. Bassett works with Colas to strategize how she can use her
platform to amplify other young athletes like her who train with

prosthetics. She even dared to appear nude in ESPN's 2019 annual Body Issue, revealing powerful images of her highly conditioned body and the prosthetic blade she runs with in her record-breaking sprints. By securing a lucrative Nike campaign for Bassett, Colas hoped to help her create even more visibility for the largely ignored Paralympian community worldwide. They also made a deal with American Girl, who created a doll with a prosthetic limb to be featured with Bassett in a photo shoot for their line of Team USA doll clothes. As a child, Bassett had the lonely experience of being the only person with a disability in her Michigan community. This simple partnership with American Girl was a poignant gesture that would help empower so many other children with prosthetics who might rarely see representations of themselves in media.

In Colas's negotiations between Nike and her client WNBA star Maya Moore—who famously took a two-season hiatus from being one of the WNBA's top performers to dedicate herself exclusively to criminal justice reform work—Colas managed to establish maternity contract language that Nike then institutionalized across all sports. During the 2018 Academy Awards Colas had a lightbulb moment when actress Frances McDormand famously schooled the audience on the new notion of the inclusion rider, which is a contract demand an actor makes to insist that a film's hiring practices for the cast and crew maintain a specific percentage of gender and racial diversity. Colas was watching McDormand's speech, and immediately imagined the implications of using inclusion riders in the sports world. What if her athletes could stipulate as part of their endorsement deals that the partnering company must include more women and people of color in their creative and hiring processes? She immediately sought out USC Professor Stacy Smith, the woman who introduced the inclusion rider concept for

Hollywood, and asked her to help adapt the concept for a new industry. Colas then used the new inclusion rider language while negotiating an endorsement contract with TYR Sport, a top swim brand for her client Olympic swimmer Simone Manuel, who is the first African American woman to win individual gold in Olympic swimming. TYR promised to "extend meaningful opportunities to traditionally underrepresented groups" and to ensure diversity would "be reflected in the creative efforts she pursues with the brand." The move created countless headlines in the sports world and helped Manuel fulfill her vision to improve racial and gender representation in sports media.

In an industry where a gaping, ugly pay disparity still exists between men and women, Colas fights to equalize not only salaries, but also resources, airtime, sponsorships, magazine coverage, and brand campaigns for her female clients. She pushes back on the hotly contested notion that there isn't a market for women's sports—an idea that is often used as an excuse by media and sports brands who choose not to air women's games or pay to use their likenesses to sell merchandise. "Why aren't there signature shoes for female athletes? It's not just because the market doesn't warrant it," Colas explained. "The big dogs need to take responsibility for how they *create* the market." Colas makes it her own personal responsibility to do everything she can to create a better world for women who both play and watch sports. She pushes major brands to amplify female athletes, not only because she wants to elevate her own clients, but because she knows there are thousands of fans out there who are uplifted by the cultural celebration of female athleticism as well.

As I sit here making final edits to this book, I'm struck by how many female athletes continue to inspire me. In the last few years alone, Megan Rapinoe, Ibtihaj Muhammad, Serena Williams, and

Aly Raisman have all motivated me—and likely millions of other fans—to think more critically about topics as wide-ranging as pay equity, motherhood, inclusion, representation, and social justice. In the very weeks of 2020 that I'm writing this, several female athletes are publicly sitting out of games and matches in the name of protesting police violence to the Black community. The WNBA has dedicated their entire season to the #SayHerName campaign and in memory of Breonna Taylor, the twenty-six-year-old Black woman from Louisville, Kentucky, who had committed no crimes but was fatally shot five times by police officers in her own apartment during a botched raid, in which many believe law enforcement's actions were deeply negligent and symptomatic of a broader disregard for Black lives. Dedicating their season to Taylor in order to keep her name in the media is one more reminder that these athletes are more than just tennis players, basketball heroes, and Olympic runners. They are ambitious changemakers who, as WNBA veteran Sue Bird told me, are using the game they love as a platform to ensure their voices are amplified. As for Colas, by encouraging her clients to do more of this—to bring their authentic selves into the spotlight—she exhibits that amplifying women can be a whole new form of huddling. By empowering this dynamic group of groundbreaking leaders, Colas is not just updating the traditional rules of engagement as a sports agent, she's changing the entire game.

PUTTING WOMEN AT THE CENTER OF THE STORY

Around the same time I was dreaming about creating *American Woman*, Reese Witherspoon launched her female-led multimedia company, Hello Sunshine (the same company that created the Film-maker Lab for Girls I discussed earlier in this book). Hello Sun-shine quickly became known for creating TV shows including *Big Little Lies*, *The Morning Show*, and *Little Fires Everywhere*, but what was extraordinary about the company is that it was one of the first production companies solely devoted to putting women "at the center" of all their content. After a lifetime working in Hollywood (and counting herself among one of its top-earning actresses), Witherspoon told me via email she was "tired of making movies where [she] was the only female lead, and seeing scripts where there was only one badly written female role." She wanted to use her immense success to amplify the stories of women in film and TV—and while she was at it, she created a multimedia company that put the spotlight on women in a variety of mediums including podcasts, audiobooks, newsletters, and even a good old-fashioned (digital) book club.

A little after the launch of Hello Sunshine, Witherspoon wrote an essay for *Glamour* explaining that Hello Sunshine allowed her to "seek out women from all over the US, to hear about their joys and struggles, and encourage them to be storytellers in all kinds of mediums." A new model was necessary, she told me, because the current system wasn't empowering enough women to become content creators. "If women are relegated to paper-thin roles in stories by men about men, we aren't giving them the full power of storytelling," she explained.

Witherspoon's definition of storytelling goes beyond just award-winning entertainment. A powerful storyline in a television show, for example should change the conversations viewers have after watching. Engaging the viewer—even making her a *part* of the storytelling—is at the forefront of the Hello Sunshine operation. Witherspoon herself uses her personal Instagram account to *listen* to other women who watch her shows. She harnesses the famously self-serving medium to pose questions and start conversations. I remember watching her Instagram Stories religiously every week after a new episode of her HBO show *Big Little Lies* aired. The way she'd pop in and discuss last night's episode could almost fool you into thinking she was just another gal watching along with you instead of the lead actress and producer of the whole show. *(Ya'll! Can you BELIEVE how mad Renata got last night? What do you think is going to happen next?!)*

This is a woman who sees storytelling as a two-way street—a TV show becomes more than just a finished product for a viewer's bingeing consumption. Instead, a TV show serves as a vital conversation starter that can *bring women together.* Every TV producer wants to spark those coveted "water cooler conversations" among their audiences, but Witherspoon has taken it a step further by encouraging women to discuss issues that have divided and isolated them for years. After the airing of *Big Little Lies, The Morning Show,* and *Little Fires Everywhere* viewers and critics were discussing with renewed energy themes of domestic violence, marital power dynamics, motherhood, aging, and sexism in the workplace. Success for a television show might typically be measured by the revenue, ratings, or number of Emmy nominations—all of which Hello Sunshine is also bringing in—but the company is clearly targeting additional metrics: they want to improve women's lives by building community and conversation among them. It's essentially one big sunny huddle that puts women's stories at the center of all their enterprises—whether it's their films, television shows, animation, or book club picks.

When I visited the Hello Sunshine headquarters in Santa Monica, I heard more about the company mission from CEO Sarah

Harden, but not before I got a tour of the cozy, sunny space shared by the forty-plus employees—most of whom were female. Almost all the decor was sky blue or sunshine yellow, and a double-wide garage-like door at the entrance remained open, bathing the whole space in natural light and fresh air. But the most striking thing upon entering was the massive eight-foot yellow triangle painted beneath a white pendant light that hung just so, creating the cheerful cartoon illusion of a spotlight shining down on whomever stood in front of it. The wall made for a great selfie backdrop and seemed to suggest that every woman deserves to find her light.

As I admired an impressive array of colorful books that dominated an entire floor-to-ceiling wall, Harden reminded me the company takes their book club just as seriously as its higher-profile film and television deals. "We did a lot of research on the history of book clubs and realized that women have been gathering around books for years." She outlined a reality familiar to many women—that so many of us are overworked, wearing multiple hats as professionals, caretakers, and homemakers—and often left with little time to connect with each other. "Women are facing a loneliness epidemic," Harden explained. "And Reese's Book Club provides a shared experience. Even if members are not physically in the same room, we are all reading the same book and talking about it online together."

Not only does Witherspoon dedicate time to chat on Instagram about the book each month with her huddle of book lovers, the company is also hiring a librarian-in-residence, and book-to-TV or film adaptations continue at a steady pace, with productions of book club picks and bestsellers *Daisy Jones & the Six* and *Where the Crawdads Sing* currently underway. Because the book club picks are chosen by Witherspoon herself, her promotion of any given book to her 22.5 million Instagram followers can instantaneously elevate sales. When I asked Witherspoon why she chooses to so often dedicate resources to adapting other authors' books versus developing her own original scripts, she said that highlighting these "incredible authors" was "just as important" to her as creating new content.

She also seemed highly intentional about what she was doing for the female authors whose books she selects for her monthly book club pics: "By amplifying their voices and introducing them to my book club community, we can bring people together to celebrate these diverse voices every month," she said. "It's a fun and exciting way to amplify women's narratives off the screen." Books can bring women together, and when chosen strategically, they also signal-boost the messages of authors who might not otherwise reach as many of the readers who are truly hungry for more female-centered content.

Harden described the deliberate choice to produce only female-centered projects. "We saw a white space in the market that was so big you could drive a truck through it," she exclaimed. The company had also recently launched an animation division targeted for children ages three to nine, because even in that demographic, female characters are rarely "nuanced or specific," according to Claire Curley, head of the kids and animation unit. "The prevailing theory in kids' television has been that girls will watch boy characters on TV, but boys will not watch girl characters," she explained. This is exactly the kind of logic that leads investors and creators to want to maintain the status quo. But if all the heroes and lead characters continue to be boys, girl viewers are repeatedly left without affirming representations of themselves. Curley reminded me how much influence content creators have on young children, which made the urgency of her mission clear: "Every kid's show we create will have a *lead* female protagonist. Not the sister of, not the neighbor of, not the daughter of."

Harden told me when she and Witherspoon created the company, they were equally focused on how the company would function behind the scenes. They were intent on putting women at the helm, ensuring that women played significant, majority roles at every level of the company. "The audience we care about has to be threaded all the way through our company," Harden explained. "From our board, to our executive team, to our employee base, to the projects we say yes to, to the narratives we champion, and the authorship process in our writers' room. It's all linked."

After interviewing several of the staff, I got the sense that this wasn't all just talk coming from the founder and CEO. There was a common thread of huddle ethos woven through all the conversations I had with Hello Sunshine staff. The employees I spoke to told me they felt trusted and empowered in this unique work setting— and that this was rare in their industry. Lauren Levy Neustadter, the head of the TV and film division, who has worked in television for nearly two decades in what she assured me were mostly supportive environments, made clear that the Hello Sunshine mission remains unparalleled. "It's like I ordered off the menu with this job," she said with authentic, bubbly joy. "I didn't even know this was possible in Hollywood."

Liz Jenkins, the head of finance, who worked on Wall Street before beginning her career in film financing, told me that men in Hollywood behave even worse than men on Wall Street. While perhaps this is due to the fact that Wall Street had its toxic-male reckoning a few decades before Hollywood did, it's worth noting that the industry with the most influence to shape the way women see themselves is also the industry led by a congregation of men— with notorious sexual predators among their most powerful. In other words, seeing female empowerment and authenticity on screen isn't as likely to happen if all the content creators are men (and sometimes even outright abusers at that). Jenkins sighed about the system, which she said "has been built up over time to insulate people who were very powerful and who behave in a way that's everything from boorish to felonious." She recounted the number of blow job pantomimes and rape jokes she'd endured in her interactions with male peers in the industry, and her requisite relief in working at a place like Hello Sunshine that is not only largely female but that is also driven by the goal of specifically uplifting women. Feeling safe and free to be oneself in the workplace, she suggested, is not something every woman gets to experience. Jenkins had often been one of the only African American women in her finance jobs, which burdened her with the task, she told me, of constantly making others feel comfortable with her difference. "But at Hello Sunshine," she explained, "because we have such a strong shared vision that's bigger than all of us, we have more trust in each other when the hard conversations come up. I've never felt this degree of comfort, because I know we all have each other's backs."

The implications of this affect anyone who views the content Hello Sunshine creates. When this degree of attention and care is paid to honoring women's points of view, the product will reflect this authenticity in spades. I'd much rather watch a television show about women's relationships, for example, that was produced and written by a huddle of women who actually care about each other and prioritize their working relationships.

When I asked Harden—a fast-talking, whip-smart Australian with an impressive corporate resume and a long history of working alongside powerful men—how a majority-female environment suited her, she immediately gushed about the palpable huddle energy. About a year after Hello Sunshine was launched, the #MeToo and Time's Up movements erupted and inspired broad conversations about change for women everywhere, which meant that Harden was a part of several huddles both on and off the job. "It has been the biggest joy of my professional career," Harden said. "I do not take this for granted. Women haven't been gathering like this for most of the past twenty-five years." She described the male-huddle structure inherent in most places where white-collar women have worked for decades. "Just five years ago, we were complaining about how women weren't invited to the golf weekends, but the narrative has finally shifted." She paused and brought it all home for me: "We aren't asking for a seat at the table anymore. We're making our own damn table." She was quick to qualify her excitement, noting that white women like her should not be the only beneficiaries of this change. "We have to do this from an intersectional feminist perspective. If we merely replace the patriarchy with white women, we change nothing."

She went on to tell me how she believes the act of amplifying women by providing female-centered content is one of the primary keys to accelerating female power in society. "We believe we are uniquely capable of expanding upon the cultural fabric women draw from when they ask themselves who they are and what their potential is." It goes back to what Witherspoon had mentioned about the "full power of storytelling." When it centers on women, storytelling can not only honor the real and lived experiences of women, it can also amplify the complex dilemmas of their lives using a full palette of colors to illustrate their struggles and potential. Harden explained the connection perfectly when she said that showing women authentic depictions of themselves on screen can truly "change the way they walk through the world."

WOMEN TELLING WOMEN'S STORIES

After the behind-the-scenes look at Hello Sunshine I was excited to see how the huddle-tastic logic played out in a writers' room, so I happily met up with a group of writers from *Little Fires Everywhere*. I know how to write a TV script for a news show, but for scripted shows in Hollywood? I had no idea. I pictured a pensive male writer all alone in a room, madly typing his masterpiece script. But as it turns out, television shows are actually written by committee. Learning this made me even more excited to meet these writers. After all, I'd spent many hours of my life writing my daily TV pieces in dirty trucks with camera dudes who on occasion sat way too close to me. I would have loved to sit in a room with several other women talking about big ideas and even bigger feelings. I imagined laughing, lunching, and building amazing stories together.

But (record scratch) my little fantasy of a roomful of female scribes almost never happens. Because—surprise, surprise—television writers' rooms are predominantly made up of (mostly white) men. According to the advocacy organization Women and Hollywood, only 35 percent of TV writers are women, a number that has improved by only 5 percent in nearly a decade. And while that number might not sound too terrible (the number of top one hundred *films* written by women is worse, at just 20 percent), what it actually means is that any particular writers' room will likely have seats for only a few women—at best. Most writers' rooms include zero women, and an *all-female* writers' room in Hollywood almost never happens. I searched high and low for one to interview for this book and confirmed their rarity with the showrunner of *Little Fires Everywhere*, an equally rare woman named Liz Tigelaar. Tigelaar had been responsible for assembling the all-female writers' room—the only exception being her trusted colleague Harris Danow who, interestingly enough, she said has a knack for writing teenage girl characters exceptionally well.

Tigelaar has been working in television since she cowrote her first episode of *Dawson's Creek* a few decades ago and was first described to me by her fellow *Little Fires* executive producer Lauren Neustadter as a unicorn. "Her voice is equal parts authentic and brilliant," Neustadter said. When I met Tigelaar a few months later in her home in Venice, we sat in her backyard next to her five-year-old son's playhouse where she served me and the other writers a well-balanced brunch of bacon, eggs, pastries, green juices, and champagne. After she said goodbye to her wife and son, who were heading out for "an adventure," she kicked off her flip-flops and sat cross-legged in her chair.

She was relaxed and gracious in addressing my curiosity about how a writers' room works. *Do they write on index cards? Do they all huddle around one laptop? How exactly does writing become a group activity?* "In the best writers' room, you're drawing on personal experiences and thinking collaboratively," Tigelaar explained. "And ideally when you throw a ball—even if your pitch is imperfect and lobs off to the side—you're throwing it to people who will dive in order to catch it." As someone who has pitched ideas to men who didn't move a muscle in response, this sounded pretty incredible to me. The group went on to explain that very quickly, writers who work together end up getting vulnerable with each other, often sharing details from their own lives as they work out characters' perspectives and wider story arcs. If the group clicks, everyone gets to know each other well, and the writing process can become more seamless.

"It's oddly intimate," said Nancy Won, a Korean American TV

writing veteran who Tigelaar described as much sought after in the business. Tigelaar expanded on Won's comment: "We end up knowing so much about each other that when we have wrap parties or events with each other's spouses, it actually feels awkward. We end up standing around acting like polite strangers until we're back in the writers' room again." Won, who told me she has been the only woman *and* BIPOC in many writers' rooms, recalled working in more emotionally stunted groups where she'd find herself intentionally pulling people aside and asking to see photos of their kids—anything to get their guards down. Raamla Mohamed, an African American writer who is best known for her work on *Scandal*, added, "And if I share something terrible about myself, I need to feel that you're going to share something terrible too." In a business where the exploration of emotional nuance is your currency, vulnerability seemed critical.

When I asked how an all-female (plus Danow) writers' room compared to working in a room with mostly men, I heard two predominant answers: more pee breaks and fewer verbal interruptions. "Male writers cut you off a lot?" I asked.

"One hundred thousand percent," exclaimed Won.

"Constantly," Mohamed added. "I don't even think it's always intentional. I read some study that men literally can't hear women's voices as well." This drew some laughter, and then Won hit on a point that I still think about almost every day. She described a certain calculus of energy required of women and especially BIWOC who must constantly calibrate their emotions and reactions to suit the dominant white male perspectives in the room: "I'm always monitoring myself thinking, *Okay, I don't want to be too strident, but then I don't want to be too quiet. If this man keeps cutting me off, should I express my anger? Then I'll become the crazy angry* lady. *How am I being perceived right now and is it because of my race or my gender?*"

Won shared this inner monologue in a way that drew vehement recognition from everyone in the room, myself included. "That internal conflict was literally taking up 70 percent of my energy!" Won said as she gestured emphatically. On the other hand, she explained, when a room becomes a place where the writers feel safe to be vulnerable and authentic, there is a sort of "atomic release of energy" that frees them to do their jobs better.

Everyone seemed relieved by the aptness of Won's revelation. Tigelaar was raising her hands to mime an amen from across the room. "Yes!!!" Mohamed added. "And removing that internal conflict frees up your creative thinking, which is why this writers' room is so great: *Our minds are actually free to think about the show.*" Everyone continued to exclaim a *yessss* and *ohmygoddddd* and *I knoooow* about this idea. As I was sitting there soaking up this point, I too was shouting an internal *hallelujah*. While I had been privileged enough to never experience the added layer of self-consciousness about my race, I knew exactly what Won was describing in regard to gender. What woman doesn't? I've been blessed to work with some extraordinary men in my career, but I have certainly spent, or rather *wasted*, a lot of my time worrying about how I'm being perceived by a powerful male coworker and then expending further energy on ridiculous mental gymnastics, including trying to work my way out of feeling like I'm being "punished" for not being enthusiastic enough about his idea; not emailing him back fast enough when he's asking a question; or performing the verbal jiujitsu required to present an idea of my own in such a way that he can claim some ownership of it too, and thus allow me to execute it. Like these women, I am *so* frustrated and exhausted by this dynamic. Why can't I just focus on the thing I love: *doing my job?* Hearing these women describe exactly what I've felt but rarely voiced was a real "come to Jesus" moment for me, as we say down South.

It was clear these writers had waited a long time to be in the presence of people with whom they shared so many mutual feelings, where they felt safe, understood, and free to be themselves—no filters or self-monitoring required. And the sense I got was that this level of realness shouldn't be so rare and unexpected—it's actually the condition in which storytellers can do their best work. And just as I related to their struggles, I was also reminded of the role huddles had played in my own professional life, helping nurture my talents, but more important, often serving as the only place I could go where I could speak honestly, irreverently, and authentically, without fear of being evaluated against male standards.

Tigelaar went on to recall several painful anecdotes to illustrate Won's point about constantly checking her true feelings against the male perspective she was drowning in. Her career had been filled with men in more powerful positions stealing credit for her work, excluding her from awards, or changing her scripts in ways that felt dehumanizing to women. She'd witnessed white male showrunners correcting Black women in the writers' room about how Black female characters should be written. On the first TV pilot she created, she was the only female producer—and a twenty-nine-year-old one at that. She recalled feeling crushed when a dream-sequence scene she'd written, consisting of teenagers playing dodgeball, was reshot to feature girls in short skirts throwing balls at women until they exploded like glass. She was completely defeated that something she'd created had taken a turn into "misogynistic male jerk-off" territory. Later on, as the production was about to shoot a date rape scene, a male mentor of hers strolled past her on set and breezily asked, "What's wrong? You don't seem very happy . . ." The subtext being (at best) *Why aren't you more grateful that we're all shooting your pilot right now?* or (at worst) *What's the big deal about rape?* Tigelaar's perspective as the creator of the pilot was completely discounted, and her sensitivity to the female characters in her script was used against her. Even worse, she felt that her voice had been erased from the conversation.

"I do think it can be so hard to find your voice as a woman in this business," Tigelaar said, pausing and smiling about the understatement of the year she'd just offered.

Perhaps this is why, when she was asked to serve as showrunner for *Little Fires Everywhere*, she filled her room with women who could protect each other's energy and nourish each other's unique perspectives. It was a huddle designed for better storytelling.

It's hard to imagine the typical writers' room (with the typical mostly white and male makeup) properly honoring Celeste Ng's incredible book, upon which the series is based. Tigelaar knew that in order to tell the story about four different mothers—two white, one African American, and one Asian American—she'd need a roomful of women who mirrored the characters and could truly speak for them from a place of real-life experience. So in addition to hiring a few white women, she also hired Won, Mohamed, and two other African American writers, Attica Locke and Shannon Houston. And because the show tackles issues of adoption and motherhood, Tigelaar hired three writers who had been through the foster care system (as she had been herself) and several mothers as well.

When I asked if she'd hired Danow—the one man in the group—to serve as the perspective of the Caucasian male characters in the show, Danow looked at me side-eyed and assured me, "I don't have the confidence of a white man. I really wish I did."

Less sarcastically, he went on to comment on the rampant inconsistencies of white men in their industry who proclaim themselves to be allies to people of marginalized genders and races while their actions remain consistently oblivious to bad behavior. This is precisely the reason why hiring people of marginalized genders and races to write the characters of marginalized genders and races (imagine that!) might yield more authentic stories. It feels like stating the obvious, but somehow it hasn't become obvious enough to the people who hire writers in Hollywood.

In *Little Fires Everywhere*, four main female characters with four radically different experiences of motherhood weave in and out of each other's lives. The script neither villainizes nor idolizes any of the individual mothers, whether they are adoptive mothers, biological mothers, reluctant mothers, or mothers afflicted with fertility struggles or postpartum depression. The common thread is that a mother's love is rife with sacrifice and complication, and the end result is a thought-provoking feast, particularly for viewers who live in a culture like ours that often pits mothers against each other or erases their experiences entirely.

"We wanted to show that there are all different types of mothers and that none are the 'right' kind," Won explained. The group hoped to present mothers who were not in the typical binary relationships (good vs. bad, old vs. young, hot vs. dowdy), and they were proud that the main story lines of both lead characters were simply that they were mothers. Motherhood was the central tension and plot in the story, not just an accessory to the main action as it might typically be in film or TV. "I really can't think of any other shows or movies that have such huge stars playing mothers," mused Won, referring to Reese Witherspoon and Kerry Washington, who portray the lead characters, Elena and Mia. "Unless the mothers are really gorgeous spies or detectives, or really hot moms who have sex in public bathrooms or something," she laughed and rolled her eyes.

"We want to show the viewers that motherhood doesn't have to be attached to something else to make it interesting," said Tigelaar. "A story about mothers is in and of itself a story worth telling."

To illustrate her point about women's stories being inherently important, Tigelaar reflected on that beautiful domino effect that can happen when one woman in a room tells her birth story. "Birth is such a crazy thing," she began, with that emotional glaze in her eyes of someone speaking from recent experience. "It's so crazy, that you can't believe you're not talking about it *every second of every day for the rest of your life.* So as soon as someone shares their birth story in a room, you think *Oh, I can talk about my birth story too!* So you tell your story, and then suddenly everyone is telling their birth stories." She paused. "I want this show to have that same effect. When one person's story is worthy, it makes everyone else's story worthy too."

...

On the car ride back to my hotel from Tigelaar's house, I scrolled through some headlines and happened to see a press piece for the upcoming release of *Little Fires Everywhere.* Reese Witherspoon and Kerry Washington revealed that their partnership for the show was born out of their collaboration on Time's Up. How encouraging that such a massive activist huddle could inspire this offshoot artistic collaboration. I wondered how many other female-affirming projects were born out of Time's Up as I popped in my earbuds and blasted the Highwomen's tune "My Name Can't Be Mama." It's a funny and heartfelt song with three verses, each written by a different member of the female country supergroup, providing some real talk about motherhood. In the first verse Brandi Carlile bemoans parenting a toddler while hungover. In the second verse Amanda Shires demonstrates the tug-of-war of guilt and ambition felt by so many working moms on a daily basis. And in the third verse, which happens to be my favorite, Maren Morris celebrates the traveling, free-wheeling, childfree life. The multiplicity of perspectives represented in that song feels important and all too rare—kind of like Tigelaar's invitation to mothers to share their birth stories. It made me want to get to work amplifying more women—to give them center stage, plug in the mic, and crank up the volume.

six

FROM SOLITARY TO SOLIDARITY

The privilege I enjoy of being able to amplify inspiring stories comes with the difficult responsibility to also bear witness to so much brutality and tragedy. I wish there were another way to put this, but being an American journalist means you become very well versed in mass shootings and gun violence. I've covered nearly every single mass shooting since Virginia Tech in 2007, oftentimes because I happen to be in the anchor chair in the middle of the afternoon when many of these gut-wrenching stories break. I'm always live on air when school lets out and parents are reunited with their children after a shooting. And no matter how many times this happens in America, our country is always shaken to the core. As the journalist covering these tragedies, it never gets easier. Just like so many other Americans, I always feel furious for the victims, furious this keeps happening, and furious that we aren't doing more to stop it.

It's a horror played on repeat, and it's happened so many times in my career. I'll be in the middle of my show, speaking with a guest. My executive producer will get in my ear from the control room telling me in a calm but firm voice, "Brooke, there's been a shooting."

I take a breath. The teleprompter goes blank.

I thank my guests but quickly cut them off and look right into the camera. The breaking news animation rolls and I talk to the world about what small amount of information we have to go on. For the next two hours, I pivot from eyewitnesses, reporters, law enforcement—all the while, I'm constantly adding new information confirmed by CNN. I have to be calm, sensitive, and above all accurate. I often travel the next day to the site of the shooting to cover the story in person and meet with those innocent families and victims whose lives have been changed forever.

I'll never forget the shooting at Sandy Hook Elementary School in Newtown, Connecticut, in 2012, where twenty first graders were murdered. I interviewed hardened firefighters who told me they would be forever haunted by what they saw. I remember the tiny white caskets. After, I went home, sat in the darkness, watched the sun set, and wept for the children who would never see the sun set again. In 2015, I sat in the Emanuel African Methodist Episcopal Church in Charleston, South Carolina, where nine Black parishioners were killed by a white supremacist whom they had welcomed into their Bible study. I was there in Orlando in 2016 where forty-nine people had been murdered in a gay nightclub—which would only carry the awful distinction of being the nation's deadliest mass shooting for a little more than a year before a new record was set by the 2017 rampage in Las Vegas that resulted in fifty-nine deaths. One year later, in 2018, I cried on camera with Representative Ted Deutch as we were standing outside Marjory Stoneman Douglas High School in Parkland, Florida. We had just heard a mother's screams as she learned her daughter was one of seventeen killed at the school that day.

I've never known any of the victims personally, but the more shootings I started to cover live, the more I started getting to know families of victims. I don't have the grace to express my outrage other than to say *enough is enough*. I can't believe how many people have lost loved ones to gun violence in America. I can't believe how many parents have lost a child. And as the world moves on after each shooting, so many of these people have become friends to me. They volunteer to speak on my show about gun violence when a new shooting happens or when the topic of gun violence resurfaces in the news. I've interviewed them time and again, and sometimes when news of yet another shooting breaks, they text me or send me prayers and peace: *Brooke, hang in there . . . I know this is tough for you too. I'm so sorry.* They empathize with *me*, while their own wounds are ripped open over and over again.

I have no idea what it means to survive this kind of tragedy—to move through the anguish and find meaning in the loss. But I've observed this very thing in so many survivors of gun violence. Being in the unique position of knowing so many of these people myself, I became compelled to do something to help. I wanted to bring them together in the hopes they might find strength in each other. I wanted to help create a huddle for them and give them the platform to articulate their unified message that this senseless violence must stop. Several times I produced segments to bring them together. Whether they had survived a school shooting, or lost a loved one in a movie theater, on the street, in the workplace, in church, or by suicide, their stories were all equally devastating. In one segment I brought together survivors of Parkland with survivors of Columbine—two school shootings that occurred two decades apart. In another segment, I interviewed a group of forty people in a town hall—all with deep wounds and a clear message they wanted to bring to Washington. I asked them to hold up photos of their loved ones so the viewers would not be able to look away. These people deserved to have a platform, a real voice, and the strength they might find in each other.

During that forty-person town hall, I witnessed mothers embracing each other, fathers who were complete strangers reaching out to hold the hands of the person next to them who needed their support as they cried and told their stories. Gun violence does not discriminate by gender, and the men there were just as affected as the women. But what was most memorable and instructive for me was hearing how some of the mothers who had lost children had initially met online or via letters they'd written to each other. They were strangers who lived in different parts of the country but suddenly had something terrible in common. They had connected through their isolating trauma and grief to form inspiring friendships and support systems that would become engines of action to change gun laws. Like many other huddles I've observed through the process of writing this book, a powerful pattern emerged. When one woman throws a line out to another—when she is bold enough to share her pain and demand change out loud— she is also *summoning her huddle*. The act of singing a solo can sometimes make you part of a choir.

America is vibrating with change, and many significant change movements have been organized by huddles of women and girls who have reached out to find each other when urgency demanded it. They are often regular women—not celebrities or people in any position of power—who have been activated by their experiences in their own lives or communities to help make the world a better, safer, and more just place. What's more, they are often doing this work without fanfare, as one of many in a large group where recognition of their leadership matters far less than the cause at hand.

SERVANT LEADERSHIP AND #METOO

Tarana Burke, the founder of the #MeToo movement, is a great example of a woman who created a seismic huddle without centering herself as the leader. Burke birthed the #MeToo concept in 2006, more than a decade before Hollywood celebrities hashtagged it into a viral phenomenon during the Harvey Weinstein reckoning. But Burke wasn't concerned with toppling one monolithic man when she created the concept. She wanted "to not only show the world how widespread and pervasive sexual violence is, but also to let other survivors know they are not alone." By asking women to come together and sing the same refrain (those two simple words "me too"), she hoped to pave the way for what she calls "empowerment through empathy." It was a means for women to publicly comfort each other, but also a way to organize a rallying cry to let the world know that sexual assault would no longer be tolerated.

On her Twitter bio, Burke calls herself a "servant leader" and a few days after #MeToo blew up in 2017, she told the *New York Times* that neither she nor the Hollywood celebrities who made the concept viral should be centered in the movement, since it was truly meant to be "about survivors." She had been working for years as an activist to make change for marginalized girls and women who experience sexual assault, but she didn't expect to singlehandedly manifest that change all by herself—nor did she ask for all the credit she rightfully deserved for the international movement taking shape. Instead she gracefully reminded everyone to keep it intersectional, and she celebrated the potential for many voices to affect the change she had dreamed of.

Besides very much admiring her style here, I think Burke's story illustrates how women can be so effective at moving the dial for change. We do not make it about ourselves. We make it about *everyone*. Resources are not poured into building up a singular hero who will save the day—but instead, we, together, *are* the resource. Huddles are assembled and we count the strength in our numbers.

I spoke to Burke on my show shortly after she spent her day in Washington sitting behind Christine Blasey Ford, who gave her testimony about allegedly enduring sexual assault by Supreme Court Justice nominee Brett Kavanaugh. A year had passed since the #MeToo movement had exploded online, and Burke was still placing the focus on survivors. She told me she was hopeful that the movement was changing "how we treat and think about [women], how we see women, how we believe women, how we hear women when they come forward." Undoubtably, her movement brought about awareness of sexual assault, and it encouraged women to heal, but it also changed the way this country *listens to women*. In refusing to center herself, Burke had helped to center *all women*. We are undoubtedly amid a cultural shift thanks to the #MeToo movement. The way men and women converse every day is changing; the way policy is created in government is affected; the way workplaces function has been altered, and even how women prioritize their own pain and healing is transforming.

"LEADERFUL" MOVEMENTS AND BLACK LIVES MATTER

When I first met Alicia Garza and Patrisse Cullors—two of the three founders of Black Lives Matter—I had no idea the movement they were building would become the global force it is today. Garza and Cullors appeared on my show in December 2014 to sit in the studio with me and give their *very first* televised interview to a national audience. They were gracious enough to educate me and my viewers about systemic racism and the "pattern of police abuse and police violence against Black communities" that so many white Americans remained woefully ignorant of at the time. Until I met them, I had been unaware that this profound movement was actually a huddle—that all three of the Black Lives Matters founders are women, yet another example of women organizing themselves around the cause of human life and dignity.

In the year they made that first appearance, I had reported on the deaths of Eric Garner, Michael Brown, and Tamir Rice. Each of their tragic deaths had stirred and compelled protesters to insist on a basic demand: that the lives of Black people have inherent value. They *matter*. It was and still is a plea so literal—as heartbreaking as it is alarming to many white Americans who are waking up to vast injustice, myself included. Our nation would continue to hear this plea time and again—after the unjust deaths of Freddie Gray, Sandra Bland, Alton Sterling, Philando Castile, George Floyd, Breonna Taylor, and so many others.

Cullors's book *When They Call You a Terrorist: A Black Lives Matter Memoir* details the way she and Garza along with Opal Tometi came together to found what many now consider one of the most potent international movements for racial justice in modern history. In July 2013, after George Zimmerman was acquitted for killing the unarmed sixteen-year-old Trayvon Martin, Cullors and Garza—who already were good friends—were grieving and processing the tragedy together online. After a Facebook post by Garza in which she said, "I continue to be surprised at how little Black lives matter," Cullors instantly recognized the poignance of Garza's statement and created the hashtag #BlackLivesMatter.

Soon after, Tometi connected with Cullors and Garza, offering to build out the various digital components necessary to build on the hashtag. And with these online measures in place, they had summoned their huddle.

The three women continued to carefully and intentionally grow their coalition consisting "mostly, although not exclusively, of women," many of whom were queer and trans women. The movement was specifically designed, her book explains, to ensure "that the Black Lives Matter network is a Black woman-affirming space free from sexism, misogyny, and male-centeredness." Cullors's book goes on to detail how the movement gained more media attention particularly after the weeks of protest in Ferguson, Missouri, following the shooting death of Michael Brown by police officer Darren Wilson. Cullors's words about the role women played in Ferguson are powerful:

> Women, all women, trans women, are roughly 80 percent of the people who are standing down the face of terror in Ferguson, saying We are the caretakers of this community. It is the women who are out there, often with their children, calling for an end to police violence, saying We have a right to raise our children without fear. But it's not women's courage that is showcased in the media.

She continues:

> Like the women who organized, strategized, marched, cooked, typed up and did the work to ensure the Civil Rights Movement, women whose names go unspoken, unknown, so too did this dynamic unfold as the nation began to realize we were a movement.

Beyond this moving argument about the wrongful erasure of the women on the front lines of the movement, Cullors seems unbothered by desire for her own personal recognition. She cares more to assign credit to *all the women* who came together in the movement. This style of leadership stands in bold contrast to what we've typically seen in American change movements, where one heroic leader often emerges as the figurehead of the coalition. He is often lionized, martyred, and quoted years after his death. He becomes the "face" of the movement. When I interviewed Garza in 2020 for this book to learn more about the huddle of women who founded Black Lives Matter, she told me that people still often assume one of their male allies helped create the organization. "The viewpoint about how change happens is often filtered through the lens of men—and white men at that," she told me. "So when it comes to Black folks and Black movements, everybody's looking for the man who's leading it." But because Black Lives Matter didn't have a heroic man in charge, they were quickly dubbed "a leaderless movement."

But "leaderless" is not how they thought of themselves.

"We described ourselves as a leader*ful* movement," she explained, "full of leaders who are women and queer and trans, and people who frankly have been left out of social movements that are supposed to include us."

Being "leaderful," she explained, provides a way to put agency and power into the hands of more people—a recipe that can actually drive change much more effectively. "Change movements are only successful when people adopt them as their own," she told me. She recalled for me her years of work as an activist prior to founding Black Lives Matter, in which she'd put in hours of effort and invisible labor within coalitions that didn't include her, much less acknowledge her leadership or contributions. "At a certain point, you start to think, is this really *for* me?" But when a group is leaderful, on the other hand, it offers a strong decentralized structure that prioritizes the will of each local chapter, allowing members to help shape the organization and become empowered within it. In this way, Black Lives Matter became much less a traditional organization, and more a flexible and expansive *movement*. It not only honored participants' shared trauma and grief over the assault on Black lives, but it also activated them into demanding policy and cultural change in their society.

This leaderful structure not only engages more activists—it also ensures the long-term viability of the movement. "Every movement that has been headed by 'one person' has been obliterated," Garza explained. She pointed out that the Reverend Martin Luther King Jr. and Malcolm X, respectively, whose movements were actually brimming with leaderful members, were still thrust into the spotlight—at the peril of the organization. "When they were assassinated, in a lot of ways, the movement faltered. It took a long time to regroup, because the movement had really been organized around one person." A leaderful movement like Black Lives Matter, on the other hand, does not depend on its heroes as much as it depends on the huddle.

Leslie Crutchfield's book *How Change Happens: Why Some Social Movements Succeed While Others Don't* supports the notion that leaderful movements are also more successful at moving the needle toward progress. Crutchfield points out that these organizations "build trust between individuals and work through networks . . . to create a whole greater than the sum of its parts." Thus, large change movements such as Black Lives Matter might be so successful precisely *because* they organize themselves in huddle formations. Like a circle, where any entry point is never too far from the center, everyone is central to the mission, and everyone's voice is equally crucial. Effective leaders, Crutchfield says, "share power, authority, and limelight," which reminds me of Cullors, Garza, Tometi, and Tarana Burke too, in their fierce devotion to the movement itself instead of their own power within it.

In the end, as I've discovered speaking with so many women for this book, successful organizations are often run more like huddles, led by those who are able to let go of ego, "lead from behind," and place "cause and mission ahead of personal or organizational power." Crutchfield doesn't address gender specifically in her book, but it interests me greatly that women might be more likely to build these "leaderful" circles as opposed to the more ascendant-male leader on top of a pyramid configuration we see so often. Garza told me as women "we actually don't get anything from leading like men do. *We* get the benefit of leadership by leading like people who know what it's like to be left out and left behind." Women in her circle, she told me, don't compete or try to "essentially be like men." Instead, they have chosen to, as her mother put it, believe that "the only way forward is with your sisters. We are all in the same boat."

To be clear, I'm not arguing that *only* women are good at organizing themselves as a huddle—just that women are *especially* good at it. So many of the women I interviewed for this book—regardless of their age, race, religion, or profession—attested to this time and again. Why are we more likely to organize in leaderful circles? Perhaps because we have experienced more marginalization that leads us to prioritize collaboration, or perhaps we are better at diplomacy, as Secretary of State Madeleine Albright told me without hesitation. When I asked Garza for her take on this, she didn't mince words: "This is what women do," she said. "And I don't say that in a symbolic way or in an essentializing way. But when you are excluded from the basic things that you need to be well, and you share that condition with other people . . . there's an element of mutual benefit. Our survival is deeply intertwined with each other."

The stakes, as Black Lives Matter has made so clear in this country, are very high. And perhaps, over generations of gathering to care for our communities, nurture our loved ones (and each other), huddling is not only our strength, but our mission.

THERE'S NO SUCH THING AS OTHER PEOPLE'S CHILDREN

In the moment Shannon Watts decided she wanted to help stop gun violence in America, she knew she wanted to do it "in the presence of women." It was one day after the Sandy Hook Elementary School shooting in Newtown, Connecticut, where a twenty-one-year-old shooter killed six adults and twenty first graders with a semiautomatic weapon. Watts was devastated, sitting alone in her house, with her five kids in school. She had no experience on this issue, but she knew she had to do something.

When she opened her laptop and couldn't find the "nationwide grassroots army" she envisioned existing, she decided to create one herself. She wasn't well informed about how gun laws worked in America or even the full extent of the gun violence problem, but she knew she'd be up against the National Rifle Association (NRA) and could sense that an army of moms would provide "the moral and emotional counterbalance to the gun lobby's bluster and posturing." So even though she only had seventy-five Facebook friends and an inactive Twitter handle, she created a Facebook page to announce a new group that would eventually become Moms Demand Action for Gun Sense in America.

Within a few years, the organization has become what is most likely the largest female huddle in America. With six million members, more than three hundred thousand active volunteers, Moms Demand Action has a solid record of passing what they call "common sense gun laws" by winning battles against "the most powerful special interest that's ever existed in America."

I met up with Shannon Watts in my hometown of Atlanta, joined by one of Watts's coconspirators and friends, Representative Lucy McBath. McBath's home district (Georgia's 6th district) was less than ten miles from where we sat at the OK Cafe, a classic Atlanta diner with checkerboard floors, old-fashioned uniforms, and delicious home cooking. Even though my favorite item on the menu will forever be the biscuit with apple butter (I spent a lot of pre–high school breakfasts there back in the day), I told everyone the squash soufflé was also worth ordering. McBath took me up on that idea, but not before we exchanged a big hug.

McBath and I had first met in 2015 at the town hall I hosted where I had interviewed forty Americans touched by gun violence. McBath, who is African American, was a part of that big interview because she had lost her seventeen-year-old son, Jordan, in 2012 when a white man shot him in a parking lot for playing his music too loud in his car. During the town hall McBath had held hands with Reverend Sharon Risher, who just three months prior had lost her mother and two cousins in the horrific and racially motivated Charleston church shooting. Although they were in different stages of their grieving, the women were clearly strengthened by each other's presence. The tears and physically wrenching experience—as raw as it was—also painted one of the most touching displays of solidarity I've been honored to witness. These women had bonded over not only their grief, but also their belief that their voices belonged in this fight. The reverend had talked openly about the difficulty of forgiving the shooter, the rawness of her pain so visible as she struggled to say, "The God I believe in is patting me on the back, saying *take your time.*" And just to her right, it was McBath who was patting her on the back, squeezing her hand, and crying along with her.

Out of this painful survivor experience, McBath had turned her grief into action and joined Watts to become a powerful spokeswoman for Moms Demand Action. She was so activated by her experiences meeting people across the country affected by gun violence that she decided to run for U.S. Congress, and won in 2018. McBath is soft-spoken and sweet—and displays the effortless poise that no doubt carried her through her former career as a flight attendant. Watts is a slight, brunette, white woman and self-described introvert. She is extremely steady and calm for someone who often has to travel with bodyguards due to the death threats she receives for the work she does.

In my discussion with them at the OK Cafe where I interviewed them for this book, I learned that Watts and her organization have racked up countless victories against the gun lobby—at the ballot box, in state legislatures, and in corporate America. To name a few, Moms Demand Action has helped pass state legislation to require background checks on all gun sales, and they have helped to pass a number of red flag laws, which allow families and law enforcement to ask a court to temporarily suspend a person's access to guns when there is evidence they pose a serious threat to themselves or others. They've defeated dangerous gun-lobby-backed bills, including bills that would arm teachers. They work at the community level with business leaders to encourage a culture of responsible gun ownership. Volunteers work to educate their communities about the importance of secure gun storage to prevent unintentional shootings by children. They've also managed to crush open carry in places like Starbucks, Walmart, Target, Kroger, and CVS—mostly by applying pressure and conducting "momcotts" until retailers change their policies.

And when they aren't changing laws, they're stymieing bad ones. ("We have a track record of stopping more than 90 percent of bad gun bills every year. In 2018, we killed hundreds," Watts told me.) And on top of all that, they're also *becoming* the lawmakers themselves. In the 2018 midterm election, they outspent and outmaneuvered the NRA, electing over one thousand "gun sense" candidates across the country, sixteen of whom were volunteers and survivors from within the organization. "We also flipped the makeup of six state legislatures who've already gone and passed stronger gun laws," Watts explained, speaking of the 2018 election. This momentum continued in the 2020 election, when Moms Demand Action volunteers registered more than 100,000 young voters nationwide, and more than thirty Moms Demand Action volunteers across the country won races up and down the ballot for everything from positions on school boards to roles in statehouses and the U.S. Congress. The volunteers, or "Moms" as they call them, advocate year-round across the country at the local, state, and federal level by showing up en masse in their red Moms Demand Action T-shirts, often going "eyeball to eyeball" with lawmakers "as if to say *not in my community, not in my state, you won't pass this,*" Watts told me.

She pinpointed further why moms make good activists: "Being a mom is about setting boundaries, being a moral authority, holding people accountable—which is what you do with your kids too." She shared her favorite moment from the past year when volunteers lined the stairs where Arkansas senators were heading into chamber right before the lawmakers tried to pass stand your ground laws for the second time. Mothers, apparently, are people lawmakers can't ignore, even if the gun lobby gives them more money. But all finger-wagging, tough-love mama jokes aside, there was a great deal of reverence at the table for the power and potential of mothers who take action together. Watts reminded me of the old saying *There's no such thing as other people's children*, and most movingly, McBath shared that even after losing her only child, motherhood is still her "ministry"—a calling to serve self-lessly for the children she cares about. It brought to mind the image of mothers on the front lines of Ferguson when the Black Lives Matter movement was taking shape.

Being an actual mother is of course not a membership requirement. Watts also spends a lot of time talking about her "soul sisters" in the movement, pointing out that friendship is tantamount: "The bonds between volunteers make us feel like we're in this together. This work is a marathon, and it isn't going to happen overnight, so you might as well like the people you're in the trenches with." The connection that forms when they phonebank and visit legislators together takes on an even deeper relevance when you consider how many gun violence survivors are active participants in the movement as well. The mutual obligation and commitment women feel in this work is palpable. Both women recounted for me the various friends they've made over the years and the particular ways women show up for each other when they believe in a common cause.

"These are people I can pass the baton to at any moment," Watts told me, recounting the time when one of her daughters was experiencing health problems and she often had to cancel flights and speaking engagements at the last minute because she was needed at home. "I knew the work would still be done, because we have this tribe and this ability to support one another." McBath called it a "sisterhood network," recalling the times when Moms showed up in their red shirts to support her on the campaign trail and at two trials for her son's killer, who tried to use stand your ground laws to defend his heinous act. With its widely distributed network, in which female friendship becomes a major benefit of volunteering, Moms Demand Action certainly qualifies as a grass-roots operation—something Crutchfield has determined in her book to be far more instrumental to change movements than large coffers or mighty influence.

But what struck me as most extraordinary about this massive huddle was the lack of ego in the founder, as well as the willing-ness she exhibited to revise and improve the organization in order to build an even more robust and truly grassroots movement. Both in her book *Fight Like a Mother* and in this interview, Watts gave a great deal of credit to McBath and other Moms for significantly expanding the organization's reach and scope and making it the powerhouse it is today. Case in point, when Watts met McBath, the movement was largely made up of suburban white women who were concerned with school shootings. McBath, who had been serving as a spokesperson giving talks about her experience in losing her son to gun violence, decided to take a leap of faith and write a heartfelt letter to Watts to point out the organization's biggest shortcoming—that it wasn't addressing other forms of gun violence outside of school shootings, including the kind that dis-proportionately afflict BIPOC families in their homes and on the streets. McBath recalled the contents of the letter that would go on to change the face of the organization: "I just said, 'Shannon, listen, I'm really grateful for this opportunity that you've given me to elevate not only my story, but the stories of so many oth-ers like me, but I really believe there are some missing links. We have to integrate the faith community and communities of color in this organization, because everybody is affected by gun violence.'"

Watts's response to the letter was to promptly thank McBath for her ideas and ask her if she could join the team to expand their mission and reach. After years of "building a bigger tent," as Watts calls it, today the Moms Demand Action staff is 40 percent BIPOC, and their volunteer base has ballooned to include communities of faith and color and even various political perspectives—all of which have broadened and deepened the movement.

McBath, who remembers being a child and watching her mother plan actions for the civil rights movement, deftly explained the power of a more expansive female huddle that incorporates the experiences and perspectives of Black women: "Women have always mobilized, organized, and galvanized support of each other—especially Black women, who have always been the center of our households because of the nature of slavery and the nature of our families having been broken, with fathers and husbands taken away to other plantations. Today we still see a lot of broken homes in our community, so women are always the focal point, doing it all." But unlike McBath's mother, who often spent hours strategizing and planning, only to be forced to take a back seat to the men who got to stand in the front lines in public marches, McBath's role in this movement is much more visible. And this is an exciting manifestation of Watts's initial vision: "What I've seen over and over again in other organizations is that women do all the menial labor around organizing—the chair setting up, making snacks, finding venues—and then men get to set the strategy and take the spotlight. In Moms Demand Action, it is the women who lead," said Watts. The "women" in her sentence was very decidedly plural, and I never got the sense that any of these women *wanted* the spotlight. Instead they wanted a sisterhood that shows up en masse to move mountains. It is clearly a leaderful movement—and one that has proven able to make constant, incremental changes, thanks to the true grassroots nature of their huddle and the genuine bonds shared between the members.

People sometimes refer to them as "the David to the NRA's Goliath," but the metaphor seems ill-suited to me, especially now that the number of Moms Demand Action members has surpassed the number of NRA members by at least a million. They are no longer "small and mighty." On the contrary, they are large and powerful, and they have fanned out in ways that would terrify any Goliath. These Moms don't need a slingshot; they've got him surrounded.

A PRAYER FOR THE VOICELESS

The more I investigated these change-making huddles that were active all around me, the more remarkable it seemed to me that their origin stories were often the same. One person would speak into a seeming void—only to find she was not alone. Whether it was Shannon Watts posting to her seventy-five Facebook friends or Alicia Garza expressing her urgent grief online, one single voice can set a movement in motion. Hundreds of women who had never run for Congress—many of whom had never even had a career in politics—were deciding their voices were needed to make changes in government. These women often started out without any sort of coalition behind them. Many of them were like Representative Chrissy Houlahan. She had no idea how to run for public office, but she was inspired and motivated, so she sent an email to EMILY's List and summoned her huddle to get the coaching, networking resources, and fundraising advice she needed.

After the 2018 midterms, when Houlahan joined the record number of 102 women in Congress, she became one of 89 Democrats in the House. The media celebrated the "pink wave," often glazing over the fact that things weren't so rosy for women on the Republican side. There were only thirteen Republican women in the house, and one of them, Representative Elise Stefanik of New York, was very alarmed. Leading up to the elections, she had worked to recruit one hundred other Republican women who might join her in the House, but only one of them was victorious on Election Day. Stefanik told me she saw this as a "huge opportunity" to ensure her party was prioritizing "supporting Republican women, recruiting them, building an infrastructure around them, and educating male colleagues as to why we need women's voices and seats at the table."

But she felt unheard. So she sounded the alarm in a GOP meeting: "Take a look around," she told her mostly male group of colleagues. "This is not reflective of the American public. We need to do better!" She was met with something worse than crickets. She got pushback. So like many solo women before her, she broke out on her own and founded E-PAC to help nurture and develop female Republican candidates—without the support of her party. Two years later, after the 2020 election, her efforts to huddle with other Republican women paid off, when her "sisterhood of conservative women in the House grew by double digits."

Another lone ranger during this same time was Greta Thunberg, the fifteen-year-old Swedish climate activist who began skipping school every Friday to stage a one-person protest to demand the Swedish government—and the rest of the world—reduce carbon emissions. She was literally a solo voice, standing outside her school on her own in the cold, and she managed to summon a sizable huddle. It was inspiring to watch the way American teenagers responded to Thunberg's quiet gesture. Some girls, such as thirteen-year-old Alexandria Villaseñor in New York, began skipping school on Fridays just like Thunberg, and in Colorado, a twelve-year-old girl named Haven Coleman cofounded the Youth Climate Strike U.S. along with Villaseñor and sixteen-year-old Isra Hirsi in Minnesota. This huddle of girls—working across state lines via text messages and social media—ended up coordinating with teenagers around the world to help organize the massive global climate strike in September 2019 that brought four million children and adults into the streets worldwide and welcomed Thunberg to the United States, where she spoke to the United Nations (giving her famous "How dare you!" speech). It shouldn't have been surprising to me by now that scrappy huddles of girls were behind this unprecedented movement, but I have to admit, I was surprised—and bowled over by their bravery. When I saw their young, serious faces on my monitor that day at work as they marched through the streets of Manhattan, I was inspired by their willingness to shout into the void of adults they feared would never listen to them.

A few weeks later, Thunberg traveled across the country to the Pine Ridge Indian Reservation in South Dakota to meet with a girl three years her junior, Tokata Iron Eyes, who many people credit with starting the 2016 movement against the Dakota Access Pipeline on the Standing Rock Sioux Reservation. While more than three hundred tribes and thousands of people had camped on the reservation in protest of the pipeline—making headlines around the world—the people who started the movement and attracted the masses to their cause were small groups of girls, women, and two-spirit youth (the term used by many North American Indigenous tribes to identify people with "both a male and female spirit within them" who are "blessed by their Creator to see life through the eyes of both genders"). Iron Eyes made a YouTube video in April 2016 asking the world to "respect our water, respect our land, and respect our people." The campaign and petition she started—

along with the work of the International Indigenous Youth Council (also led by "womxn and two-spirit" youth)—attracted much of the early attention to Standing Rock. Anna Merlan, reporting for Jezebel.com in 2016, states: "It's not an exaggeration or flattery or romanticism to say that women built the Standing Rock movement, and will sustain it through whatever fight is yet to come." Merlan details the efforts of the women of the Indigenous Environmental Network as well as the work of LaDonna Brave Bull Allard, who was the first to establish a camp on the site, inviting others into prayer and protest.

When Thunberg visited Iron Eyes, it wasn't just to lead a rally and march in Rapid City with her. She also had a message for the world: "Indigenous people have been leading this fight for centuries," she told the crowd. "They have taken care of the planet and they have lived in balance with nature, and we need to make sure that their voices are being heard." It was a clarion call for those who had idolized Thunberg, reminding everyone that she was a relative newcomer to an effort that Iron Eyes and her ancestors had been tending a great deal longer. And in the end, this movement was never about the leadership of one girl. The planet wouldn't be saved by one superhero, but rather it required a huddle of women reaching across nations and generations to solve this problem.

Just as I had learned from several interviews that African American women have been huddling for generations, I wanted to learn more about the ways Indigenous women had been working together to protect the planet. I called Paulette Jordan, a forty-year-old politician and activist in Idaho. As a member of the Coeur d'Alene tribe, she had been the youngest person ever elected to her tribal council and went on to defeat a Republican incumbent in 2014 to become a Democratic state representative in a very red district. I had met her in 2018 when she ran for governor of Idaho.

She ultimately lost her race, but not before making waves across the nation, running on a platform of environmental justice, education, and health care, and raising nearly half of her campaign funds from supporters and admirers *outside* the state. If she had won her race, she would have become the first female governor of Idaho and the first Native American governor in the nation. Later, in 2020, she also fought a very respectable but uphill battle, ultimately losing the race for a Senate seat against a two-term incumbent, Senator Jim Risch.

When I caught up with her before the 2020 election, she told me her loss in 2018 had led her to take stock of her future. Shortly after the election, she attended a winter ceremony—a tradition in her tribe in which people can connect spiritually with their ancestors. It was here that she received a message from an ancestor who spoke through a relative participating in the ceremony that day. The ancestor's message to Jordan reinforced her purpose: she was here to defend the rights of nature. The scene Jordan set for me of her experience at the ceremony was beautiful—a moment of quiet huddle with her forebearers that resulted in a call to action. "It was really humbling to receive this direction," she told me. "And to be redirected back to what matters most, which is to ensure that everyone and everything has its rightful place at the table, and to make sure nature has a voice."

The notion that nature could have a voice was intriguing, and I asked her to tell me more. She explained how Indigenous people all over the world have been fighting to give nature a "voice" by pushing governments to award legal rights to specific bodies of water or tracts of land. Granting rights to a *place*—the same way a *person* is guaranteed certain rights—is one way to legally save it from human-caused degradation or climate change destruction. It's a fascinating new tactic environmental groups and Indigenous leaders are sometimes taking to protect natural spaces. Inspired by this and the ancestor's message, Jordan spent the next year building a strategy and assembling a huddle of mostly Indigenous women to help build out her vision. She partnered with women in frontline roles at the Natural Resources Defense Council and the Endangered Species Coalition, and started several foundations, including Save the American Salmon, to protect the endangered salmon and orcas that have been threatened by the combination of global warming and the outdated Lower Snake River dams in Washington. Additionally, her Rights of Nature project was underway—a comprehensive document to propose that all tribes reaffirm their commitment to remain stewards of the land.

Jordan told me that with their centuries of experience in tending the land, Indigenous tribes continue to steward natural resources, using ancient tried and true land and water management practices that often protect and restore what the EPA and the federal government sometimes neglect or disregard. "Right now, because of the Trump administration," she told me, "the EPA is deregulating air and water quality. You can see the difference." Her Rights of Nature document would connect hundreds of tribes in a shared mission to stand up for the land regardless of the whimsies of politicians and government policies.

In addition to running for U.S. Senate, Jordan also had a leadership role on the National Indian Gaming Association, and a founding role with Idaho Voice, a nonprofit for developing leadership in women and getting out the vote. I asked her how she found the time and strength to carry out all of this work, particularly in the face of a problem as multifaceted as protecting nature. She told me her "sense of responsibility was triggered" by her huddle with her ancestors at the ceremony that day when they declared that not only would it be *women* protecting the rights of nature, it would be *Indigenous* women. "We are here to be the voice for nature," she explained. "Therefore, within these responsibilities, as Indigenous women, we have to bring humanity together and show all people throughout the world what it means to care for every living being."

Jordan's grandmother Lucy Covington was a well-known chief respected throughout the Northwest for politically advocating for all tribal sovereign status. Jordan grew up hearing stories of her grandmother selling cattle so she could buy a flight to D.C. and lobby on behalf of Indian Country—making an impression on all who encountered her. To this day, many older legislators remember her fiery short frame, dressed in full regalia as she visited Congress. "She was very keen on protecting tribal rights and environmental stewardship. If she hadn't stood for these things, I would not know my culture and language today," Jordan explained.

She could not speak of the much-beloved Lucy without mentioning her other less famous grandmother and great-grandmother. While they may not have been in the spotlight, they were still equally influential to her, she recalled. The common thread among all of them was that they taught her the importance of integrity and humility. I wondered aloud what humility had to do with fighting to protect a burning planet, and she reminded me of the women of Standing Rock who were not loud in their protest. "A lot of women there were huddled in prayer," Jordan said. It was eye-opening to hear her speak of the many Native women she admires, who, despite holding multiple academic degrees, would say their power is seated in their songs or prayer. "They carry all this knowledge and wisdom within them," she said, "but they don't have to yell." Unjust as it may be, it is not surprising that our leader-focused culture has not given these intentionally humble women the widespread credit they deserve for starting the highly visible movement at Standing Rock in 2016, or for being the water and earth protectors they have been for generations. They do not yell about their leadership. They do not idolize or center individual voices within their movement. On the contrary, they huddle with the spirits of their great great-grandmothers, and become the collective voice for an entity (nature) that does not speak except through them.

Before we said goodbye, I thought back to the beautiful view from Jordan's porch in Coeur d'Alene, Idaho, where I had visited her on her family's ranch when I interviewed her for *American Woman* a few years prior. She'd taken me and a favorite horse on a walk out in the brush, which was full of brambles that somehow penetrated the boots and jeans I'd carefully chosen to wear that day. Yet, Jordan, standing six feet tall, her shoulders back and her head held high, led the horse calmly through the thorns without so much as wincing. I followed along, listening to her steady voice, unsurprised she was steely enough to run for governor at the age of thirty-eight in a place where she was so politically outnumbered. Her strength was clearly derived from the generations of women who'd come before her, who'd assured her, she told me, "this is our time to rise up together. We have our prayer in place."

seven

MULTIPLYING RESPECT

One of the few times I ever cut someone's mic live on air occurred shortly after a sports radio host said the following to me:

"The only things I believe in are the First Amendment and boobs."

Yes, that's right. He said *boobs*.

Let me set the scene for you. It was 2017. I had invited this man whose name I'd rather not print (it's not a recognizable name anyway) onto my show to discuss something President Trump had tweeted. Trump had called for ESPN to fire Jemele Hill, an African American journalist who had called the president a white supremacist in a tweet. Hill's tweet came shortly after Trump had refused to fully denounce the white supremacist and neo-Nazi groups who were rallying to "Unite the Right" and save Confederate statues in Charlottesville, Virginia. At that time in America, two years after the Charleston church shooting where nine Black people had been murdered by a white supremacist, several cities in the South were reconsidering their dedication to Confederate statues—and this inspired the Unite the Right rally. It was one of the most public gatherings of hate groups in a very long time, and before it was over, a thirty-two-year-old woman named Heather Heyer was killed when another attendee deliberately drove his car into the crowd where she and many others were holding a counterprotest to stand up to the white supremacists.

Virginia governor Terry McAuliffe publicly called out this "hate and bigotry" but President Trump, on the other hand, remained silent for two days, refusing to denounce the rally's organizers. The nation was hurt and angry. After the president finally spoke up and rebuked the hate groups, he equivocated soon after, noting the "very fine people on both sides." This pandering to the neo-Nazis and white nationalists set off a flurry of criticism from several media sources and public figures around the country. And yet, as I pointed out on my show that day, Trump's retaliation was directed mainly at this one Black woman, Jemele Hill. I had brought on ESPN senior editor Keith Reed and the other guy—I'll just call him the Boob—to discuss the issue. I expected the two might have opposing viewpoints but never imagined the latter would use this moment as an opportunity to degrade women in such an inane fashion by saying *the only things he believes in are the First Amendment and boobs.*

After he said it, I did a double take. "Hold on, I just want to make sure I heard you correctly. As a woman anchoring the show . . . did you say boobs? As in b-o-o-b-s?"

"Yes, boobs," he said with a smirk and a self-satisfied look on his face that reminded me of a high school boy who had just managed to prank the teacher, or a child who felt giddy because he had just derailed an adult conversation.

My male producer was in my earpiece assuring me the word I was hearing was *booze*, not *boobs*, that it was okay to move past the comment. My boss—another male—also called in to the control room to essentially say the same. To be fair to them, no one could imagine a grown man would say this disrespectful garbage on live TV—particularly to a female anchor. Everything was moving so quickly. Meanwhile the Boob repeated his asinine remark a few more times while I collected myself, listening to the continued assurances in my earpiece that I should move on. As a woman in a male-dominated profession where opinions and perceptions fly fast and furious, I often find myself second-guessing my instincts or questioning if I'm overreacting. But I knew what I had just heard and I didn't want to let the comment pass.

"I just want to make sure I'm hearing you correctly," I said, to cover my bases one last time. "Did you say *booze* or *boobs*, because as a woman—"

"Boobs . . ." he cut me off and continued sucking up more airtime. The sting set in and I grasped what was happening in real time. We were discussing one of our nation's deepest wounds; Americans were being targeted for their religion and the color of their skin; a president was giving the impression that he was permissive about white supremacy; and a Black woman's job was on the line. But this man on my show wanted to humiliate me—and this very urgent topic—with his junior high–level sexism, to reduce me and all women to a body part. It didn't threaten me in the way he probably intended. Instead, it flipped a switch in me.

"I'm done," I said, following my gut. "This is done. Conversation over. Yanking mics. Bye. See ya." In that moment, my team disappeared him from the screen, and I apologized to my viewers that I hadn't yanked him off the air even faster.

In the grand scheme of things, it wasn't really a big moment in my personal or professional life. It wouldn't be the first (or last) time a guy was disrespectful to women in my presence. And all things considered, I feel pretty lucky to have gained the level of respect I enjoy at my job every day. Sure, I've brushed aside plenty of comments about my weight or "surprising intelligence," but that pales in comparison to what women just one or two generations before me had to endure as a matter of course. Secretary of State Madeleine Albright once told me that at her Wellesley College graduation ceremony, the commencement speaker, Secretary of Defense Neil McElroy (whose daughter was in Albright's class) told the all-female audience that their main responsibility as college graduates was to go get married and raise children. "The fact that we kind of sat there and listened to it is amazing, in retrospect," Albright mused. She joked that she attended college "sometime between the invention of the iPad and the discovery of fire," which made me laugh, but in reality, it wasn't all that long ago. It was 1959—just ten years before Hillary Clinton would graduate from the same college and be selected to give the commencement speech herself. And even though Clinton delivered what the *New York Times* called "a public rebuke" of a condescending male Republican senator who had spoken just before her, I'm sure she'd probably be the first to say that these kinds of abysmally low expectations of women are still very much in circulation. Whether it's being intellectually underestimated or sexually harassed, millions of women deal with this kind of disrespect every day. Tale as old as time.

But one month after I yanked the Boob's mic, the #MeToo movement erupted on social media. Suddenly women everywhere were speaking up about the sexual assault and everyday indignities they'd been enduring at the hands of men for their entire lives. Conversations were happening everywhere, and I joined in on my show, expressing my solidarity with all the women telling their #MeToo stories and speaking up for women who had been overlooked, abused, or demeaned. I used my airtime to demand the president respect the African American female staffers, politicians, and journalists he had been name-calling, and I said "enough is enough" after covering a series of powerful men in the news who had been accused of trafficking and abusing young girls and women. Almost every woman I knew recognized herself as part of the #MeToo movement. It was a powerful demand for accountability, reckoning, and respect. Most of us had lived a lifetime in which humiliation of women had been normalized, and we were all collectively done with it.

Out of this roiling boil, another huddle quickly assembled. The Time's Up movement was premised upon a simple insistence of "safe, fair, and dignified work for women of all kinds" and was grounded in efforts such as a multimillion-dollar legal defense fund, legislation advocacy work, and a research arm that would help elevate and protect all women—everyone from corporate CEOs to migrant farmworkers. The three hundred women in Hollywood who initially launched Time's Up were still standing in the very bright spotlight they'd attracted to their industry with the Harvey Weinstein allegations, and they sought to share their privileged platform with blue-collar women whose complaints were far less likely to gain attention. The letter they published in the *New York Times* to announce the movement called out the unsafe conditions for nurses, janitors, health aides, and factory and domestic workers, who deserved pay equity and freedom from harassment just as much as the high-profile celebrities did. It was a stunning show of solidarity across class lines, but it was also a profound example of how one huddle can engender another.

Inspired directly by #MeToo, the Time's Up movement sought to turn the raw, emotional hashtag storm into direct action. According to Maria Eitel, a co-chairwoman of the Nike Foundation who helped facilitate some of the earliest Time's Up meetings, the original Time's Up members "didn't come together because they wanted to whine, or complain, or tell a story or bemoan. They came together because they intended to act. There was almost a ferociousness to it, especially in the first meetings." The productivity of Time's Up might not have happened without the very crucial work accomplished by the #MeToo movement. To me, this was a lesson in how one huddle emboldens another; how iron sharpens iron—and even multiplies its power; and furthermore, how one huddle's efforts to disrupt the status quo can have a multiplier effect on the sum total of change generated well into the future.

Imagine the ripple effects of one powerful man telling that entire graduating class of Wellesley women in 1959 that their job was to go get married and have babies. The ramifications of such a statement are probably impossible (and too depressing) to quantify. But more optimistically, on the other hand, imagine the multiplier effect of introducing just one female secretary of state into the history books. And not long after Madeleine Albright served her term came Condoleezza Rice. And then right after Rice, enter Hillary Clinton. And pretty soon, you're hearing girls like Albright's eight-year-old granddaughter say things like, "So what's the big deal about Grandma Maddy being secretary of state? *Only* girls are secretary of state." I'm not a social scientist, but by my calculations this is pretty good evidence that change begets change. When multiple women command respect, they provide a foundation for all women to demand respect.

LEAVING THE TEAM BETTER THAN THEY FOUND IT

When I met Megan Rapinoe at a totally unpretentious hotel restaurant in midtown Manhattan in late 2019, the topic of respect was very much on her mind. She had spent the previous evening at an event where she was lauded as the 2019 *Sports Illustrated* Sportsperson of the Year, something that had only been awarded to individual women three other times in its sixty-five-year history. A few days before that, she had been named the recipient of the Women's Ballon d'Or, yet another distinction, after she helped lead her team to victory in the 2019 World Cup. The *Sports Illustrated* honor was a monumental one—and the party had been a good time, she said—but she was preoccupied with something else as she sipped her coffee. She wanted to know if I'd listened to the much buzzed-about Howard Stern interview with Hillary Clinton that had aired just a few days prior. There was a dull roar around us as tourists helped themselves to the breakfast buffet, seemingly unaware they were in the presence of one of soccer's biggest and loudest icons. Rapinoe spoke over the noise, her signature pink coif obscured by a Supreme white ballcap that read in ghosted white letters the words "FUCK YOU" for anyone who got close enough to make them out.

She was annoyed that the 2019 Hillary Clinton who spoke to Howard Stern was able to be so much more relaxed, frank, and authentic—and, well, likable—than the carefully calculated and unrelatable Hillary Clinton who ran for president three years prior. Rapinoe's frustration wasn't directed at Clinton herself, but rather the forces at play when a woman occupies such a public role and is forced to perform a personality that will conform to masculine norms and offend exactly no one. She bemoaned what so many of us have recognized as a catch-22 for women in power: if you act like a woman, you get no respect. If you act like a man, you're considered a cold, unfeeling bitch.

Rapinoe's empathy for Clinton wasn't surprising, given that Rapinoe had become known for expressing herself, standing up for her beliefs, and quite literally taking up as much space as possible with that famous post-scoring pose she'd strike, in which she spread her arms out as far as possible—as if to challenge the world to embrace her *exactly as she is*. She was one of the first prominent soccer players to come out as a lesbian and the first white American athlete to support NFL player Colin Kaepernick by kneeling during the national anthem in peaceful protest of police brutality against Black lives. She also didn't mince words when she told a reporter that she wouldn't be visiting "the fucking White House" if her team were to win the World Cup. Trump responded with a tweet admonishing her to "win first before she TALKS." He also chastised her to "never disrespect our Country, the White House, or our Flag"—which was most likely a dig at her earlier show of solidarity with Kaepernick, an act that made her the focus of much MAGA ire. Rapinoe seemed mostly unbothered by the tweet in the days that followed as she went on to "finish the job" (to use Trump's terminology) and score the game-winning goal in the final match of the World Cup and promptly become an American hero. For Rapinoe, trying to be everything for everyone else was clearly not the path to progress for women, and she was not in need of a Twitter lecture about respect.

Respect, after all, was something she'd been grappling with heavily since 2016 when she and her teammates registered a complaint about pay equity with the Equal Employment Opportunity Commission. In 2017 they negotiated a new collective bargaining agreement, and on March 8, 2019—International Women's Day— she and her twenty-seven teammates filed a lawsuit against the United States Soccer Federation claiming gender-based discrimination.

But Rapinoe and her teammates were not the only professional female athletes raising the banner for fair treatment. Within the same span of a few years—when so many women outside of sports were also huddling for change nationwide—similar battles in the Women's National Basketball Association and the National Women's Hockey League had come to a head. Although the situations were different within each sport—the basketball players were fighting for a better collective bargaining agreement, while the hockey players were boycotting their league entirely—the underlying crisis was much the same. Women in all three sports were paid significantly less than their male counterparts (even when they won more games, in the case of the soccer team). They were also given shoddier working conditions and benefits and were universally underestimated for their ability to advance their respective sports to future generations of athletes and fans. More than just equity, it was a matter of respect and dignity for these women.

Sports leagues and federations not only determine the amount of their athletes' paychecks and the quality of their locker rooms and travel accommodations, they also designate the level of investment to make in their athletes via corporate sponsorships and marketing opportunities. Oftentimes these kinds of investments—a signature athletic shoe in an athlete's name or an ad campaign with a major sponsor—can lead to greater visibility and celebration of the athlete, not to mention the higher earning potential that comes along with the elevated profile. Without these perks, it can become a self-fulling prophecy that female athletes aren't popular enough to warrant sponsorships or the kind of reverence their male counterparts receive by corporate entities—regardless of how beloved they might actually be by the fans.

Rapinoe painted a picture of this drastic underinvestment thusly: the popularity of the U.S. Women's National Team (USWNT) grew immensely after the 2011 World Cup, in which Rapinoe crossed the ball forty-five feet to Abby Wambach, who then scored in the

122nd minute—a feat of teamwork that is largely considered one of the greatest moments in Women's World Cup history. After this win, the team went from playing to crowds of two thousand to twenty thousand overnight. The following year, in 2012, they took gold at the Olympics, and they followed that win with two more World Cup victories, in 2015 and 2019. In short, they had become some of the most beloved soccer players in the world—celebrated by everyone. Everyone, that is, except their own federation, the U.S. Soccer Federation. Even though they had created an enormous surge of momentum and attention for the sport, their federation gave them very little credit or compensation. "The federation made so much money," Rapinoe explained. "All our victory tour games were crazy popular, and we were feeling that all around us. But there was no way to actually participate in the show that we were putting on for everyone else." According to Rapinoe, the federation didn't capitalize on the team's massive popularity, and when corporate money did come calling, the federation wouldn't leverage sponsorship deals in ways that would maximize benefits to the players themselves.

"We're not asking for the moon," Rapinoe's teammate USWNT center back Becky Sauerbrunn told me. "We're asking for basic standards so that we can perform as professionals." As one of three members of the soccer players association executive committee (the group that represents the league in contract bargaining agreements), Sauerbrunn filled me in on some of the team's demands. They included such gleaming luxuries as showers in locker rooms, properly turfed fields, a stated minimum of players on the roster for away games, and one full-time athletic trainer per team to handle injuries. I think I'm like most people in that when I imagine the glory and spectacle of a professional soccer game, the celebrations and inspirational feats of physical excellence, I do not also picture the star athletes having to drive to a second location to rinse off afterward.

Nneka Ogwumike, the power forward for the Los Angeles Sparks and president of the WNBA Players Association, told me about similar indignities within her own sport prior to the collective bargaining agreement (CBA) she and her fellow league players had just signed in January 2020 when I spoke to her. Besides fighting off constant false perceptions that "no one watches us and no one takes [us] seriously," Ogwumike described the shocking discrepancy in childcare provisions between the WNBA and its parent league, the NBA. The wives and girlfriends of the men in the NBA, she explained, actually have better childcare options than WNBA *players themselves* do. She described her teammates bringing their children on the road, seating the kids in the bleachers during practices, cramming family into one hotel room.

Sue Bird, who serves alongside Ogwumike as a vice president of the Players Association, is widely known as the oldest active player in the WNBA. At the age of forty, she had just finished her eighteenth season with the Seattle Storm and had a lot of institutional knowledge of working conditions over the years. She told me about other hard-won provisions in the new CBA, including an increased salary max for top players, which might finally help disincentivize playing abroad in the off season—something that most top players have been forced to do to earn closer to their potential. Bird, who revealed publicly last year that she froze her eggs (on her own dime), also described the new maternity and family planning benefits. These provisions, she explained, are crucial to female athletes for whom pregnancy and child rearing are especially challenging, particularly for those who work overseas in the off season. With the new CBA, players are given 100 percent pay during maternity leave and are provided a stipend that can be applied toward freezing eggs, adopting a child, or treating a fertility issue. "It's all in the name of having options," Bird told me, "which was something female basketball players in this country really didn't have before."

The situation for America's female professional hockey players was perhaps the most dire of all. In May 2019, just two months after the women in soccer filed their lawsuit on International Women's Day, two hundred of hockey's most elite and accomplished players from around the world came together to form the Professional Women's Hockey Players Association (PWHPA). Independent of any league or existing federation, this group of athletes announced they were "coming together not as individual players, but as one collective voice" to announce a full-on boycott of their entire league. With salaries as low as two thousand per season and no health insurance, the players announced they would not play in any professional league in North America until they received the resources "that professional hockey demands and deserves."

It had already been a long road to get here. In 2017 the national team had announced a boycott of the world championships as part of their demands for resources that were equitable to those received by the men's team. Much like the soccer and basketball teams, the hockey players were asking for better (though not equal) pay, equitable transportation and hotel accommodations, and reasonable amounts of training time on the ice. The boycott resulted in a new four-year contract with better conditions for players, but after they brought home the gold in the 2018 Olympics, they remained frustrated with the conditions of their regular seasonal association, the National Women's Hockey League. Even though women's hockey had become the fastest growing sport in North America, and more little girls than ever were playing, most people had no idea that these Olympic gold winners didn't even receive a living wage in their own league. In fact, most professional hockey players had to take on second or third jobs just to make ends meet.

Thus the call by hockey stars Hilary Knight, Kendall Coyne-Schofield, and Shannon Szabados to lead what they called the #ForTheGame movement that initiated the league boycott and birthed the PWHPA. Not being able to play professional hockey was painful for many players who were sacrificing the prime of their careers and had just gotten used to finally having a league of their own (the NWHL had only formed in 2016). "There are bad days," Knight told me, "but this is 100 percent the right move. This is not only about us. It's for the next generation."

Knight and the PWHPA weren't content to just sit out on the sidelines during the boycott, however. They took a page from the legendary Billie Jean King's book and created their own tournament, the Dream Gap Tour, to keep players on the ice during the walkout. And just like the tennis icon who banded together with eight other women to break away from the tennis establishment and create her own tournament that highlighted gender inequality fifty years ago, the women in hockey spent the rest of the 2019–2020 season playing games around the country for the Dream Gap Tour. And they organized it entirely themselves. Meaning, in addition to providing a thrilling spectacle on the ice, they also ordered jerseys, coordinated practice times, hired coaching staff, and hosted fundraising events—all while building their new players association and setting intentions for the future of women's hockey in America. If there is a more stunning example of the way a women's huddle can multitask to conquer both the tedious logistics and all the visionary work at the same time, I can't think of one.

Knight told me about sitting on a bus after practice in Finland one day, heading to the airport and sharing air pods with her teammate Kendall Coyne-Schofield and talking to Billie Jean King's partner and tennis great Ilana Kloss about how to create a players association and a tournament of their own. This was just one of dozens of moments several athletes shared with me, revealing how frequently they were all crossing sporting lines to support one another in their individual battles.

To me, this is what the multiplier effect looks like. When women in one sports league huddled to demand respect, the women in other leagues were inspired and empowered to do the same. Just as the #MeToo movement had provided a springboard for Time's Up, America's female professional athletes had been building on each other's momentum for several years. Bird (the basketball player) and Rapinoe (the soccer player), who are in a relationship and live together, were of course exchanging notes with each other about how to frame their teams' demands within the context of their respective sports. Ogwumike (basketball) provided advice to Knight (hockey) about how to effectively engage the large group of women in her players association to keep them all on the same page during negotiations. Knight told me she also sought advice from retired soccer player Heather O'Reilly, and when she found herself riding in a golf cart with WNBA star Sue Bird, a personal idol of hers, she found herself wanting "to soak up everything she said."

"Even though we are in our silos in many ways," Knight told me, "our sports are so connected. I look at the WNBA and U.S. Soccer and think, we're still like twenty years behind those girls . . . but having access to different people in their industries is extremely important to hopefully cut that learning curve." Sauerbrunn and Rapinoe both told me the athletes from different sports leagues were constantly rooting for one another and there was a steady stream of love and solidarity expressed between them, whether in person at events or via supportive shout-outs on social media.

This bond was so public and obvious over several years that other journalists were writing about the contagious fervor and mutual support among the various women's teams.

My favorite example of this multiplier effect came from USWNT and North Carolina Courage midfielder Sam Mewis, who recalled working out in a gym during her off season in her hometown of Boston and finding herself training side by side with a bunch of hockey greats, including Olympian and team captain Meghan Duggan. Mewis was inspired by the hockey team's confidence to demand the respect and equity they deserved—not to mention the legwork they were doing to make it happen. Meghan Duggan had told Mewis about the hundreds of phone calls she personally made to every single hockey player and every Division 3 up-and-comer in the nation, asking them not to cross the picket lines in advance of the 2017 boycott. Mewis mused that if someone like Abby Wambach or Megan Rapinoe (the soccer-equivalent icons to Meghan Duggan) had called her as a Division 3 player to urge her to fight for something bigger than her own hockey career, she would have been pretty moved by it as well.

Fighting for something bigger was another common thread among these athletes, even if it meant adding an unwelcome tedium to their schedules. There was much talk of crammed meetings in hotel rooms, late-night phone calls, learning the complexities of legal negotiations and collective bargaining, and keeping up on detailed text chats on top of an already busy training schedule. Every athlete I spoke to (all of whom were leaders in their players associations) told me about the disruption caused to their physical regimens. No one wants to take off three or four days of work to, as Rapinoe put it, "fight with our employer about our job." Dan Levy, Rapinoe's agent, told me that despite all the coverage the soccer team has received during its historic cry for equality, the one thing that remains "underreported" is this level of collaboration and hard work the female athletes have put in behind the scenes to make it happen. Huddling isn't always easy work, but these women saw the inconvenience as worthwhile. They were doing it for the game, for their dignity, and for the athletes who would come after them.

"We're fighting for something way bigger than just our own lawsuit," Mewis told me. "Filing on International Women's Day was a message to say we're not just fighting so our own paychecks go up. We want everyone to feel like they can fight for that too." When I asked Billie Jean King for her take on this, she told me that 96 percent of women in senior management positions at companies identify as athletes. "And I guarantee you, those business leaders are following this story. . . . This is no longer purely a sports story. It's a pay equity story." Her point was well taken. I felt like so many stories I was reporting during this time were different versions of a soccer huddle story—all variations on a theme of women making demands to be paid, to be seen, to be heard, and to be respected.

Rapinoe told me she saw her teams' demands as part of a larger nationwide call for dignity for all women and BIPOC—a cry she saw coming from other movements like Black Lives Matter, Colin Kaepernick's movement, #MeToo, and Time's Up. Bird's take was similar, but with a touching nuance from her own personal life. She shared with me that she had only recently become more vocal about her beliefs after she came out as a lesbian to the public a few years ago (she had been out to her friends and family for several years). Bird said she had learned through experience that when women share their stories, it can have an "amazing trickle-down effect." The #MeToo movement, she suggested, had a multiplying effect on everyone: "It all started with women being empowered

to share their stories," she said. "To open people's eyes to what
the walk of a woman is. This empowered one woman after the
next . . . and now people are taking notice of how we have been
treated differently or unfairly."

There's a legendary motto among the soccer players that Mia
Hamm of 1999 World Cup fame drilled into the head of Abby
Wambach, who then passed it down to the current generation of
players: "Leave the team better than you found it." All the players I
spoke with were acutely aware that they belonged to a huddle that
had been formed over decades. They had deep respect for their
athletic elders, so to speak. Mewis talked about soccer great Julie
Foudy fighting the same fight for the team a generation ago. Bird
spoke of seeking advice from her friend and basketball legend Rebecca Lobo, and Knight admired the work of her friend Cammi
Granato, the ice hockey Hall of Famer who waged the same battle
for women's hockey nearly two decades before Knight did—only
to be shut down. Like their predecessors, the current players are
also focused on the next generation—none more than thirty-year-
old Hilary Knight, who grew up in Illinois in a time not so long
ago when there weren't any girls' hockey teams for her to join. She
told me stories of being bullied by the parents on her co-ed team,
being called a bitch or asshole—as a child!—for taking one of their
sons' spots on the team. It reminded me of Hillary Clinton telling
Howard Stern that when she showed up to take the Harvard law
school exam, she was shamed for potentially banishing men to the
Vietnam draft if she passed the test and "took their spot." Or like
the story of the late Supreme Court Justice Ruth Bader Ginsburg,
who dealt with queries from her Harvard law school dean in the
1950s about "why she felt entitled to take a man's spot in her class."

Regardless of the fact that Knight may never reap the benefits of a better hockey league during the prime of her own career,

she feels confident she's going to leave the game better than she found it for all the girls out there playing today. When I asked her if she ever catches a girls' game herself—something that is now far more widespread than when she was young—she told me about hockey clinics where she'd had the chance to work with young girls directly. But mostly, she told me, she just enjoys sitting in the bleachers and watching. "There's just little pig piles of girls all over the ice," she laughed. "Little bodies flying and running into each other, swinging at pucks, sometimes hitting pucks, *not* hitting pucks . . ." Being a spectator to the next generation, she implied, was already reward enough.

RESTORING DIGNITY TO "WOMEN'S WORK"

Tega Toney has a saying she tries to live by: *You can't pour from an empty cup.*

As a public school teacher in Fayette County, West Virginia, she has to remind herself of this belief regularly. Toney teaches eleventh-grade history and social studies, and like most teachers in America, she never stops working. Her friend and fellow teacher Angie Turkelson from a few counties over explained that teachers "are always thinking about a better way to spark an interest for our kids." Turkelson teaches math, science, algebra, and zoology in a special education department to students in various grades. Like most women I met in West Virginia during my three years living there in my twenties, Turkelson and Toney are passionate, strong, and kind. They are the kind of women who do things like buy food, shoes, clothing, prom tickets, and caps and gowns for their students—many of whom come from poor families. "My faculty has passed the hat to help with a kid's parent's funeral costs," Toney added. These stories are similar to those of so many public school teachers I've met over the years in my reporting. In addition to merely instructing students, teachers are often the kind of folks who will spare no expense to preserve a child's dignity, to uplift their spirits and discreetly provide them with the most basic needs their families might not be able to afford.

They go above and beyond the call of duty, and yet this generosity isn't always extended back to them. In addition to working beneath state governments that continuously ignore the seeding of their salaries, health care plans, and pensions, public school teachers today work in a system where buildings are underfunded and classrooms are overcrowded. Nationwide, the system increasingly favors standardized testing over teacher autonomy and privatized schooling models that many argue undervalue the assets an experienced educator brings to the classroom. All of this contributes toward making a teacher feel unappreciated for her talents.

Toney, whose state ranked forty-seventh in the nation for salary rates in early 2018, recalled, "There was just a general feeling of being overworked, underappreciated, and devalued." To add insult to injury, health-care deductibles for teachers had increased by 500 percent in West Virginia without any corresponding raises. "It actually amounted to a giveback," Toney exclaimed. Many teachers, who were already working side gigs to make ends meet, were worried about being able to pay for essential medicines for themselves and their families. "I know teachers who have had to foreclose on their homes because of health-care expenses," Toney explained. "These are people with master's degrees and full-time jobs." She sighed and earnestly continued: "We're doing this work for the love of the profession and the love of the children. But at the same time, we cannot be expected to continue to be martyrs."

One month after American women began calling "Time's Up" on workplace inequalities, a nationwide labor movement erupted across the country, and it all started with a nine-day strike by thirty-four thousand workers in West Virginia in February 2018. The sight of so many teachers there demanding respect for their profession had a multiplier effect on other teachers in other states across the country. In the months that followed, similar work stoppages were initiated by educators in Oklahoma, Arizona, Kentucky, and North Carolina. In 2019, teachers in several large cities followed suit, including in Los Angeles, Oakland, Denver, and Chicago. Randi Weingarten, president of the American Federation of Teachers, told me, "The teacher uprisings [in 2018–2019] have laid bare the frustration over insufficient resources, deplorable facilities, and inadequate pay and benefits for educators." And yet, "it's not just the underfunding," she explained. "Teachers are frustrated and demoralized and really stressed. The lack of classroom autonomy and discretion have supercharged that dissatisfaction."

In a fascinating opinion piece on the US teacher strikes for the *Guardian*, Tithi Bhattacharya, a professor of history at Purdue University and the national organizer of the US International Women's Strike, outlines the ways that teaching has been culturally demoted as "women's work," and as such has been stripped of its "dignity and security." In other words, the education crisis is fueled by an epidemic of disrespect for teachers, roughly 80 percent of whom are female.

In Boone County, West Virginia, Carrena Rouse, an English teacher serving her thirtieth and final year before retiring, told me that the disrespect directed at female teachers for so long served to unite them. And many, she shared, were angry that this storm in their profession had "robbed education of its sweetness." This love for her vocation shone through when she told me about one of her favorite projects with students that encouraged them to read banned books. "Watching ideas coalesce," she explained in her deep southern West Virginia accent, is something "all teachers know and love." So when her county suffered a loss of coal tax revenues and the legislature decided to withhold a portion of teacher pay to make up the difference, Rouse said she got "snarly." Anger began to foment as teachers exchanged stories in a Facebook group that they actually made less money than they had a decade prior after adjusting for inflation. The stage was set for a walkout and most teachers were ready.

As tensions heated up, and Governor Jim Justice famously called the fed-up and majority-female educators "dumb bunnies," Rouse went to Walmart and bought out all the bunny ears she could find for her teacher friends to wear to the capitol. Meanwhile, in Putnam County, Turkelson set up what she called "hallway huddles," where she gathered teachers for five minutes after class to empower them with the talking points they needed to speak to their legislators. When Rouse and her friends arrived at the capitol to join the thousands of other educators who'd assembled there, she told me she prayed over the Senate chambers and then proceeded to "talk the ears off" of any representative who would listen. She and her friends fanned out to meet with as many elected officials as possible. A somewhat less holy experience, Rouse recalled, was joining in the massive chant (directed at recalcitrant Senate President Mitch Carmichael) inspired by the Ludacris song: "Move, Mitch! Get out the way!" Rouse laughed when she recounted how a younger teacher had to fill her in on Ludacris's original lyrics.

Most teachers, I'm told, lined up at the capitol or picketed outside their schools all nine days in the chilly February air. The mood among many, Toney told me, was "determined and angry," but the healing camaraderie turned out to be a "once-in-a-lifetime spiritual experience." In the end, the teachers were granted all five of their demands, including a 5 percent pay raise. And the eyes of the nation were upon them.

Meanwhile, in another deep red state, Oklahoma high school English teacher Jackie Rasnic and her fellow educators were feeling "an electric current" to see their West Virginia counterparts standing up for themselves. "We had been whispering about a walkout for years, but when we saw what West Virginia was doing, it definitely gave us strength," Rasnic explained. The conditions in Oklahoma were starkly similar to those in West Virginia—except here, the undertaxed natural resource was oil—not coal, and instead of "dumb bunnies" the insult of choice by Governor Mary Fallin was to compare the teachers to "teenage kids who wanted better cars." At forty-ninth in the nation in pay, the Oklahoma teachers hadn't been given a raise in ten years, and seasoned educators like Rasnic were often working side jobs to make ends meet. Rasnic remembers crying at the humiliation of the moment she finally cleared the $40K mark on the pay scale, with two master's degrees under her belt and fifteen years of tenure.

"Morale was awful," she recalled. "You give your heart and soul to your students and it's demoralizing to not be able to pay your bills. No one prepares you for students who want to kill themselves, for students who are traumatized by sexual assault, by abuse, by hunger, by unchecked mental illness. Parents want the best for their children, including the best teachers and best educations; however, no one seemed to care that I didn't have enough money to buy gas or groceries. No one seemed to care that I couldn't afford to support my own children."

After the West Virginia strike blazed across social media, a teacher in Oklahoma started a group on Facebook to rally the state, and within twenty-four hours, it had thousands of followers, gaining thousands more each day, according to Rasnic. "It was like wild-fire. Teachers across the state were ready," she recalled. So along with thousands of her peers, Rasnic and her husband, Mike, who is also a teacher, took their kids to the capitol in Oklahoma City to participate in the walkout and let their voices be heard. Despite the unseasonably cold April weather, a group of more than one hundred teachers in Tulsa conducted a three-day, 110-mile walk to the capitol, arriving to find tents erected and food and shelter to greet them. Torie Shoecraft, a kindergarten teacher in Oklahoma City, recalled her favorite moment of the ten-day demonstration in the capitol rotunda, when hundreds of teachers decided they wouldn't allow Governor Fallin's patronizing insult slide. The so-called bratty teenager teachers jingled their car keys at Fallin as she made her way into her office, ignoring the crowd.

"It was honestly the best ten days of my life," recalled Shoecraft, noting the number of parents and students who showed their support at the rallies. Their solidarity was a great relief to many teachers who worried their rebellion would be viewed as neglectful. This level of commitment, dedication, and agony was expressed by every teacher I spoke to. "It was incredibly hard for us to walk out of our classrooms," recalled Rasnic. "You are made to feel like a degenerate the second you walk away from your responsibility to teach your students. They use our kindness against us."

In the end, the teachers' resolve paid off. The legislature folded and granted teachers $6,000 raises and nearly $500 million in additional funding. But perhaps the greater victory came seven months later in November 2018, when teachers and parents across the state voted out more than a dozen of the more notoriously unsupportive state representatives, adding fifteen women to the house—many of whom were former teachers—a record for Oklahoma. The state even elected a woman to U.S. Congress, Democrat Kendra Horn, who was only the third female ever to be represented by the state. The teacher walkout not only bolstered statewide perception of the value of women who teach, but it also prompted stronger political engagement within these very women who no doubt contribute most to shaping the state's future.

In frank discussions with her students, Rasnic told me she often asks the teenagers why they think the football coach who leads five sections of weightlifting classes makes more money than the teacher who helps them write their college admission essays. "But the real question," she said, "is why do we disrespect women's work?"

•••

After a year of meeting women in such seemingly opposite professions as education and professional sports, the parallels stood out more than the contrasts. And even though these women had all shaken things up considerably by standing up for themselves, in the end, most of their battles were still unfolding—and would likely continue to do so for years. Several months after I interviewed the soccer players, their claim of unequal pay in the lawsuit against the federation had been dismissed by a federal judge. The hockey players were staring down yet another year without a league as their 2019–2020 Dream Gap Tour came to a close. And in West Virginia, teachers had initiated yet another two-day strike in 2019, this time to protest state Republicans' continuing efforts to privatize education. One year later, in 2020, as COVID-19 raged through the nation, these teachers were being asked to do the impossible once again—to deliver lessons both in-person and online, risking their own health to show up for scores of confused and scared children. Meanwhile, the WNBA players dedicated their entire season to Breonna Taylor and partnered with the #SayHerName campaign to bring awareness to the fact that Black women are killed by police violence at alarming rates— while their names are often erased from the increasingly public dialogue about police brutality. Year after year, these athletes and teachers remain at the forefront of a quest for basic dignity for all women—regardless of their profession.

In their battle to demand respect, the target is probably constantly moving. But there is always victory in the huddle. And if these athletes and teachers are any indication, the promise of multiplying that victory seems well within reach. Already they had influenced the hearts and minds of so many across the country. They'd served as a reminder that women can and do have each other's backs—and this energy is contagious. "You never really do anything alone," Billie Jean King had told me. "Each one of us is an influencer, and if we stand together, we can influence more people."

My mind flashes back to the ticker tape parade New York City threw for the USWNT after they won the 2019 World Cup. I wasn't assigned to cover the parade that day for work, but I raised my hand to ask my boss to let me go anyway. My twenty-something producer Randi, who I work with very closely on my show, had played soccer her whole life and her hand shot up as well. We'd been watching some World Cup games together, which worked out well for me, because she taught me more about the game— plus, her excitement was infectious. Randi is brilliant at her job, working side by side with me, making me sharper and smarter every single day. So it was a thrill to be there at the parade that day together—both of us geeking out to see the soccer team and soaking up the energy of what felt for me like a pint-sized women's march. We interviewed little girls (and boys!) who explained to us with sports-fan-level excitement what the team had taught them about equality. It was remarkable: kids were almost as excited to talk about equal pay as they were to see their favorite soccer stars in person.

I remember that day almost in slow motion. I paused long enough in between live shots to look around at all those little girls. I'll never forget their faces as the floats full of their favorite soccer stars cruised by in a flurry of confetti and celebration. Randi and I couldn't stop smiling. We smiled so much that day our faces hurt. For one moment, our entire city—and really most of the country— had set aside our differences to pause and cheer for women. It was truly contagious.

eight

HEALED BY
THE HUDDLE

People always ask me how I stay sane working a job that requires me to process so much death and destruction every day—not to mention the political division. More than a few times, my joking response has been "alcohol helps." But the truth is, some days, there's no amount of tequila that could wipe away the stubborn residue of stress, emotion, and information overload that can build up in my psyche. And it's not just journalists affected by this conundrum. So many Americans consume information that simultaneously compels and exhausts them. According to a set of surveys by the Pew Research Center, two-thirds of Americans reported having "news fatigue" in 2018 and again in 2019. I'm sure any studies to be done on the concept of "doom scrolling" in COVID-era America will reveal fatigue levels to be off the charts. Even before COVID-19, so many of us have been perpetually tethered to mobile devices, so the scrolling never stops. We are constantly seeking and receiving new information and feedback on our phones—whether we are on the train, at the beach, or in bed. After a while, the never-ending input takes a toll. Our minds and bodies can become hijacked by this morning's controversial headlines and tomorrow's projected worries. It becomes surprisingly difficult to live in the present.

This predicament is what initially brought me to The Class—a group "mind and body workout" that combines "simple, repetitive calisthenics and plyometrics" with mindfulness and breathing. Three times a week—before COVID hit, of course—I would head out the door at 7 a.m. and make my way up to the third floor of an unassuming building in Tribeca. The building doesn't have one of those massive windows displaying a row of sweaty warriors on stationary bikes or ellipticals. No giant assault of bold-faced words marching across the side of a building challenging you to come inside and get physical. In fact, you'd probably miss The Class headquarters if you didn't know it was there.

By the time I head over, I'm usually fresh off the first phone call of the day with my executive producer, having run through the big stories for today, discussing which interviews we will book, and predicting which stories might develop in real time before the start of my show that afternoon. This is how I spend the first segment of my day—quite literally obsessing about the past and the future. But when I ring that buzzer to the three-story building for The Class, I'm ready to jump into the present with myself.

After I've climbed the first flight of stairs, my senses are already waking up to the moment. I start to smell the burning palo santo wafting from upstairs. I take a deep breath and keep climbing. When I reach the third floor and open the door, I feel immediately more relaxed. Just entering this place provides a sort of sensory relief from the chaos of light, color, noise, and speed on the New York City street from which I just ascended. Everything inside The Class is cast in warm light, neutral colors, and good energy. The adornments in the decor—in the form of a few crystals, candles, and orchids—are minimal. It is a welcoming and calm womb-like environment.

I wander into the large, airy, naturally lit space where the workout takes place, and the second I step onto my mat and lay out my two towels (because there will be a lot of sweating), I begin to notice what's going on with my body. I have become better at noticing my present physical baggage and the deep contrast the room presents. I recognize that I have arrived in my body a tad groggy, with tight quads and a neck stiffened from hovering over a computer that morning. Meanwhile, a lovely mix of mostly women begins to stream in—all ages, body types, and dispositions—and I feel safely surrounded by these open and thoughtful people who are just as focused as I am on sixty-five minutes of healing.

Soon enough, Taryn, the founder, or one of the other instructors—Natalie or Jaycee—wander in, dressed in earth tone–colored workout wear, headset on, greeting us calmly, giving hugs, checking in with newcomers ("anyone have any injuries?"), and asking us to stand to begin. After the reassuring reminder that any modifications to the moves are welcome—that you cannot do any of this wrong—the music begins and we are suddenly enveloped in it, with our eyes closed, breathing together in our resting position: one hand on our hearts and the other on our bellies. The first song is often instrumental, an electro-charged palette of drums, chanting, and rhythmic patterns, designed to help us "drop in" to our bodies. We do deep squats to warm up our legs, and the music often picks up, maybe something from Nine Inch Nails, Sofi Tukker, or Beyoncé. With each new song, a new plyometric move is introduced—something like burpees, jumping jacks, lunges, or high-impact dance moves. The instructor will remind us to "get out of the mirror," stop looking at our neighbors, and focus instead on how we feel, how we are breathing. While our bodies push through these repetitive motions, releasing perspiration and anxiety, we are asked to witness our own resistance to discomfort, to observe the present moment we are moving within, to truly connect with what's happening *right now*.

Between each song we close our eyes again, placing our hands back on our hearts and bellies in resting position, making physical contact with the now racing, pulsing life force that demands the brain to unbusy itself. The workout is challenging enough for me that sometimes it's all I can do during the rest position to just simply breathe and behold myself exactly as I am—a gasping, wincing, free body in space. As the workout intensifies (I always soak through both towels), the instructors invite us to "make sound" to express any sadness, rage, celebration, joy, or grief we're holding. We moan, groan, yell, cry, woop, or emit whatever noise we feel we must. It is vulnerable and incredibly intimate to make these noises or to cry in the presence of strangers. And yet, the sounds of other women's voices remind me I am not alone, that we all have bodies we want to more fully inhabit, embrace, and enjoy. That we all have pain and trauma that can sometimes keep us detached from this opportunity our bodies offer us. The session closes with a "heart opener" in which we sit down, bringing our arms forward and away from our chests, as if to more fully invite and receive the experience. By the time the sixty-five minutes are over, the mirrors are fogged and I open my eyes, feeling more elated and clearheaded than I will for the rest of my day.

What a gift to be a part of this, to shed what Taryn Toomey calls the "residue" or "sludge" of life, to center myself in the morning before I go out and brave the world with all its sensory assaults and distractions. When I first began attending, I knew the mindfulness focus of this workout would be good for me. But I was caught unaware by just how vital it is for women to "drop in" to their bodies on a daily basis, to "stay in your body, stay present" as the instructors are always telling us throughout the workout. This kind of "somatic work," Toomey told me, can become an act of "unlearning" or rewiring the brain, to help dismantle the negative thought patterns and behaviors that "destabilize our mental and emotional health." I realized I needed this mindfulness-based sweat session not only to clear away the workday static constantly buzzing in my brain but also to deconstruct a lot of damaging narratives about my body that I had been collecting and repeating my entire life.

Maybe those narratives began with being that child my parents called "sturdy," the girl who ended up being too tall for gymnastics, getting called out by the petite athletes on my team for my comically profuse sweating. Maybe it was growing up in a home where thinness was something to be proud of, where I was the only family member with meat on their bones. Maybe it was being surrounded by schoolboys who called me "fat," "giant," or "Amazon," or maybe it was that Halloween night in sixth grade when my parents surprised me in the den where I was still in my Halloween costume, meticulously sorting my stash of M&M's, Reese's Peanut Butter Cups, and candy corn. My mother told me years later that she had hated every second of what happened next when she and my father sat down next to me, a concerned and united front: "Brooke, we want you to know, you can eat all the candy you want tonight, but after that, we're taking you to Jenny Craig." I was eleven years old and deeply ashamed that my body had been the source of so much scrutiny by the people I trusted, that it would be dragged to a diet center, weighed on a scale, and monitored closely for several weeks moving forward. And like so many other young women in America, I went on to grow up in a body that was constantly compared to the bodies of impossibly beautiful women in magazines, and despite my obvious mental toughness, despite my strong, grizzly shot put–throwing self, I still cried at the slightest weight gain in high school and college. Not surprisingly, none of this was a very good foundation for what would come next: a career—my dream job—where men literally lit my body parts for maximum effect; where male bosses, colleagues, and viewers constantly commented on my weight, on my arms, my legs, and my ass; where makeup, clothing, and shoes became essential collateral to my worth; where on any given day, I could find hair extensions and false eyelashes floating around in my purse like disembodied doll parts.

The outcome of all this—a lifetime of body scrutiny and management by parents, media, men (and let's face it, sometimes myself)—is that I became disconnected from my own body. I came to conceive of my physical being as something that wasn't *for* me. It was, instead, for being pretty, or being thin, or "worth watching" on television. But it wasn't for *me*.

Experiences like The Class helped me reconnect with my body, to see it as something *meant for me*, something that brings me joy and sustains me. And the methodology of the "somatic work" Toomey designed allowed me to feel more at home in my body, freeing me from some of my body shame. According to Bessel van der Kolk, MD, author of the seminal text on trauma *The Body Keeps the Score*, "One of the clearest lessons from contemporary neuroscience is that our sense of ourselves is anchored in a vital connection with our bodies." Furthermore, he says that physical activity or somatic work can offer a way to "utilize the brain's natural neuroplasticity" by "allowing the body to have experiences that deeply and viscerally contradict the helplessness, rage, or collapse that result from trauma." Though they make no claims of being medical professionals or therapists, Toomey and her VP Natalie Kuhn (who is also an instructor) have studied the concept of neuroplasticity and put its benefits to the test by designing intentionally repetitive movements in The Class that allow your brain a break from remembering difficult choreography. The ease of repetition in the movements literally requires less brain activity. As the motions become familiar and easier to perform without thinking, your brain can develop new grooves and pathways and body-positive connections, crushing the old familiar loops of self-loathing and shame. As Toomey always says, "What you repeat, gets strengthened."

Doing all of this—the work of healing myself—*in the presence of other women* only deepens the benefits for me. Instead of the competition and comparisons I'd often engage in during other kinds of exercise classes, The Class demands that you resist looking at your neighbor, that you hold space for yourself to connect inward. And yet at the same time, the power of moving, yelling, and breathing in a roomful of other women—who are each on a similar healing journey—is undeniable. Van der Kolk, who outlines the healing effects of yoga on traumatized women, also points out the ways that Buddhists, Muslims, Catholics, and Jews alike incorporate collective movement and music rituals as a means of creating "a larger context for our lives, a meaning beyond our individual fate." Yes, I'm comparing an expensive exercise class to a religious ritual, and it rings very true to me that most women (because so many of us do suffer individually from varying levels of shame and trauma) can find healing through music and movement that we perform in the presence of each other. And it doesn't have to come from a $40 class in a fancy studio. It can happen wherever women gather with the intention to love and care for themselves. It's deceptively simple, and it applies to almost every woman I know in America.

Because so many of us are riddled with trauma. One in four American women have experienced severe physical violence by an intimate partner; one in five women are raped in their lifetime;

and one in nine girls under the age of eighteen experience sexual abuse or assault at the hands of an adult. Beyond these forms of life-altering violence, as many as 77 percent of all women experience verbal sexual assault; 51 percent experience unwelcomed sexual touching; and 41 percent experience cyber sexual harassment. And these statistics are just the most general categories of trauma, not accounting for the additional layers of trauma endured by women who move through the world in disabled bodies, Black bodies, Brown bodies, lesbian bodies, gender non-conforming bodies, or transgender bodies. Women in poor or violent communities put their bodies at risk every single day to simply feed and house themselves and their families. As caretakers, mothers, wives, and breadwinners alike, we women often place our bodies last on the priority list, and the repercussions go far beyond anxiety, high blood pressure, disassociation, or fatigue. Failing to engage our bodies is to ignore the deepest wellspring of healing we have available to us.

It is no surprise to me that innovative somatic work like Toomey's is designed and facilitated by a group of women. "I know from my own upbringing the imprint that trauma has," Toomey told me one day in a conversation I had with her and the women with whom she assembled her company, Jaycee Gossett and Natalie Kuhn. "I'm not a trauma specialist, but I know what has worked for me, and from that, we have built practices that help people feel safe enough to drop into the power of their own presence to heal themselves." Toomey shared stories of participants in The Class—roughly nine out of ten of whom are women—who inevitably approach her after they've been attending several months to share with her the ways the body work assists them in their journey of healing from the pains of divorce, death, loss of children, or sexual trauma.

Besides providing these practices to wealthy women in big cities,

Toomey has also begun implementing a plan to deliver her healing practice to middle schoolers in Harlem who, statistically speaking, are subject to more trauma and stress than the average American child. Regardless of the audience—whether you're talking about a middle school girl in an underserved community or Jennifer Aniston (who is a known fan of The Class)—everyone needs healing, and Toomey calls this her "medicine." When COVID removed the option for women to come to the studio in person, Toomey realized she could provide this "medicine" virtually to a much wider audience of women if she offered a dramatically reduced monthly fee option. During the pandemic when women were bearing the brunt of so much additional caretaking and labor, they needed a healing space for themselves more than ever before.

While I feel more than privileged that I had been able to expend the time and money to participate in The Class before COVID happened, I was so grateful to stay connected through the virtual experience of the Class Digital Studio. The daily workout via my laptop has been no less powerful in helping me take care of myself through the quarantine—and even as I recovered from my own bout with COVID.

Although I had already experienced it for myself—I asked Toomey, Gossett, and Kuhn, who interact like emotionally supportive sisters, why the mostly female group setting is so effective at advancing the healing process. "Seeing someone cry," Toomey answered, "gives you the permission to have your own experience. And seeing somebody next to you continuing on gives you the strength to continue too." To this, Kuhn added, "Our culture has often pitted women against each other, but we were not ever meant to do that. We were only ever meant to raise the barn together as a village."

"We all know what women have had to rise up from," Gossett

chimed in "what women have had to overcome since the beginning of time." She told me about growing up in a house with five boys, being bullied by girls at school, and finding solace by herself in dance. It wasn't until she was in her twenties that she learned about the importance of what she called the "sacred bond with women."

"I had no idea how magical and incredible women were, and what could happen when they came together."

AN ARMY OF SURVIVORS

While the #MeToo choir certainly normalized the phenomenon of women speaking up about sexual assault, it was a quieter, solo voice that forced us to contemplate the depth and expanse of trauma that plagues the lives of so many American women. In September 2018, Dr. Christine Blasey Ford, a fifty-one-year-old psychology professor, stood alone to testify in front of a largely male Senate judiciary committee who were gathered to hear her allegations that Trump's second Supreme Court nominee, Brett Kavanaugh, had sexually assaulted her when the two were teenagers. After detailing her memory of being pinned down by Kavanaugh while another boy watched, of being grinded under the weight of his body, of attempting to scream, of struggling to breathe with his hand over her mouth, Ford endured a litany of questions from the senators about the clarity of her memory of an event that had taken place thirty-six years prior. She was asked why she couldn't remember the date the assault took place or how she got home that night. She was questioned about how certain she could be that it was Kavanaugh who had assaulted her in the first place. Her memory seemed to be on trial, and when Vermont senator Patrick Leahy asked her, "What is the strongest memory you have of the incident, something that you cannot forget?" her response unleashed a new conversation in America.

"Indelible in the hippocampus is the laughter," she said through tears. "The uproarious laughter between the two and their having fun at my expense."

Indelible in the hippocampus became an oft-repeated phrase in both the media and regular conversations between women who were suddenly participating in a widespread dialogue about the physical and mental realities of trauma. Ford's entire testimony was like a lesson on the neurological context of trauma and the ways in which memory is affected by fight-or-flight moments. She used clinical words like "neurotransmitter" and "sequela" interchangeably with her raw emotional offerings. In a single breath, she presented as both an accomplished psychology professor and a terrified fifteen-year-old girl. Many in the media remarked that she served as her own expert witness, and Connecticut senator Richard Blumenthal told her, "You have given America an amazing teaching moment."

Women across the country who had carried similar trauma weren't so much experiencing an "amazing teaching moment" as they were being retriggered and punched in the gut with the reality that trauma is lonely and enduring—a powerful force with recalcitrant, invisible tentacles. I remember the sheer number of texts and phone calls I received that week from female friends young and old who had been through similar assault experiences and were having visceral responses to Ford's testimony. There was something about seeing a fifty-one-year-old woman with more than three decades between her and her assault—a woman who had undergone therapy and understood quite literally the scientific inner workings of her trauma—and observing how unmistakably the aftereffects still gripped *even her*. The tiny muscles in her face still crinkled in pain. The cruel laughter still echoed in her brain. If the #MeToo movement had shown us that speaking up can be empowering and necessary, Dr. Ford's testimony showed us that trauma is isolating and indelible.

In the face of such widespread pain, it can sometimes seem like the cultural response is to avoid despair, to focus instead on the victories. We tend to celebrate moments when abusers are arrested or called out. Our sense of justice is usually adequately riled for some period of time, but when the cancel culture megaphones are set aside, countless traumatized women are still left with overwhelming work to do. When Olympic gymnast Aly Raisman bravely provided a victim impact statement at the sentencing of her abuser, the infamous USA Gymnastics and Michigan State University physician Larry Nassar, she told the courtroom what many survivors of sexual assault know: "There is no map that shows you the pathway to healing." When I spoke with Amanda Thomashow and Morgan McCaul, two other women who gave impact statements in the Nassar sentencing that day, they told me that although there is indeed no roadmap for healing, huddling can be a very important part of the process.

Alongside the elite household-name gymnasts Nassar abused were young women and girls like Thomashow and McCaul who sought Nassar's treatments at Michigan State University. Thomashow, who was a twenty-four-year-old student at the time of the abuse, had sought help for lingering high school cheerleading injuries, and McCaul was a dancer who was abused by Nassar on multiple occasions between the ages of twelve and fifteen. By the time of the sentencing, Thomashow was twenty-eight and Mc-

Caul was eighteen, but despite the decade of difference in their ages, the two women became fast friends. Both had delivered searing statements in the courtroom, McCaul's calling out the university for protecting Nassar, and Thomashow's delivering a line that would be repeated continuously in media coverage around the world: "Larry, the thing you didn't realize when you were sexually assaulting me and all these young girls is that you were also building an army of survivors."

The line came to her the night before the sentencing, she told me, when she had reluctantly attended a pizza party organized for all the women who would give statements the next day. Thomashow hadn't wanted to attend for fear of not quite belonging in this group of survivors who were mostly younger than she was. "I had let the abuse isolate me," she told me. After reporting Nassar to Michigan State University in 2014 and being brushed off, Thomashow had felt even more alone when the story finally became public. "All the victims were elite gymnasts, many of them young girls or teenagers, and I was this twenty-four-year-old woman," she explained. But the pizza party ended up being a positive experience for her, allowing her to shed her guilt about being older than the other survivors and connect with several other women. She felt reassured that she was indeed not alone in her trauma. McCaul, who was also in the room that night but didn't meet Thomashow, felt happy about the instant camaraderie among the large group as well, but told me she also left feeling "disturbed by what eighty-eight bodies in a room looks like, knowing the violence that culminated in that space." Throughout our conversation, McCaul, who seemed wise well beyond her years, articulated so clearly the physicality of the experience of trauma, and both women outlined for me the nuanced version of huddling they developed to help each other through the delicate process of healing they began after the sentencing.

After meeting at a press conference where they had bonded over their shared anxiety of speaking to a wall of cameras and reporters, the two women created an intimate safety net to help each other move forward. Sure, they joined the private Facebook group for the five hundred–plus victims of Nassar's abuse, and they connected with women around the country who they'd met through the sentencing hearing and the weirdly public experience that ensued, but it was their unique commitment to "showing up for one another" that helped them most.

"Healing is such an individual experience," McCaul told me, describing the seemingly random pattern of ups and downs trauma tends to inflict. Weathering this, she explained, requires an on-call support system in a friend like Thomashow who not only understood her trauma but gave her space to experience it at her own pace while nurturing her in a gentle, consistent way. It sounded a lot like self-care, but administering it to your sister instead of yourself. For example, they described the ways they and a few other sexual assault survivors on a group chat check up on each other on a daily basis, and how they escort each other to doctor's appointments, even reminding each other to eat, drink water, or try to sleep.

"We have this rule more or less that you always call back," Thomashow said. She gestured to McCaul: "She'll call me back anytime, any day, at 3:00 in the morning. She'll walk out of class to call me back and make sure I'm okay—and if she can't, she'll text me exactly how many minutes before she can return my call." Traumatized people, they explained, often have trouble showing up for themselves, but having a small group of friends who are simply present in their day-to-day tasks and headspace can make a world of difference. "People without our background might think,

Well, Amanda seemed fine the last time I talked to her," McCaul explained. "So if you are not familiar with the dynamics of trauma, you can let people slip through the cracks."

Expanding upon this supportive framework they created, Thomashow also cofounded a nonprofit organization called Survivor Strong to provide other survivors of gender-based violence a variety of educational and healing opportunities with a "trauma-informed victim-centered approach" and a focus on community. Beyond tackling an array of educational and advocacy initiatives, the organization also offers what they call #SimpleSelfCare to their constituents, such as providing healthy recipes or care packages, or forming self-care circles where they can participate in "activities rooted in self-expression, self-compassion, and self-love." They have also partnered with another like-minded local organization, the Firecracker Foundation, to offer trauma-informed yoga and meditation.

This partnership with the Firecracker Foundation was very important to Thomashow, who told me they hoped Survivor Strong could help "fill in the resource gaps and build more community" among survivors and other resource networks in Michigan. While there are many national organizations that women can call for around-the-clock emotional support, for example, Thomashow wanted to be able to provide very practical resources for local survivors as well, such as the addresses of LGBT-friendly crisis shelters, or the names of sympathetic local nurses who could administer rape kits and provide plan B to women in crisis situations.

I couldn't help but admire the astonishing resilience of these women—so young, and yet so fiercely devoted to taking care of themselves while helping others heal too. Through Survivor Strong, they had transferred their intricate devotion to each other's well-being into a much larger effort. "We've been through the fire," Thomashow said, "and now we get to show other people how to get through the fire too."

When I asked them if the trauma they share in common has proven to strengthen their huddle, McCaul made a beautiful and important clarification: "It says nothing about who we are, to have been victimized by the same human being, pretty much at random." She paused, thinking it through. "We were *brought together* by this trauma, but *bonded* by how we supported each other in its aftermath."

WHERE TWO OR MORE
ARE GATHERED

The guidebook for GirlTrek, America's largest health movement for Black women, begins with an Audre Lorde quote:

Caring for myself is not self-indulgence; it is self-preservation. And that is an act of political warfare.

By rallying women to walk together in their neighborhoods for thirty minutes a day, the founders of GirlTrek invite Black women to participate in what they call "radical self-care." Facing the grim statistics—that "Black women are dying younger and at higher rates than any other group of women from preventable chronic disease"—founders T. Morgan Dixon and Vanessa Garrison, two former college friends now in their forties, want to help Black women address this physical health crisis. But they also want to unite Black women to solve problems in their communities, while honoring the ancestral "army of freedom fighters" who walked for justice before them.

"We did not create this concept," Garrison told me. "We are

continuing a tradition that has already been established," she said, recounting for me the ways Black women in America have engaged in walking for generations to reclaim their freedom, safety, and livelihood. Whether it was abolitionists like Harriet Tubman, who literally walked herself and others North into freedom, or the women in the civil rights movement who marched in Selma and the Montgomery bus boycotts, Black women have a legacy of coming together to walk. "For so many years," Dixon explained, "we weren't legally allowed to have proximity to one another, or to gather, which had been our strength culturally for generations prior to slavery." Coming together can be an act of resistance, "a direct response to folks telling us we couldn't gather," she explained.

With Dixon video-calling in from Ghana, where she was visiting for an extended stay, and Garrison in Washington, D.C., I learned more about the ways these women have applied the powerful blueprint of their communal legacy to the present-day crisis their sisters face. They shared with me stories of growing up in large extended families—Dixon in Kansas and Garrison in Seattle—where caretaking was shared freely and joyously among matriarchs, grandmothers, aunts, and cousins alike, who all considered themselves "collectively responsible for each other's well-being." Garrison explained that this tradition "has literally been the foundation and crux of Black folks' survival in this country." And yet, no matter how much it may have been historically prioritized, today, huddling can sometimes feel inaccessible to Black women, given the resources and space it requires to connect, not to mention the work and family obligations that leave so little time to spare. "And although Black women often gather for faith services," Dixon observed, "we haven't been gathering for healing. In fact, outside of church, community has become a luxury." But in that spirit of church, Garrison and Dixon realized Black women should also be gathering "in the name of powerful healing."

In his book *My Grandmother's Hands: Racialized Trauma and the Pathway to Mending Our Hearts and Bodies*, Resmaa Menakem examines the body as a kind of receptacle that has collected the trauma of our parents, grandparents, and their ancestors before them, each of us receiving an imprint created by centuries of racism and violence. Like van der Kolk, Menakem explores how we can heal our bodies from trauma using somatic work, including tools that "settle our bodies" like meditation, humming, as well as chanting, singing, or walking in groups. "The traumas that live in many Black bodies," he explains, "are deep and persistent. They contribute to a long list of common stress disorders in Black bodies, such as post-traumatic stress disorder, learning disabilities, depression and anxiety, diabetes, high blood pressure, and other physical and emotional ailments." By encouraging Black women to gather and practice self-care together, Garrison and Dixon hope to address these physical ailments as well as their attending underlying traumas. Their project is also extraordinarily hopeful and joyful in tone and approach, considering the very systemic obstacles Black women are presented with in this country. "This crisis Black women face," Garrison told me, "is a direct reflection of the environments in which we live and the policies that have been created in our communities. We don't have leisure time or physical activity. We don't have access to fresh fruits and vegetables. We have a labor force that receives sixty cents on the dollar to what a white man is getting." Dixon added to this list of barriers a reminder of the extent to which Black communities are overpoliced and separated from each other by incarceration at rates far higher than other communities.

If you were ever under the illusion that GirlTrek is a gimmicky weight loss club, you realize very quickly that these women are not just looking to change numbers on a scale. They are looking to revitalize the support networks Black women deserve, drawing from the deep stores of strength and resilience in their DNA. They are looking to build a culture-shifting paradigm to show up for each other. With GirlTrek now approaching one million members—a milestone goal they'd set at their inception—the organization has not only brought women together to experience communal joy and better physical and mental health; members around the country have also been activated to solve countless local problems, curbing violence in their neighborhoods, advocating for political change, and addressing everything from pothole-riddled streets to the reclamation of green spaces in their cities.

When I spoke with GirlTrek member Shaka White from the Seattle chapter, she told me that before joining, she had never seen a group of Black women gather to spend time outdoors. White grew up in Buckley, Washington, as the only Black child in her entire school. She was accustomed to longing for community. When I inquired about how she found GirlTrek in the first place, she told me she had been reading in 2016 about the life and tragic death of Sandra Bland, the twenty-eight-year-old Black activist who was pulled over for failing to signal a lane change in 2015, and was subsequently brutalized by Texas state trooper Brian Encinia and found hanging dead in her jail cell three days later. Bland had been vocal about her support of Black Lives Matter and had experienced pregnancy loss and untreated depression in the year leading up to her death. Like so many Black women in America, she carried a great deal of pain, trauma, and hardship without enough support. She was also a member of GirlTrek. "I saw pictures of her walking with a bunch of Black women in blue T-shirts," White told me, "and I thought, what is this about? I have to find out!" A few internet clicks later and White had signed up for a GirlTrek special event in Yosemite, which meant that she and her twelve-year-old niece would drive thirteen hours *each way*—just for the opportunity to spend *one day* hiking in the presence of other Black women. It was the first time she recalled so openly discussing self-care with other Black women, and it sparked a journey that led to weight loss and the creation of a safety net that would prove to be vital to her in one of the darkest seasons of her life.

In 2018, with more than two years of walking with her Seattle GirlTrek sisters under her belt, White's eighteen-year-old autistic son endured a mental health crisis and went missing. Because he was past the legal threshold of being considered a minor, law enforcement told her they couldn't help her find him, regardless of the fact that he lived in her care and had been so clearly in crisis when he disappeared. But White's GirlTrek sisters, who were midway through a 365-day walking challenge with her, rallied to look for her son. They created flyers and assembled a search party, walking the streets of Seattle and nearby towns for two weeks. When he finally turned up two states away in California, White agonized over how to get to him. "I had $27 in my account," she told me, but within a few hours of White learning the whereabouts of her son, word had traveled through the GirlTrek networks and Garrison called to offer White full financial assistance to book flights, rental cars, and hotel rooms to bring home her son.

A few months after White's son was safely back in her care, he was diagnosed with paranoid schizophrenia, and one dark night, he attacked White out of nowhere, stabbing her more than forty times. While receiving treatment for her serious injuries in a hospital, White was horrified to learn that her son was taken directly to jail, where he ended up serving fifteen months without receiving any of his typical mental health care. The ordeal was harrowing for White, as it would be for any mother. But through it all, she told me, it was her GirlTrek sisters who helped her care for herself while her physical and mental wounds were healing. They brought her food, and a birthday cake the day she turned forty-four; they prayed for her and checked in on her as regularly as they had walked with her. "And when I worried who would ever love my son after what he did to me, my GirlTrek sisters were the ones who prayed for him and accepted him," she told me through tears.

When I discussed White's story with Dixon, she pointed out to me how remarkable it was that during White's time of extraordinary crisis with her son, she never gave up on the 365-day walking challenge. *Until she was literally hospitalized with stab wounds and unable to carry herself out of bed, White kept walking.* Dixon reminded me of the ways that so many women are forced to move through trauma "without a circle of support," rendering them not only mentally scarred but physically affected as well. When trauma or crisis halts the regular rhythm of our lives, we often stop exercising or taking care of ourselves, so our crisis only compounds. "But when Shaka White reached the other side of her trauma she was actually physically healthier than she was before the trauma began," Dixon said. "Clearly, we are not just a fitness organization." Walking together with your sisters, she explained, can be a stabilizing and life-protecting ritual.

When I asked Dixon and Garrison about some of the group's memorable triumphs, like the moment when Michelle Obama joined GirlTrek and amplified their message nationwide, or when they brought together Dr. Bernice A. King and Ilyasah Shabazz—the daughters of Martin Luther King Jr. and Malcolm X, respectively—for their first public discussion, they shifted the focus entirely.

"GirlTrek is about the power of everyday women," Dixon said. "Whether you are struggling with addiction or whether you're the preacher's daughter, you are welcome here," she added with a smile. "We believe you don't need a PhD to be an activist," she said, underscoring the fact that this group of doctors, lawyers, nurses, teachers, mothers, and artists are all highly qualified to be their own healers.

But one of their greatest achievements, it seems, is their ability to summon each other to experience communal joy—to provide each other not only the healing that comes from huddling, but also the levity required to move through the "oppression and muck" Dixon says they face every day. They recalled for me a memory of organizing a trek in 2017 in the tiny four-block town of Ruleville, Mississippi, in honor of its native daughter Fannie Lou Hamer, the civil rights activist, on what would have been her one hundredth birthday. "It's an incredibly impoverished community, where there are no jobs now that cotton fields no longer need labor. All the porches are gone, and there's lots of payday loans," Dixon recalled. GirlTrekers had traveled from around the country to be there and gathered in their blue T-shirts in the middle of an old cotton field. "We literally had to talk to the grandson of the plantation owners," Dixon said. "It was real healing, American style." From the plantation, the group marched to the courthouse where Fannie Lou Hamer's daughter still works and proceeded to their endpoint at Hamer's grave. The picture Dixon and Garrison painted for me of this mass of joyful women making their way through the streets, laughing and engaging locals along the way, was so clearly reminiscent of their favorite scripture, which they paraphrased thusly: "Where two or more are gathered, that's where God is also."

In the midst of this scene, women chatting, moving together

with the town's one proud police car following behind them, the trekkers suddenly heard the cries of a woman who had spotted them from the window of her little shotgun house. "Wait!" she hollered. "I've been waiting for you! Hold on! Let me get my T-shirt!" As she emerged from the house dressed in blue, she yelled and laughed toward her sisters: "Oh my God, my tribe has arrived!"

nine

TEND AND
BEFRIEND TO THE END

In the summer of 2009, I was lonelier than I'd ever been in my entire life. I was twenty-nine years old and had moved back into my childhood home with my parents in Atlanta to pursue my life-long dream to work for CNN. I'd spent the last eight years scrapping for airtime on TV stations in Virginia, West Virginia, and D.C., living alone in tiny apartments (at one point with my baby brother) and bunking with sympathetic friends. It was hard to say if getting my old high school bedroom back was a step up or step down. But given that I was about to turn thirty, I can tell you I did not feel cute. I knew I was lucky to have a big, beautiful home to live in that would cushion me during my time of career transition (and believe me, my mom has a lot of cushions placed all over that house), but sometimes it still felt like a move in the wrong direction. The plan was to work my ass off and freelance my way into a permanent job at CNN. But after a year of these efforts not paying off, I was getting more than a little discouraged.

I am not a quitter, but for the first time in my life, I thought about quitting.

To make matters worse, my boyfriend of three years had recently cheated on me, and I was so defeated I'd taken him back, which only compounded the indignity of my situation. Did I mention he also had a full-time job with CNN? I jealously watched him clock in for the life I wanted every single day. Meanwhile, my parents' marriage of forty years was dissolving before my very eyes. I was literally there to witness its death, surrounded by my old cheerleading photos. It felt like the ground was shifting beneath my feet, or like someone had pulled one of the many rugs my mother was constantly vacuuming out from under me.

One day that summer, in what my mother and I still refer to as the "yellow chair moment," I wandered into my parents' bedroom and slumped into that soft seat the color of sunshine—and cried my eyes out. My mom had been fussing over something in her closet, but she dropped everything to help me like she always has, and we shared a moment I will never forget. She talked me out of wanting to quit and reminded me that my strengths would see me through. She may have also consoled me by quoting some Disney lyrics, and for that I love her anyway. She helped me pick myself up and keep pushing. I'll never be able to express my gratitude for having a mother like her. I was her first child, and she quit her teaching job to be a stay-at-home mom so she could devote everything to me and my younger brother, Ryan. Raised as one of five sisters, she must have learned something about supporting other women during her lifetime, but I never much witnessed her enjoying close female friendships during my childhood. Her marriage, as it turns out, hadn't exactly been a fairy tale either. But she still gave everything and more to her children.

I knew I was fortunate to have her in that moment—every woman deserves the soft landing of her mother's support and affection—but when I rewind the tape and hit pause, there's also something really wrong with this picture.

Why wasn't I leaning on my female friends in this time of young adult crisis?

Where was my huddle?

I did have close friends who were scattered around the country, as well as a few work friends and high school friends around Atlanta. It's not that friends weren't important to me, but I had been working so hard, with few vacations for the past eight years, that I hadn't really prioritized my friendships as much as I would have liked. While other twenty-something women from my generation were getting through their dating and career struggles side-by-side in big cities together, I spent my days in more random places, shooting the shit with older male photographers in freezing news trucks. My weird work hours sometimes made it hard to even talk on the phone with my girlfriends, and technology hadn't yet fully transformed all of our lives with ubiquitous smartphones and the nonstop texting and social media check-ins they afford us today. My oldest and closest friend (since ninth grade), Aki, was living across the country in San Diego, in the throes of new motherhood, learning to parent her daughter, Curren, while working a full-time job.

It's never a bad thing to cry to your mother, but I think most twenty-nine-year-old women having a yellow chair moment ought to be able to turn to a friend—a peer, someone who isn't bound by family ties to be on your side, someone who doesn't view your success or failure as a reflection of their parenting, someone whose only investment in you is their sheer dedication to your happiness. But in that moment of floundering, it hadn't occurred to me to turn to a friend. I didn't truly see friends as resources quite like I do today, and sadly I wasn't investing in them as much as I was expending time, money, and attention to career, self-improvement, family, and my marriage aspirations. A quick browse through my journal at the time reveals that my energies were divided by the constant drive to "land" my career and manage my concerns about my parents and getting engaged (even though it is painfully clear today that I was essentially screaming at myself in that journal, *Brooke, break up with this guy!*). What strikes me most looking back at this is not only the lack of friendship in this picture, but also the fact that my plight wasn't entirely abnormal.

In Kayleen Schaefer's book *Text Me When You Get Home: The Evolution and Triumph of Modern Female Friendship*, Schaefer points out the ways that women have traditionally been directed by cultural norms to sidestep friendship as a resource worth cultivating in their young adult lives. "We're made to believe that at some point we will have to distance ourselves from each other, whether that's to find romantic mates, raise children, assist elderly parents, or go after promotions," she says. But Schaefer, who published her book in 2018, lights a fire under all of us to consider an alternative option: "We're pressing back on this notion. We're caring for each other—loudly and continuously—for no reason besides wanting to. We're saying and showing: Our friends matter as much as our other attachments."

Schaefer isn't the only one in recent years to make bold statements about the importance of friendship. Two years after her book was published, besties Aminatou Sow and Ann Friedman wrote a brilliant memoir of their friendship that doubled as an instruction manual for women who want to invest in each other. In *Big Friendship: How We Keep Each Other Close*, Sow and Friedman contend with many of the same career and young adulthood struggles in their twenties and thirties that I did, except they calculated ways to prioritize each other in the process. They managed to do this while dealing with added layers of adversity, such as the sometimes-tricky dynamics of their interracial relationship and the difficulties of making a long-distance friendship stick while running a business together (the much beloved Call Your Girlfriend podcast). These friends go the distance for each other. They don't just schedule regular phone calls, BFF vacays, and twinsie tattoos, they have created annual rituals to celebrate their "friendiversary." They discuss writing friends into wills or naming them as medical proxies. And when their own resentments and unresolved conflicts overwhelmed them, they addressed them the same way married people do. They went to couples therapy—even driving there together each week, which was a surprisingly touching detail to me. And while they acknowledge that it might seem "weird" or "radical and extravagant" to pay a professional to help save their friendship, they refused to consider the alternative. Maybe I'm just speaking as the still partially heartbroken adult child of divorce, but it floored me when they explained that going to therapy was far less ridiculous than having to admit to themselves: "We didn't do everything we could to save our friendship." If you sometimes think in emojis like I do, picture with me right now the little yellow face just full-on ugly-crying those waterfalls of tears.

This decision they made to not only do the work but also to reveal it to the world in such a vulnerable fashion is as poignant as it is radical. Their example confirms that friendship is something women absolutely have the power to shape and define, to flex like a muscle—and we'd be stupid not to, because it can strengthen and transform our lives. Before they wrote their book or had their own relationship drama, Sow and Friedman were known for the concept they invented, Shine Theory. Although it is often and rightly applied to women supporting each other in workplace settings, Sow and Friedman say Shine Theory began as merely "an operating principle for their friendship" defined as "an investment over the long term in helping a friend be their best—and relying on their help in return." Shine Theory is deceptively simple and a necessary prescription for any feminist friendship: "It is a conscious decision to bring our full selves to our friendships and to not let insecurity or envy ravage them. It's a practice of cultivating a spirit of genuine happiness and excitement when our friends are doing well, and being there for them when they aren't."

It seems to me that this elevated level of intentionality around friendship, despite whatever amount of "work" or time it might require of us (it's something Sow and Friedman say both parties have to "continually opt in to"), can provide so many long-term benefits. Friendship is, after all, not just about cocktails and girls' trips. It can provide a lifelong safety net that carries us through adversity and crisis in ways that other relationships can't. The absence of friendship is never so strongly felt as when a significant other lets us down or a family structure falls apart. And no matter how much I love my work, I know it doesn't love me back. Simply put, I can't afford *not* to invest in my friends.

However obvious all of this might seem (having friends is important—who doesn't get that?) many people—particularly women—are not centering friendship in their lives. The recent spate of publications on the topic makes it all the more clear to me that a mandate has been issued to all of us. Lydia Denworth's 2020 book, *Friendship: The Evolution, Biology, and Extraordinary Power of Life's Fundamental Bond*, presents an unignorable mountain of scientific evidence that friendship is neither a "choice or a luxury" but rather "a matter of life and death" that is "carried in our DNA" and has the "power to shape the trajectories of our lives." On the heels of Denworth's book was U.S. surgeon general Vivek H. Murthy's *Together: The Healing Power of Human Connection in a Sometimes Lonely World*, which reveals the increasing body of scientific evidence that connects loneliness to ailments as varied as heart disease, high blood pressure, stroke, dementia, depression, anxiety, lower-quality sleep, immune system dysfunction, and impaired judgment.

There is even science (though not a lot) about the power of female friendships specifically. In what is considered the largest and longest-running study on health and wellness ever (the famous Nurses' Health Study conducted by Harvard Medical School beginning in the 1970s and continuing on today), data shows that women who maintain friendships are healthier over their lifetime and less likely to die of specific diseases like cancer.

And while all of this is compelling, what caught my attention perhaps the most is the scientific study in 2000 that looked at the ways humans evolved to react in times of stress. While the well-known fight-or-flight reaction to stress has been more prominent in scientific research, researcher Shelley Taylor and her colleagues at UCLA identified another important phenomenon—the tend-and-befriend response to stress. Taylor's study found that while both males and females "share the capacity for fight-or-flight, females seem to use it less" and are more likely than males to tend children and befriend each other in times of stress, due to their hormonal makeup (as well as the reinforcing factors of learning and socialization). Meaning, when under duress, women are actually genetically disposed to locate other females (and children) and begin connecting with them and caring for them—as a soothing and healing mechanism. (Taylor points out that this finding shouldn't stereotype the sexes but rather help explain the ways our biology interacts with other "social, cultural, cognitive, and emotional factors.") Regardless, it's a stunning revelation: women are actually hardwired to huddle, particularly in our most difficult moments.

Nearly four years after the Women's March, as I write this last chapter of my book, I wonder if it makes sense to reframe that fateful day as one big tend-and-befriend moment for American women. A rightful criticism of the Women's March is that it attracted a lot of performative activism by white women who just wanted an Instagrammable moment in their pink hats. This is a point very well taken—and one I don't dispute—but I also can't help but wonder if many of these women who attended the march were motivated less by political activism than by the need to merely soothe and be soothed by fellow women. Many white women there were feeling for the first time that they were not safe or valued in their country. Their new president had made disturbing comments about women, and suddenly the relative privilege they had taken for granted as white women had been obliterated. BIWOC, on the other hand, had felt this unsafe for generations. It must have been frustrating for them and all the other seasoned activists who had been doing the work for years to see so many new faces show up without a productive fight in them. But if we see that moment through the lens of Taylor's tend-and-befriend study, it can look a lot like a nationwide expression of women's impulse to reflexively take care of each other in hard times. (Sidebar: Group hugs are great and absolutely necessary, but we also need to follow the examples of BIWOC and seasoned activists and *do the work* to get shit done.)

I'm amazed by all the huddles in this book who have done exactly that—gathered to solve a problem, to resist collectively, to put their lives and well-being on the line to make change. But it's also profound to me how intensely women can serve as a resource to each other in our more private and personal struggles. After that fateful yellow chair moment with my mom petting my hair and wiping my tears away, I picked myself up and did my best to carry on. As fate would have it, just a few weeks later, I got my first call to fill-in anchor at CNN on the weekend. It would still be more than a year before CNN gave me a permanent job, but something else very beautiful happened in the meantime.

An old friend from high school, Kathryn, moved back to Atlanta. Kathryn was retooling her career too and she was very deliberate about making time to get together with me, and some months later, she brought along another old friend, who had been a grade above us in high school, Allison. Shortly thereafter, I planned my first real vacation with my BFF Aki to Cabo—to take place during what would have been my honeymoon. (Yes, I actually allowed myself to get engaged to the cheating dude who ended up doing even worse things, but I finally came to my senses and kicked his ass to the curb.) This was a turning point for me with prioritizing friendship, and little did I know at the time, I had just planted the seeds for what would eventually blossom into my first official huddle as an adult about a decade later.

• • •

When I got the incredible opportunity to see Oprah interview her BFF Gayle King for the first time, I thought of it as a master class in female friendship. Oprah told the audience of fifteen thousand people (mostly women) who had gathered for the Oprah 2020 Vision tour stop in Denver, Colorado, that she had never stopped to analyze their famous forty-year friendship, that it "just is"—as if it were as effortless and sacred as the air she breathes. But she went on to reveal the obvious upkeep in their relationship, noting how they'd managed to speak to each other *every single day* for decades—minus that one day Gayle's mother passed away and she didn't want to disturb Oprah's special dinner with Denzel Washington to break the news. Then, Oprah—who has never been one to hide her belief in the legitimate value of therapy—explained the reason why she had never sought it herself: "All these years, I never needed therapy, because I had you as my friend. All those years I was coming home [to you], downloading, downloading, downloading." Gayle's immediate response was to reassure her BFF that it had never felt like one-sided downloading. In fact, she replied, "I've been to five therapists—when I was married, and nobody has been a better therapist than you. It's good we can do that for each other." They see themselves as opposites in many ways, joking that Gayle has FOMO (fear of missing out) and Oprah has JOMO (joy of missing out). And despite the fact that Gayle is an incredibly busy mother of two and Oprah is—well, she's Oprah— the two have always found a way to support each other's extremely different set of challenges throughout their parallel lives. And it seemed clear that the key to this was a lot of intentionality— deliberate commitments made—to consider each other as a priority each and every day.

When I interviewed the Olympic fencer Ibtihaj Muhammad about her sports agent Lindsay Colas, we also talked a bit about Ibtihaj's sisters, especially her younger sister Faizah, who became a fencer and trained along with Ibtihaj for the 2016 Olympic qualifiers. The siblings, who describe themselves as close, also run a conscious clothing line called Louella along with their other sister, Asiya. Having not grown up with sisters myself, I asked Ibtihaj what it was like to have siblings play such a significant role in so many aspects of her adult life. I wondered how sisterhood in those contexts compared to a more noncompulsory relationship with a friend. She fixed her gaze on me with her sabre-fast focus: "My sisters feel like anchors. They are very real with me in ways that friends do not always want to be. Friends can sugarcoat things, but sisters don't do that." Her distinction between less-authentic friends and sisterly realness made a strong impression on me, because it's something I'd been trying to ask of my own friends— that they always tell me the unvarnished truth the way real sisters would.

VIRTUAL VULNERABILITY WITH NEW MOMS ON THE INTERNET

My sister-in-law, Wrenn, reminded me of another facet of this struggle to remain authentic with ourselves and our friends when she told me about her foray into a private Facebook group for new moms. When she gave birth to the cutest baby in the world (aka my nephew Bridger), she was blindsided, like so many first-time moms, by how difficult, consuming, and exhausting new motherhood can be. During pregnancy, she had every expectation she would enter into "one of the most incredible, beautiful, amazing experiences ever," but instead, she felt deep guilt about how difficult it was to bond with a tiny baby. She wasn't "overjoyed" every day as she'd seen other new moms describe on social media, and she often felt confused about how it was possible to feel such great highs and terrible lows all at the same time. The draining work of nursing around the clock while trying to learn the rhythms of infant sleep was exhausting and contributed to what Wrenn describes as "a very cloudy season" in her life.

"Even though I had all the help anyone could ask for—my husband worked from home and my mom came to visit—I still felt very isolated with these private thoughts I was having." She became terrified of having a second baby, which had been part of the plan, and she felt a nagging fear and anxiety about it constantly that she wasn't discussing with anyone—not even her own friends. When I asked her why not, she explained her fears that her emotions might be a lot for them to take on, and she didn't want to scare them from becoming mothers themselves. Sometimes, we want to save our dearest friends from our most vulnerable selves because the crisis we're wading through is either so nebulous or intense that we're afraid it might overwhelm others.

Wrenn was passionate about breastfeeding Bridger, and when the time approached for her to return to her teaching job as a special educator, she began having a "tremendous amount of anxiety" about being able to pump enough milk throughout the day at work. She managed to mention this concern to a friend who invited her to join a private Facebook group called Working Moms Who Make Pumping Work and her whole experience of motherhood changed from there on out.

If you're not versed in the realities of pumping breast milk (and I'm not, but lord knows my girlfriends and female colleagues are), I can confidently relay to you that it's not for the faint of heart. In order to provide enough sustenance for a three-month-old baby, most employed American women have to lock themselves in whatever weird, random closet their employer has designated as the "pumping room," and then proceed to fasten small (but mighty powerful) suction cups around their nipples and sit there being "milked" for fifteen to twenty minutes. Then they have to protect that little bottle of liquid gold like it's the creamy holy grail and convey it carefully to a communal work fridge, hoping their male coworkers don't wince at the sight of it. For most women, this process must be repeated two to four times per workday. The whole affair requires an extreme amount of stealth, creativity, and perseverance—because there's still a job to do between pumping sessions too. To make matters worse, often, the mother's physical distance from her suckling baby confuses her body, so her milk "dries up," which means her baby might not get enough to eat. And that's a fate worse than death to a sleep-deprived and over-worked mama bear. (Have you hugged a working mom lately? Because if you haven't, you really should.)

Despite the daunting task she was faced with every day, Wrenn didn't want to give up. Enter the Working Moms Who Make Pumping Work Facebook group, which saved her a million times over. Not only did they provide tips about pumping at work and increasing milk supply, they also offered a digital safe space where Wrenn could vent about all kinds of new mother issues. "We were able to bond over these common interests without the added stress of sorting the logistics to be in the same room or the same time zone," she told me. She was able to ask the kinds of questions that were too obscure for her child-free friends and too distracting for her extremely busy mom friends. She remembers feeling unembarrassed to type a post about whether or not she should let Bridger keep napping past 4:30 p.m. one day, even though it might lead to a rougher night of sleep for him later on. ("Yes, let him sleep, and drink some wine, mama!" they said.) She also remembers them talking her off a cliff when she wanted to stop pumping altogether one day. And after she suffered a few painful miscarriages, this massive group of women she didn't know IRL provided empathy and encouragement. "It was a lifesaver," she reflected. "I realized people on the internet can sometimes show their vulnerability where they might otherwise feel uncomfortable doing so in person." The group normalized what felt like taboo issues to Wrenn such as miscarriage, extended nursing, postpartum depression, and co-sleeping. "It felt like the heavens opened up," Wrenn said, "and I was never denied the space to mourn, vent, celebrate, or ask more questions."

Not only did the Pumping Moms Facebook group help Wrenn successfully achieve her pumping goals, she also got over her fear of having a second baby (and later gave birth to my nephew Hudson, who ties with Bridger for cutest baby ever). Most amazingly, though, she says this online refuge allowed her to relax more fully into her real-life friendships. Even after she had moved through her difficult postpartum phase, she found herself unable to leave the Facebook group. She wanted to stick around and lend an ear to other new moms, and she was grateful for the ways this new relationship with thousands of women she'd never met in person had helped her become a better friend to her real-life pals who were starting to have babies. She wanted to make them feel safer to be vulnerable with her if they needed to ask for help, or confident to trust their guts regardless of what they chose to share.

Wrenn's Facebook group sounded like a massive virtual tend-and-befriend space, and it also served as a great reminder that vulnerability sometimes takes practice. And maybe flexing that muscle over the internet can warm us up for the face-to-face version of it. And regardless of the environment, vulnerability can be contagious. If you are willing to share your struggles openly with others, you not only create space for them to reciprocate, you also initiate a chain of events that can end in another woman resolving her crisis or solving her problem. Who would have thought the internet could provide more than just a gaping void to yell into? It can be a divisive place, to be sure, but it was nice to hear that it also facilitates such an exquisitely purpose-driven huddle.

THE HUDDLE RIGHT UNDER MY NOSE (AND HOW IT GOT ME THROUGH COVID)

Little did any of us know before March 2020, we would all need to embrace the idea of virtual huddles. When the COVID-19 pandemic hit America (as I was nearing the end of writing this book), suddenly everyone needed to learn how to connect online. When I contracted the virus myself just a few weeks into the pandemic, I'd never been more grateful to have a solid huddle of female friends. Suddenly I was sicker than I'd ever been in my life, and I was trapped in my bedroom, under strict warning from my doctor to stay away from my husband, James, and beloved sixteen-year-old pug (easier said than done). James slept on a futon in our spare bedroom with the pug and I cried myself to sleep many nights as the fever and aches would descend on me with a vengeance. As most people reading this will know by the time this book is printed, COVID-19 is an unpredictable and relentless virus. I was lucky my lungs were spared and that I had a husband who brought soup and toast to my door for every meal, but it was still an incredibly isolating few weeks.

As a journalist I was hurting for my country—so many Americans were struggling to make ends meet, or they were forced to put their bodies into harm's way to provide essential services like mail, groceries, garbage collection, and health care. It wasn't fair that BIPOC Americans were so disproportionately affected by the virus, and I just wanted to be on the air, doing my job, helping to connect Americans to the information they needed in such a troubling time.

But I was stuck in my bed, so I turned to my girlfriends a lot. They were always there for me via text, Zoom, or FaceTime. All told, I was mostly healed after about fifteen days (though my senses of taste and smell took a while longer to recover), but the experience of ailing alone in a room for that long pushed me to stretch the limits of my vulnerability. One day, I decided to share what I was going through on Instagram, and the outpouring of love and kindness was a game changer for me. Here's something I wrote in a CNN.com essay after I recovered:

> I realized that sharing my own vulnerability with others online and receiving positive energy and well wishes back brings me the gift of connection. I quickly discovered how grateful I was to all of these people showing me love. It didn't take long for me to learn to lean in and receive it. In my darker moments, I would log on to Instagram just to be lifted up by love. It was overwhelming in a way I have never felt in my life. And it showed me how—even when the world stops and takes a collective breath—we're all capable of showing up for one another.

I realize just how lucky I was to not only have had such great health care and family support during my illness, but also to benefit from this wealth of human connection. I was in touch with so many amazing people—most of them strangers who helped radically change my outlook. One day, when I was feeling a little stronger, I reread a favorite Brené Brown book, and found her words imbued with so much more meaning upon this reading:

Staying vulnerable is a risk we have to take if we want to experience connection.

Those words made me look back on the last four years that I'd spent researching and interviewing women for either my CNN Digital series *American Woman* or this book, and I realized the process of witnessing so much vulnerability, so much leaning and convening, had truly been contagious. It had helped me tighten my own bonds with my friends. Even though I had consciously started spending more time individually with my female friends after that infamous yellow chair moment a decade ago, it wasn't until several years later, at my bachelorette party in 2018, that I intentionally brought all these amazing women together in one place. I remember thinking, *How am I only experiencing this just now for the first time—at the age of thirty-eight?* This was a huddle just waiting to happen. And it had been right under my nose for nearly a decade! That glorious weekend of eating, singing, hiking, and talking around a campfire (and me proving to all my girlfriends that I really do remember every word to Salt-N-Pepa's "Shoop") sealed the deal and changed my life.

One year later, the weekend I fomented a plan to call this book *Huddle*, I started the text chain that was my life breath through COVID and on through today. It was June 4, 2019 (yes, I scrolled all the way back in my phone to find the exact moment my huddle officially formed). I count this as the moment the huddle began for me, because it was the first time I really put myself out there in my text chain with my friends Aki, Kathryn, and Allison.

"Ladies, can I call a huddle moment? I need you."

And that was the beginning of our text exchange as we know it today. It was a month before my fortieth birthday and I was having a moment with my dear husband (I love you, James—but yes, we have moments and yes, thank God for good girlfriends). The way these women jumped in so swiftly on text made me feel heard and supported. They asked all the right questions and gave me wholehearted advice on how to handle everything swirling in my world at that time. My friend Kathryn ended our exchange with this:

"I'm so sorry BB. But I'm glad you called a HUDDLE. <3"

And that was it. That was the beginning.

For my fortieth birthday, they all flew up to New York City and even snuck on set at CNN that Friday, July 12, and made an appearance live on my show right by my side (something that had never happened in my decade on the CNN anchor desk). We are all north of forty now, and take it from me, it is never too late to find your huddle.

Having this small group of very tight friends has been life-changing. Each of us has chosen to invest in this huddle in a very intentional way, leaning on one another, and choosing vulnerability to strengthen our connection. I make a conscious effort to share and listen on our epic text chain. We've already had a few amazing girls' trips and quiet weekend visits. And even though we're four very busy women with lives so full they're bursting at the seams, we make time to help each other process issues ranging from parents, dogs, kids, body, and politics to marriage, sex, mental health, and so much more. Making the choice to show up for my friends as my authentic self, and truly lean into the arms of others has been worth every "vulnerability hangover" I've experienced, to quote Brené Brown's hilariously trenchant concept. And at the age of forty-one, it's exciting to think of how my friendships might continue to evolve as I get older. I don't think of my huddle (huddles, really) as a closed loop—I imagine it more like a circle that can be widened at any time. I'm a big believer in adding to my huddle as I grow and experience more of life. Flexibility and openness are no less important than commitment.

A few days before I got sick with COVID-19, I had interviewed Emily Fawcett on my show. Fawcett is a thirty-one-year-old nurse at Lenox Hill Hospital in Manhattan, which was ground zero for COVID during the worst time of the pandemic in New York. For a few months, every single patient in Lenox Hill was a COVID case. Fawcett told me how she spent her days watching people struggle to breathe, holding up phones so they could speak to their loved ones via FaceTime (because family wasn't allowed to visit), and absorbing the unprecedented levels of anxiety among her peers while somehow managing to swallow her own.

On a daily basis new challenges presented themselves that medical professionals had never faced in their careers. One day, for example, the oxygen supply became critically low in the hospital, weighed down by the demands of so many COVID patients requiring oxygen support. "All of a sudden, we heard this crazy high-pitched beeping noise," Fawcett told me, "and ten administrators in suits ran up and down the halls telling us to transition every single patient to portable oxygen tanks." Fawcett and her fellow nurses spent the next hour moving as quickly as possible to transition every patient's machinery, terrified the oxygen supply would shut down before they were done. It sounded like the scene from some sort of improbable action movie where buff "heroic" men are defusing bombs in space or something. Except this was real life, and it was a bunch of levelheaded and long-suffering women getting it done. One thing remained the same every day—at the 7 p.m. shift change, she left the hospital to go home and unwind, alone.

In some ways, nurses might be better prepared for this kind of emotional strain than anyone else on the planet. Fawcett told me they are natural huddlers, because they define success in one way only: patient outcomes. When collaboration or triage is required to help a patient, it happens efficiently and without fanfare among nurses. But despite how accustomed they might have been to putting their heads together—and regardless of how inured they might have become to pain and suffering over the course of their careers—this situation that involved so much more death, isolation, and uncertainty proved very difficult for them. When I asked Fawcett what got her through it, she said, without equivocation, it was the support of her friend huddle—a group of seven women she'd grown up with or met in college, none of whom were nurses like her.

Not only did her huddle provide daily moral support via a text thread, they also made sure that Fawcett didn't have to go to the grocery store a single time for three months. They sent her multivitamins, spa products, hand lotion, and flowers. They wrote cards for her coworkers and patients and rotated among themselves to provide lunch for all thirty hospital staff members on Fawcett's floor. "Some days I felt so isolated and overwhelmed, but they truly gave me the strength, courage, love, and support to keep going." Fawcett says she could feel their energy behind her every day, even when things got dark. And to look at Fawcett, it's difficult to imagine her being so much as glum, much less dark. She has an energy and optimism about her that I'd absolutely hope to encounter if I were ever hospitalized with something grave. She seems unflappable and calm—but cheery just the same. It didn't surprise me when she told me that sometimes she had the instinct to protect her friends from some of the harsh realities she was facing at work. It wasn't necessarily a fear of vulnerability per se, but more a protective measure shaped by her constant consideration for other people. It reminded me of Wrenn not wanting to upset any of her friends about her postpartum struggles.

But one day, Fawcett's resolve wore thin and the dam broke. She had arrived home from a particularly hard day at work where she'd witnessed five people die completely alone. On the phone with one of her closest friends from her huddle, Anne, she suddenly began sobbing. "Anne just sat there and let me cry," Fawcett told me. "She said, 'Em, you need to cry. I'll be here on the phone for you until you stop crying.'"

When I asked Fawcett to explain to me in a medical sense what kind of bearing confiding in our friends can have on our physical health, she told me about what happens inside our bodies when we allow ourselves to express our emotions. "It literally changes the chemicals in your brain when you laugh or cry," she said. "On the other hand, when you bottle up your emotions, it can raise your blood pressure and your heart rate, which is not good for you." In her humble and cheery manner, she insisted I speak to an actual physician to get a more precise answer to my question, but I didn't need a doctor by this point to understand that vulnerability can be not only life-changing, it can be lifesaving as well.

CHOOSING DIFFERENCE

When I got the chance to tell Gloria Steinem about this book and all the women I'd interviewed for it, she told me that three things were "the source of all of our progress" as women: friendship, chosen family, and women coming together from diverse backgrounds to organize. The act of a woman calling a friend her "chosen family," she explained, is in and of itself a radical act, especially since women in her own lifetime were handed over by their fathers in marriage and required to get their husband's permission just to secure bank loans and credit cards. "Given all that—and a lot more—for women to organize together and honor each other and affirm our full human identity is a revolution in itself, and also a path to replacing patriarchy with democracy," she said.

Steinem's third point—that women must come together from diverse backgrounds—reminded me of an admonition in Sow and Friedman's book about weathering the inevitable difficulties of an interracial friendship. The outcome, they say, is worth it. Choosing friendships with people whose backgrounds are different from our own, they explained, can actually make the world less divided. "White people can't be surprised that white supremacists are marching in the streets if their own lives are racially segregated," they explain. "The choices that each of us makes every day about who we include in our lives end up shaping the larger world we live in."

Stacey Abrams, the African American politician, organizer, and entrepreneur from Georgia, told me about forming a close friendship in elementary school with a girl from Vietnam who had been part of the refugee boat lift to southern Mississippi, where Abrams lived at the time. "Since then, I've always been very personally intentional about being friends with people who aren't exactly like me, from whom I can learn and who I think can learn from me, particularly in cultural ways." Abrams shared with me that her closest friends now include an African American woman, a Southern white man, and a Chinese American woman. While these relationships have sometimes involved "pointed conversations" about cultural norms and "tropes that seep into our DNA," they have helped her immensely. "It's easy to become cavalier about the needs of others if you don't constantly engage and try to test yourself against your exposure to the world." Abrams believes that our friendships can help influence how we vote, govern, hire, and stand up for each other. "You don't vote in ways that consider others if you don't understand what the considerations mean. Familiarity may breed contempt, but it also breeds understanding, and it creates new lenses of information and access that we might otherwise miss." While I am not suggesting that interracial friendships alone can end racism in our country, I do find hope in Abrams's assertion that these friendships can be one of many building blocks that help create a less racially divided America. Simply put, she said, "It is hard to be mean to those with whom you have to share bread and life and space."

Yet another fascinating book on the science of friendship proposes the same. In *Survival of the Friendliest: Understanding Our Origins and Rediscovering Our Common Humanity*, evolutionary anthropologist and research scientists Brian Hare and Vanessa Woods, who happen to be a married couple, posit that the selection for friendliness in *Homo sapiens*'s evolutionary journey led to cognitive changes in our brains that allowed us to better communicate and cooperate with one another—thus ensuring our survival. But this friendliness feature that causes us to seek love and connection also has a dark side. "Humans became more violent when those we evolved to love more intensely were threatened," they explain, likening it to the "mama bear" phenomenon. As humans, we have evolved to love and connect with each other deeply—so deeply, in fact, that when we feel our loved ones are threatened, we attack. Thus the very thing that makes our species remarkably capable of deep bonding is also responsible for ugly tribalism, racism, and violence. Hare and Woods explain how this trait has often been exploited by white supremacists and colonizers in their campaigns to grab power. By dehumanizing those they hope to destroy (calling them animals, vermin, or monsters, and making them seem like they are biologically different), white supremacists paint the "other" as easier to hate, enslave, or exterminate. Painful examples of this phenomenon turn up throughout history in the heinous justification for enslavement, colonization, and genocide.

"Evidence for dehumanization turns up in every culture we

study," Hare and Woods state, noting the occurrence of multiple major genocides over the last two hundred years on every continent except Antarctica. And yet, "interaction between people of different ideology, culture, or race," Hare and Woods say, "is a universally effective reminder that we all belong to the same group." While there is certainly no implication that interracial friendships alone can dismantle white supremacy (that certainly requires white people make sweeping systemic changes to their power structures), Hare and Woods rightly sound the alarm about the dangers inherent in the American status quo. We are a country with staggeringly low numbers of interracial friendships, and these kinds of relationships can be very powerful in helping people see each other as being on the same side.

Over the years, I've had the privilege of meeting some extraordinary people all over the world, and of all the women I've met, military spouses came to the front of my mind after reading Hare and Woods's theories about the importance of forming friendships with people who are different from us. Although not all military spouses are wives (some of them are husbands!), the ones I'm thinking of here are, and they are women like no other I've met. They are incredibly hardy, enduring constant relocations, often moving every eighteen to twenty-four months, picking up their entire lives, their children, and starting over with new schools, dentists, hairdressers, coffee shops, communities, and friends—over and over again. They are frequently separated from their spouses during all this change, and isolated through what researchers call "a roller coaster of intense contradictory emotions." Although they are known to be one of the least studied cohorts in psychology, they suffer in unique ways that deserve more attention. Despite the limited resources available to help them with their physical and mental hardships, the military wives I've met are phenomenally resilient. They also seem to have figured out that a key component to their survival is friendship.

If you ever want a master class in how to make friends, how to find people to be friends with, how to speed date friends, or how to keep in touch with old friends, talk to a military spouse. Sharon Bright, who has relocated ten times in twenty years, moving all around the world with her enlisted husband and three daughters, seems like she should have a PhD in friendship. Over several conversations with her, she told me how military spouses were employing COVID communication techniques (like Zoom or the video-messaging app Marco Polo) since well before the pandemic. Military wives are agile and giving with their outreach and kindness, always quick to jump in and babysit each other's kids—even when they barely know each other—because they know family is never nearby. Bright also told me that military wives are more efficient than the CIA when it comes to sourcing valuable information from their vast network of peers around the world. "If you'd like three opinions about the best high school on the mainland in Hawaii for your tenth grader, I can get them for you in less than an hour," she quipped, not even joking.

But after two decades living this lifestyle, Bright, who teaches yoga and looks about fifteen years younger than her forty-something years, has learned to become more mindful about what friendship means to her. Over the years, she began to intentionally befriend spouses who were from different backgrounds or perhaps more "on the fringes" of existing social groups, and she says the decision always proved rewarding. One of her most treasured friend groups over the years—one that she still keeps up with very closely to this day, in fact—is a group of women she met through her daughters' school in England where her family was stationed in 2015–2016. This huddle included a couple of British military spouses along with some local expat civilians, including a South African, a Filipina, an Indian, and a Nigerian. "The diversity was strong, and there was magic in having broader experiences come together." Coming from a woman who has run the gamut in so many directions with female friendship, her advice seems meaningful.

And it's not at all unusual for military spouses to find comfort in someone whose life is radically different than their own. Kathy Roth-Douquet, a military spouse who cofounded Blue Star Families, an organization that strengthens military families by providing community, resources, and support, told me that "nowhere else in America do such diverse people with no other necessary commonality become connected because of the people they are married to." She told me it is not uncommon for a forty-year-old military wife with a law degree and Ivy League pedigree to share a strong sense of camaraderie with a twenty-year-old mother of two with a GED. "There's something wonderful about that," she remarked, and I couldn't agree more. In a country with so much political division, a pandemic raging, and a reckoning on race, I gather the most inspiration from people like Bright and Roth-Douquet—and Sow, Friedman, and Abrams—all women who make a conscious effort to form friendships with people whose backgrounds are markedly different from their own.

•••

During the course of our email conversation, Steinem remarked at one point, as a harmless aside, that the term "huddle" seemed "way too temporary and negative" to her, like "something you'd do only in the face of danger." Her female friends, she explained, are quite the opposite—they are instead a long-term chosen family.

Her point was well taken, and nothing about it made me bristle. She's Gloria Fucking Steinem after all and she can say whatever she wants about a word I've decided to use. But her remarks on chosen family made me think of my dearest friend, Aki. Her daughter, Curren, who is now thirteen years old, always goes surfing or out to eat with us when I swing by San Diego, where they live. I didn't grow up hanging out with my mom and her friends (though she has gotten so much closer to her sisters as she's gotten older), but Aki, who spent her early years in her mother's native Japan, grew up watching her mother interact with a socially rich and happy network of women. Her mom played tennis with her female friends and enjoyed the company of her sister and Aki's other "extended aunties" when she could. And even though I wouldn't trade my childhood for the world, I also don't think it's any surprise that Aki's emotional intelligence is through the roof. She is truly the best friend and listener I've ever met, and I think being surrounded by so much female joy in her upbringing had something to do with that.

Aki and I have become more intentional about taking Curren on our little weekend trips up to Santa Monica, especially now that she's entering the age of "mean girl" dynamics at school. When Curren was a baby, I bought her a pair of the teeniest Ugg boots to match her Auntie Brooke's. It's unbearable for me to imagine that sweet baby, or the eleven-year-old beauty who served as ring-bearer/pug-handler in my wedding, for that matter, grow up to have trouble navigating relationships with other women. With a mom like Aki, however, I don't think it would be possible. "Cultivating friendships or developing huddles is not always an innate skill that people have," Aki told me. "And it's not something you learn formally through school or training. It comes from being intentional and deliberate about it," she said. Aki wants to be sure to model this practice for Curren, and lucky for me, this means we get to take her on vacations with us, letting her in on our friendship and our closest conversations. We hope she will take from us what she can and learn from any of our mistakes as well. It gives us hope for the future, that no matter what Curren might face down the road, her friendships, when chosen wisely and tended carefully, will be a resource she can always count on.

The desire that drives me to catch every sunset I can with Curren and Aki also drove me to launch the journey to write this book. I wanted to better understand the power of women coming together, to celebrate the powerful legacy of huddling in this country and challenge myself (and you too!) to keep leaning on one of our greatest resources—our female friends, colleagues, and sisters. If you're reading this and you haven't found your huddle yet, never forget that it's out there waiting. Wherever you are most inspired, most vulnerable, and most authentically yourself, I know you will find it. And it just might save your life.

Gloria Steinem wasn't wrong. We aren't just a temporary unit, teaming up for a moment to hatch a plan or put out a fire. We are more than that. We are a permanent, chosen family. We are a huddle for life.

epilogue:
How to Find
Your Huddle

Writing this book has changed my life. And even as I type these words, I have a sneaking suspicion there are more changes to come. Learning to huddle has made me a better advocate for myself and my fellow sisters; it has encouraged me to use my platform to amplify more women; it has sharpened my senses to hear the voices of women, to really see their struggles and victories; it has made me a better student of the history of women's contributions in America and beyond; it has made me a more supportive and collaborative colleague; and it has made me a more present, vulnerable, and supportive friend.

When I started this journey, traveling around the country, interviewing these powerful huddles of women, I thought it would be a pretty straightforward process: book a plane ticket, do the interview, write the chapter—and on to the next! What I didn't realize was how much this would differ from my day job, how often the line between journalist and subject would blur. In each of these interviews, whether they realized it or not, these women were holding up a mirror to me. As they were speaking about their own plight, my inner voice started to whisper to me. Sometimes the interview would end and I'd turn off the tape recorder, only to experience my interviewees turning the tables on me. They'd ask *me* questions about my life, my career, my voice, my huddle.

The very first interview I did for this book—with the judges in

Houston—cracked me wide open. That armor I often wore at my job—the one that allowed me to cover so much death, destruction, and political division—had to come off. Even before I met the judges that day, I realized in the airport that this would be the first time in my career that I would jump in head-first to follow a story that wasn't for my employer. And the nearly three-hour conversation I had with the judges that day was so different from any five-minute live interview on my show. I got to dive into the deep end with them. Not to mention, those judges challenged me to believe in myself and this project. They brought me into their huddle, and I left feeling the spirit of something bigger. As a woman, I saw that I had access to this incredible resource, and it felt more important than ever to tell the story of this powerful phenomenon and share the lessons I was learning with women around the world.

Slowly over the months that I sat with so many women, I started coming more into my own—at work, at home, in my huddles. The process felt almost like osmosis. By surrounding myself with so many "huddle-tastic" women, I slowly began to evolve into a stronger version of *myself*. For example, things that had bothered me pre-*Huddle*—a coworker, a cause, a complaint—could no longer lie dormant within me. I had to take action. And I knew I had a network of women who would take action with me—or at least help light my way.

The idea of huddling to make my life better became contagious. I remember the weekend I got together with my closest friends and told them about this book I was going to start writing. I shared with them the concept of huddling and pitched to them the word "huddle" as the title. I was visiting my BFF, Aki, in Encinitas—waiting for our friend Kathryn to fly in from Atlanta and join us—sitting at our favorite breakfast spot, Swami's, over chilaquiles and coffee. We talked about the word "huddle" for a long while, how it's a word associated with men and sports and how cool would it be for *women* to own it. I talked about how I wanted to learn more from women who were good at huddling and get better at doing it myself. I wasn't just telling her about a book I was writing. It wasn't just a career move. I was asking her—and later Kathryn and Allison—to join me in making a choice to huddle. And from that day on, we all became more deliberate about leaning on each other. For me, it started to become second nature to huddle with other women; to trust each other; to learn vulnerability, courage, and respect for what we have to offer each other. In the end, my own huddles and the ones I interviewed for this book activated me. Little by little, I started showing up in my day-to-day life as a bolder version of myself, daring to share more of me and my truth with my colleagues, viewers, friends, and even my boss. Full disclosure: sharing your truth does not mean instant success. But little by little, I've learned that my truth really is the thing that will set me free. And learning to lean on other women helped lead me down this path. By the end of my journey, I had learned so much. I could finally answer those questions I'd asked myself in the very beginning:

Why haven't I been huddling more intentionally in my own life?

I hadn't been huddling more because it just wasn't a priority. Looking back, I was "busy"—which I'm now calling *bullshit* on. I am now very purposeful about my huddles. I make time for them. I treasure them. And I always have an eye out to add to them.

Who's in my huddle? Do I even have a huddle?

Yes, I have a huddle! In fact, I have several: my Atlanta huddle, my CNN huddle, my NYC huddle, and my wellness huddle. (And as I've learned during COVID, none of these women has to be physically present for me to lean on them. Thank you, Wi-Fi!)

Do I fully appreciate this incredible legacy of huddling I've been lucky enough to inherit as a woman?

I had no idea—until now. I'm grateful to the generations of women who've sacrificed and come before me. And more than anything, I want to pass this down to the younger generations. A woman I greatly admire, Diane von Furstenberg, says it all the time, and I really believe her: "Women can change the world."

This book was a joy to write, but I experienced many growing pains as I explored the power of huddling. It wasn't always easy for me to lean on others, to share myself or dedicate time and effort to friendships. Not to mention, I know what the depth of loneliness feels like—not just in my younger years but certainly still today. Any new habit can feel like a stretch at times. And not every woman is game for huddling. In fact, sometimes women can be you-know-whats to each other. I've made it a point not to focus on this fact in my book—you can find plenty of stories about mean girls and competitive women in so many other books, TV shows, and films. But let's be real: not all women are down to huddle. So this process of learning to huddle sometimes required me to better hone my radar and learn to identify faux friends or women who don't share my huddle philosophy. But on the flip side, sometimes you might have a huddle right under your nose and not even realize it. You may have a group of colleagues at work who just need to be more intentional about getting together. You might have several female friends who just need a push to break out of their comfort zones and connect in more meaningful ways.

I mentioned in the prologue of this book that huddle has become my religion. But maybe it's more like a practice for life like meditating or working out. It is a choice we make every single day. It's not just the moment you gather with other women. It's all that comes before and after. And it transcends physical proximity. Being together in person is certainly not required, but keeping each other in mind is a bottom line. Setting intentions to accept and give help are priorities. Trusting and uplifting each other are paramount. Huddling is not just a gathering; it is a mindset.

Regardless of where you live, how old you are, or how alone you might feel, there are ways you can access this incredible resource right in your own workplace, community, or friend group. Allow me to share with you my list of ten ways on how to find your huddle.

HOW TO FIND YOUR HUDDLE

1. BELIEVE IN YOURSELF.

You deserve to have a huddle, and there are huddles out there that need you. If you're finding it hard to put yourself out there, *I feel you*, more than you know. After all the time I spent in my twenties lonely, moving for my career to places where I had no good friends or family, I know what it is to wish for deeper friendships. I know how it is to feel shy or reluctant to put myself out there. Even if you are uncomfortable or feel like you have a lot to learn, *believe in yourself.* Your voice deserves to be heard. And other women *need you.*

From these women, I learned about believing in myself:

CLIMATE ACTIVIST GRETA THUNBERG: She was just fifteen years old when she started her one-woman strike outside the Swedish Parliament to call attention to the climate crisis. She began this effort completely alone, but she put herself out there anyway. And soon she found there were other groups of women out there—Indigenous women and teenage girls—all over the world who were fighting the same fight.

#BLACKGIRLMAGIC JUDGES IN HOUSTON: The secret to their success was that they made a choice to believe the unlikely could happen. These women believed in themselves even when their entire county and political party did not (not at first, at least!). They knew taking that photo of themselves to share with the world would inspire others to believe in them too. And they were right.

USA WOMEN'S HOCKEY PLAYER HILARY KNIGHT: She told me that her personal mantra is "dare to be," which means dare to be bold, or dare to be _____, however you choose to fill in the blank. She said her advice is to "believe in yourself and make sure you have the right people around you. For every successful person you see in the media—every celebrity, athlete, or CEO, there are ten people behind her that are pushing her up and continuing to pick her back up." For Knight, believing in yourself is synonymous with getting other people to be in your corner.

HUDDLE TAKEAWAY: Find the courage to join that movement, sign up for that volunteer position, or reach out to that friend you want to connect with. You are worth it.

2. MAKE AN INTENTIONAL CHOICE TO BE A HUDDLER.

Be deliberate about prioritizing your huddles, whether this is the group of colleagues you make a point to have lunch with once a month, an organization you give your time to on a regular basis, or just checking in with your personal friends. It's hard to believe that I was nearly thirty-nine years old the first time I got all my closest girlfriends together in the same place. It may have been a quick weekend gathering just before my wedding, but that momentary huddle (which also happened to be an incredibly soulful and fun weekend) helped me see that I needed to set an intention to make this happen way more often. So far a number of us have kept that promise, because we see the inherent value in maintaining our huddle.

From these women, I learned about being a more intentional huddler:

POLITICIAN, ORGANIZER, AND ENTREPRENEUR STACEY ABRAMS: She told me: "I am not unusual in my coalition with women; I am unusual in my *intentionality of doing so.*" Make yourself unusually attentive to your huddles.

CEO OF HELLO SUNSHINE SARAH HARDEN: She says she still gets together on a nearly annual basis with her close friends from business school who, twenty years later, are now busy with careers and families and living in different regions of the country. They find a weekend to be in the same place, where they can relax at a spa, play golf, and eat dinner together—the standard girls' weekend fare. But they also created a ritual that gave their get-together the name Life Plan Weekend, particularly in the first decade after graduating. "We did really funny PowerPoint presentations. They were as specific as, 'I want two kids. Here's all of the names. Here's the names that my husband hates, and the ones he likes. What's my strategy, girls?'"

SUPERMODEL AND KODE WITH KLOSSY FOUNDER KARLIE KLOSS: She told me about an event she had recently attended that made her realize women don't get together often enough just for the sake of gathering. "We're so busy, we don't prioritize gathering and facilitating connections. But I think there's something really powerful just about gathering *for ourselves*, without needing to have a transaction or purpose."

HUDDLE TAKEAWAY: You have to make a conscious decision to prioritize huddling, but once you do, you won't be sorry.

3. FIND A HUDDLE THAT SHARES YOUR PASSIONS.

Even if you feel alone, you are *not*. There are others out there who care about the same things. Even if online. *Find them.* One of the best ways to deepen your connection and friendship with other women is to work toward a common cause together.

Whether you're passionate about a political movement that your immediate friends and family don't support, or you just have a random hobby you like to rock—there *are* other women out there who share your beliefs and interests. It can be incredibly sustaining and motivating to find them and link arms with them. Don't be afraid to put yourself out there.

From these women, I learned to never give up on finding your tribe:

MOMS DEMAND ACTION FOUNDER SHANNON WATTS created one of the largest grassroots organizations for women in America when she couldn't look away from the tragic school shooting at Sandy Hook Elementary School. She created a Facebook post for her seventy-five followers, looking for an army of mothers to join her. Today that army is nearly six million strong.

BLACK LIVES MATTER COFOUNDER ALICIA GARZA typed a Facebook post, "I continue to be surprised at how little Black lives matter," and her friend **Patrisse Cullors** hashtagged the phrase #BlackLivesMatter. Thus, along with the help of **Opal Tometi**, the Black Lives Matter movement was born.

LESBIANS WHO TECH FOUNDER LEANNE PITTSFORD realized how few lesbians like her were represented in tech jobs, so she started Lesbians Who Tech to bring LGBTQI techies together and encourage more of them to enter the field. Now it's the largest organization of its kind.

U.S. REPRESENTATIVE LUCY MCBATH, a leader in Moms Demand Action, told me how people often feel intimidated to become an activist like her: "People say to me, 'I can't do what you do.' I'll say, you're not supposed to. You don't have to. Are you artistic? Or are you a good organizer? Or are you good at administration? Then take this passion that you have and begin to build from that. Act on what you're interested in, act on what it is that you're concerned about or you want to create."

SPORTS AGENT LINDSAY COLAS provided a reminder to be real about your own authentic interests and the huddle will follow: "It's not about the cool crowd. Seek your tribe in a way that feels authentic for you and not worrying about what people have to say. You don't do it for show or for the 'gram. It's about who is doing stuff that you're interested in. If it's Dungeons & Dragons, awesome. Do what you love and then things start to make sense. And you find each other."

U.S. SECRETARY OF STATE MADELEINE ALBRIGHT kept it real: "You don't automatically get along with every woman just because she's a woman. People have different interests. What are your substantive interests and how can you cooperate?"

FRESH FILMS INSTRUCTOR AMY CALDERONE-BLOMMER told me: "the happiest I felt in my life professionally is when I found a group of like-minded women going toward a common goal to create something good. That's impact. That's success."

OKLAHOMA HIGH SCHOOL TEACHER JACKIE RASNIC reminded me that "when you fight together for something you are passionate about, you become bonded with those people for life." After conducting a walkout with her fellow teachers to earn deserved pay raises, she told me the bonding experience was "larger and lovelier than the financial gains."

HUDDLE TAKEAWAY: No matter what your interest or passions are, your huddle is out there. When you show the world what you authentically care about, you will find your sisterhood.

4. NURTURE YOUR FEMALE FRIENDSHIPS.

Tend to your female friendships just as carefully as you tend to your bonds with your significant others or family members. Our friendships are more than just outlets for fun or blowing off steam. Friendships can sustain us, keep us honest with each other, and challenge us to contribute more to the world. And just like any relationship, you have to put the time in on a regular basis. For example, after I helped bring my friend group together a few years ago, we started a text chain to make the huddle more official. One of my girlfriends named the chain #HUDDLE: FTF. As in "Fuck Those Fuckers." (No amount of tequila will get me to spill the beans on the meaning behind that phrase!) We text about everything from: "Are we too old to wear jean shorts?" to "How can she talk her dad out of voting for Trump?!" to "This girl I grew up with is racist—how can I help widen her perspective?!" Nothing is off-limits. I trust these ladies and they trust me. We go out of our way to see each other in person. It's something we schedule on a calendar, as if it were our job. I know it sounds obvious: *Breaking news! Friendship is great!* You already knew that. But are you really making it a regular priority in your life? Are you making yourself a *daily* resource to your closest friends?

From these women (and also my own husband!) I learned more about the importance of nurturing friendship:

KARLIE KLOSS: She told me she FaceTimes with her high school besties on Sunday evenings. Even though they are all in different regions and different phases of life, their regular check-ins are vital to their friendship.

When **MADELEINE ALBRIGHT** served as the U.S. ambassador to the United Nations, only 7 of the more than 180 representatives were women. These women huddled and quickly made a pact to stay connected and work on large initiatives together. Albright told me, "We did the girl thing, and we said that we would always take each other's telephone calls no matter what. Once a male delegate came up to me and said, 'Why would you take a phone call from Liechtenstein instead of from me?' And I said, 'Well, have yourself replaced by a woman and I'll always take your phone call.'"

Also, it may sound obvious, but never underestimate the power of your phone here. So many women in this book told me they schedule weekly phone calls, annual visits, daily walks, or regular check-ins with each other. And almost every huddle I spoke with had a hilariously heated text chain. The huddle of U.S. congress-women I interviewed told me their text chain is called The Bad-asses, and they assured me that their texting is a critical component of their daily communications.

Special shout-out to **MY HUSBAND, JAMES,** on this too: When he and I first met, he was living in London and I was in New York City. Because of the distance and time zone differences, we emailed a lot. I'll never forget in one of James's first emails, he made a point about friendship—that he makes a conscious ef-fort to "never let the trail go cold." When I first visited him in London, I joked later that we barely had much time to ourselves, as James was constantly taking me out to breakfast, lunch, and dinner where I was meeting so many of his friends. It was one of the things I found most attractive about him—that he has maintained (what he calls) "back catalogue" friends from the deep past.

HUDDLE TAKEAWAY: Give time and attention to your friends on a regular basis—even if it's just a text or email check-in. Even if your life is hectic, make it a priority. Consider it an investment in your huddle, which is likely to make you a happier and stronger person over time.

5. DO HARD THINGS WITH YOUR HUDDLE.

Find a huddle with whom you can push yourself—whether physically, mentally, emotionally, or intellectually. Thank you Glennon Doyle, for reminding us that women can and must do hard things in order to grow. Furthermore, I learned from writing this book that when women do hard things *together*, they improve their skills, self-esteem, courage, and connections with each other. There is something about having a partner or a whole crew of other women that helps stoke your bravery. When I got the crazy idea to climb Mount Kilimanjaro, I called my friend Allison, who I had never even done a short road trip with, much less a journey to another continent. But I knew she embodied equal parts strength, moxie, and crazy and wouldn't be alarmed when I asked: "Hey, do you want to climb the tallest mountain in Africa with me?? We'll bunk together in a tent and won't be showering for seven days. Interested?!" It was the most physically challenging thing I've ever done in my life, and there is *no way* I could have done it without her. She might've talked me out of getting a tattoo after our epic climb, but she is now one-quarter of my closest friend huddle. We have proven to ourselves time and time again that we can do hard things— *together*.

From these women, I learned more about the value of challenging yourself within the safety of a huddle:

THE GIRLS FROM GIRLS ON THE RUN, KODE WITH KLOSSY, AND THE AT&T HELLO SUNSHINE FILMMAKER LAB FOR GIRLS: Consider the girls in chapter 3 who came together to do challenging tasks that have traditionally been dominated by boys—like running track, building apps, and making movies. They all found that even if they were slightly intimidated to try something new, it was easier when surrounded by a group of like-minded girls.

KARLIE KLOSS was so inspired by the girls who sign up for her coding camps, remarking on how much courage it took to sign up to do something outside of their experience with a room full of strangers. But, she told me, the upside is that "taking that first risk and trying something new, putting yourself in an environment where you might be challenged to grow, can oftentimes lead to meeting amazing people and growing both as an individual and as a unit along the way."

THE WOMEN OF GIRLTREK not only help each other get more physically fit when they show up to walk together every day, they also solve community problems together—doing everything from fixing potholes to restoring green spaces to fighting for racial justice in their neighborhoods. None of these tasks are easy in the lives of busy women, but together they make a commitment to tackle them as a group.

THE SEXUAL ASSAULT SURVIVORS AMANDA THOMASHOW AND MORGAN MCCAUL told me how they accompany each other to doctors' appointments. This seemingly simple gesture is actually a beautiful act of solidarity—where one sister can provide safety and comfort during a potentially triggering experience.

HUDDLE TAKEAWAY: Whatever is most difficult or intimidating to you should also inspire you to signal for your huddle. Experience hardship and challenge together. It will not only boost your chances of success—it will also strengthen your bonds with each other.

6. FUCK SHARP ELBOWS.

We live in a patriarchal society. There are only a few seats at the table for women. We are still vastly underrepresented in leadership roles and board positions—in so many fields. Shirley Chisholm famously said, "If they don't give you a seat at the table, bring a folding chair." But some of the women I met for this book suggested we should just build our own damn table. With a bigger table and a new model for uplifting each other, we don't have to sharpen our elbows and push each other out of the way. So many women in this book told me they got where they are because they subscribe to the abundance mentality— that there is room for all of us to succeed. Women from all industries—politics, sports, food, business, and media—echoed this mandate to stick together.

From these women I learned to prioritize collaboration over competition:

U.S. WOMEN'S NATIONAL SOCCER TEAM PLAYER MEGAN RAPINOE told me, "I didn't get here by myself." She used a soccer metaphor to explain: "I know very much that I don't have that cross without Abby, and Abby doesn't have that header without me, and Alex doesn't score these goals without me, and I don't get to have all of these assists without all of that. We need each other. Literally nothing can get done unless you have multiple people working on it at the same time."

U.S. WOMEN'S NATIONAL SOCCER TEAM PLAYER BECKY SAUERBRUNN preached the gospel of the abundance mentality: "It's all about changing the mindset that there's only so much success that can go around for women, which encourages us to compete with one another. That whole notion needs to be thrown out. There's enough for everyone out there, and we're all going to get a piece of it if we do it together."

RAPINOE even took this notion a step further to say, "Once you get power, give it away."

HUDDLE TAKEAWAY: Whether you are a student, an entry-level employee, or a superstar athlete, this rule applies to you. You can share your advantages with others around you. Hire women, work on a class project with other women, nominate women for roles at work, and pass along any skill or advice you have freely.

7. BE VULNERABLE.

So often we're in cutthroat environments. We're so often compared to each other. This can make us want to appear perfect—at work, at school, or on Instagram. Sometimes we don't want to allow even our close friends to see us cry. It can be difficult to admit when we are clueless or inexperienced. But I am here to tell you that you don't have to always be in control of your emotions. And you don't have to know everything or get everything right on the first try to be successful. You just have to be willing to ask for help. I've learned this lesson at work, many times over. After I shot my series *American Woman*, I wanted to hold a screening event and invite a group of accomplished women to join me for a discussion panel. Many other CNN shows get this treatment, so I was surprised when my request was denied. To be honest, I was completely gutted. But instead of sulking in my office, I decided to put it all out there to a fellow huddler in my office at the time, Kelly Wallace. She had always been a big believer in me and *American Woman*, so I felt safe being real with her about my feelings. She gave me the encouragement and advice I needed, telling me to go speak with one of the executives in charge. Turns out, the executive in question, Allison, had been under the impression the screening would be more like a party, but once she heard my pitch to make it a full panel discussion, she was in full support of it. My friend and mentor Diane von Furstenberg offered to host at her flagship store for free, and the event was a huge success! If I had been too proud to share my dejection with Kelly that day, things would have ended very differently. Sometimes the best resource is in the office right next to you if you are willing to open up and keep it real.

From these women I was reminded to be vulnerable enough to ask for help:

CLAIRE CURLEY, HEAD OF KIDS/ANIMATION AT HELLO SUNSHINE, told me: "Dare to ask for help." **LIZ JENKINS, HEAD OF FINANCE AT HELLO SUNSHINE,** agreed that "asking for help doesn't make you look incapable. There's no shame in that." And **LAUREN LEVY NEUSTADTER, HEAD OF FILM AT HELLO SUNSHINE,** shared one of her favorite jokes about the needless standards women hold themselves to: "We put so much pressure on ourselves to know everything, to be able to say *this isn't our first rodeo.* But you don't have to know everything by your second rodeo, because, as the joke goes, that's a very low amount of rodeos."

OLYMPIC FENCER IBTIHAJ MUHAMMAD provided a reminder that sometimes the benefits of being vulnerable might surprise you: "I oftentimes am so self-reliant that I'm not willing to ask for help. I'll just do it myself. It doesn't come naturally for me to ask for help. But I've learned that in asking for help, I'm actually doing myself a great service and that I'm decreasing my workload. I'm relieving stress and anxiety and learning to delegate."

NURSE EMILY FAWCETT says this lesson about vulnerability can apply to friendship as well. She said, "It's important to cry, and laugh, and let those walls down. It's important to know that you don't have to always be so strong. You can lean on other people."

FRESH FILMS INSTRUCTOR KELSEY CONLEY told me that a lot of strong women feel the need to project their strength in order to be respected and be heard. "But for me at least, the strongest female relationships I've had were the ones where I was able to be vulnerable, and we were able to share our insecurities with each other and realize that we have a lot of the same insecurities."

SURVIVOR STRONG FOUNDER AMANDA THOMASHOW advised, for those of you who might want to reach out to others but feel afraid that no one wants to be bothered by you: "Your anxiety is lying to you. They want to hear from you."

> **HUDDLE TAKEAWAY:** Be willing to be vulnerable and transparent about your fears and inexperience. Find women who make it safe for you to be real about your feelings and give you room to cry and grow.

8. AMPLIFY EACH OTHER.

Amplifying can take many forms. It can mean complimenting another woman or giving a much-needed shout-out to a coworker whose accomplishments haven't been adequately credited. It can mean celebrating the role women have played in our history or shining a light on women whose struggles have been erased. It can mean simply showing up for women, rooting for them, or merely allowing them to be their real unvarnished selves. It's one of the easiest things we can do for each other. If you have a platform, use it to uplift other women. If you have reached great heights, throw down your ladder (a great phrase I'm borrowing from Megan Rapinoe). For me it's pretty clear-cut how I can do this work. I have a TV show and I can choose to use that platform to amplify the messages of amazing women in the news.

From these women, I saw beautiful examples of using your megaphone to uplift other women:

REESE WITHERSPOON created an entire media company that would make films and TV shows to center on women's stories.

THE WOMEN OF THE WNBA dedicated their entire 2020 season to Breonna Taylor and the #SayHerName campaign. They knew the eyes of the country were on them, and they weren't about to waste that opportunity and chose to use it to call out police brutality against Black women. Amplifying problems that affect women or highlighting women whose struggles have been overlooked is just as important as calling out female accomplishments.

KODE WITH KLOSSY PARTICIPANT KYARA TORRES-OLIVARES reminded me of the capacity social media has to become an amplifying tool in the hands of whomever uses it. She told me she only follows positive social media accounts where women aren't pitted against each other. Whether you're **AVA DUVERNAY,** who leverages her account to specifically "amplify the magnificence of Black people," or you're a teenage girl who shouts out the accomplishments of her besties, you have an amplifying mechanism available to you right at your fingertips.

HARRIS COUNTY JUDGE SHANNON BALDWIN reminded me that amplifying is mutually beneficial: "We don't live in each other's shadows. We thrive in each other's sunshine."

HUDDLE TAKEAWAY: Using your energy to shine a light on other women is important and so easy to do. You don't have to be famous or run a production company to amplify others. No matter who you are, you can use your voice to shout out other women or tell their untold stories. You can give props to women you work with, put someone up for a raise, casually mention your friends' accomplishments to others, or find other small ways to spotlight the accomplishments and struggles of fellow women.

9. HUDDLE WITH PEOPLE WHO ARE DIFFERENT FROM YOU.

I'll never forget the sage advice from my friend/rapper/activist Killer Mike when I was first interviewing him in the wake of Ferguson: "Make sure you have plenty of friends who don't look like you." It is so important to form real relationships with people of different races, religions, ages, abilities, cultures, classes, and backgrounds. When white women collectively organized a hundred years ago to win the right to vote, they also silenced and excluded Black women from their movement—and their victory. They left Black women to wait another five decades before they won the right to vote—and today Black voters are still disenfranchised all over the country. We aren't empowering womankind if only the white women benefit from the huddle.

From these women, I learned the importance of diversifying your huddle:

BLACK LIVES MATTER CO-FOUNDER ALICIA GARZA pointed out to me that the exclusionary feminism of white women wasn't just bad for BIWOC. It was bad for womankind as a whole, because it amounted to a "major erosion of our base of power." She explained that "as long as women of color are not a part of this women's movement, as long as trans women and other folks are not a part of this movement, it can't be as powerful as we need it to be. Because we won't be able to make the connection that how I get left behind is tied to how you get left behind—and that we can build something that would allow none of us to get left out."

MILITARY SPOUSE SHARON BRIGHT said we have "a responsibility to try to bring other people into our friend groups." She urges that we take a look at our friend group and "if it is truly happy and content, then it is strong enough to handle more members. But if more members threaten or break you up, or cause some sort of issue, it isn't that great of a group to begin with."

HUDDLE TAKEAWAY: Yes, America is riddled with injustice and we are deeply divided, but I've seen with my own eyes—through thousands of conversations on my show—how people can grow and learn by listening to perspectives that are vastly different from their own. Look around at your huddle—if everyone looks like you and believes like you, ask yourself how you can open your circle.

10. SHOW THE EFF UP.

Whatever you put into your huddle, you will get out of it. Yes, it really is that simple. If you join a collective of activists and continue to put the time in; if you nurture that text chain among friends and never allow it to go cold; if you keep your office cubicle warm and inviting to others; if you make space for other women's struggles, then fellow huddlers will do the same for you.

From these women, I learned about the power of showing up:

U.S. NATIONAL WOMEN'S SOCCER TEAM PLAYER SAM MEWIS talked to me about the growing pains associated with serving as a union representative for her team amid the very public fight for pay equity. She told me that sometimes she found herself a little uncomfortable with this difficult and time-consuming role. But ultimately, she decided, showing up was important: "It is my responsibility and privilege to stick my neck out a little bit to benefit the whole team. I have seen such good examples of that, and it always seems so worth it." Her nod to her teammates setting an example for her is a reminder that huddle energy is contagious. When you offer it to someone, they tend to offer it back. And even if they don't, you must keep sharing it with the next person anyway.

ALICIA GARZA told me that she "shows up for other women," particularly those who most need her expertise or connections. "It's about redistributing resources equitably," she said. "I prioritize spending my time and lending my skills so that there can be more of us everywhere in these positions of deciding where the money goes, deciding who gets hired, and making our workplaces more equitable."

FEMINIST ICON GLORIA STEINEM reminded me (in a wistful moment during the pandemic when in-person contact was not even remotely advisable) of the importance of spending time around each other. "As important as the internet is," she said, "it can't replace women—or human beings and other animals—being together with all five senses. That's what releases oxytocin, the 'tend and befriend' hormone, that allows us not only to learn and understand, but to empathize." Even when we can't be together in person, as she advises, her message to empathize still applies. "Showing up" for other women isn't just about physical presence, it is also about imagining yourself as belonging to a larger huddle of women who can strengthen you and be strengthened in return.

HUDDLE TAKEAWAY: It has never been more important for women to see each other as a resource, and for women to feel safe to lean on each other. Show up for them, and they will show up for you.

acknowledgments

I am bursting with gratitude as I write these words. As with essentially anything I've ever done in my life, *Huddle* would not have been possible without the love, hard work, and belief of so many people.

First and foremost, to all the women and girls who allowed me to interview you for this book: thank you for sharing your victories, your struggles, your advice, and your tears. It was an honor to meet you, have the gift of time, and share these in-depth conversations. I learned so much from all of you as you showed me so many gorgeous examples of how women can and *do* make each other's lives better. I have been changed for good.

To my wing woman, my collaborator, and my dear friend Cayce Dumont: you are the other half of *Huddle*. I'll never forget flying to meet you and take you to dinner in the depths of a Chicago winter. Before we even finished our meal, I believe my oh-so-elegant phrasing was: "Cayce Dumont, will you accept this rose?" Fast-forward to months of travels (pre-COVID!) to interview these women: flying to Atlanta to meet my mom; introducing you to some of my closest friends and then my brother and nephews; finally landing the interview with our favorite pink-haired soccer star; eating ice cream with five congresswomen in the eerie nighttime quiet of Capitol Hill; sitting with the legendary Stacey Abrams, right across from CNN HQ; blasting The Highwomen as the soundtrack to our entire *Huddle* journey; passing Google docs back and forth on so many planes; meeting Oprah, when she grabbed me and was beyond gracious; crying listening to Dom

Crenn lovingly speak about her father; leaving every. single. interview. saying, "This one was my favorite. I just learned so much"; feeling so blessed to spend such quality time with these women. Cayce, you're a brilliant writer and storyteller, and equally important but even more rare, you're an empathetic listener. Thank you for being my rock, my partner, my girlfriend. I cherish you. And we still have many more miles to go. #HuddleForLife

To my editor, Hollis Heimbouch: thank you for believing in my book from the day we met. When I first pitched you the Huddle concept at HarperCollins, the energy around that table was electric. From the very start, you not only believed in the Huddle concept, but you embodied it yourself. Over this past year, I threw so many ideas at you, and you were so brilliant at parsing, organizing, and refining everything to help me realize this dream in writing my first book. None of us expected to be writing and editing a book during a pandemic, but you rolled with it with such professionalism and class every step of the (virtual) way. Not to mention, I never thought I'd meet someone who owned more No6 Store clogs than me! May all my future collaborations with women be as fruitful and fun as this one.

To Rebecca Raskin, associate editor: thank you for being a vital part of the *Huddle* huddle! Your insights, feedback, edits, and advice always came at the perfect time during this journey. You wowed me so often with your wisdom, humor, and attention to detail. Without a doubt, you made this a better book, and I'm so grateful. And gratitude must also be expressed that you shared Edna with us during all those Zoom calls!

To the rest of the HarperCollins team: I know it takes a village to make a book, and I am so proud to have worked with this group. Thank you to Brian Perrin and Laura Cole in marketing;

Leslie Cohen in publicity; Jocelyn Larnick and Christina Polizoto in production; Bonni Leon-Berman in design; and Victor Hendrickson in legal.

To my UTA family: this book would not have happened without you. First, to my TV agent and elegant friend, Carole Cooper: thank you for embracing all that I am and would like to achieve. I remember when you were gracious enough to pick up the phone when I cold called you so many years ago as a cub reporter to boldly ask you to represent me. Lucky me, I eventually got my wish, and look at us now. And to Albert Lee, my literary agent and fellow pug owner: I'll never forget when Carole first connected us, and you wondered aloud if I'd ever thought of becoming an author. Thank you for planting the seed that became *Huddle*. Your early vote of confidence and all the enthusiastic brainstorming sessions meant the world to me. (Also. Please never stop texting me *Golden Girls* and Beyoncé gifs.)

To Angela Baggetta: our partnership has just begun, and I'm already so grateful for your vision and support.

To Mary Ellen Matthews, who shot the photo for this book cover: you are my most generous, badass photographer hero. Sure, you've photographed all the hosts of *Saturday Night Live* for years (not to mention you can rock a mean pair of cowboy boots)—but you can also shoot me in a studio during a pandemic at a safe social distance! It was a pinch-me kind of day thanks to you. And to Claudia Pedala and Merrell Daly for your hair and makeup magic that day: I just love y'all.

To Kathryn Beane, Patricia DiCarlo, Lisa Respers France, Christine Choi, Will Banks-Blaney, and Syndee Thompson: it's one thing to write a book offering my own personal point of view; it's another thing entirely to create a narrative that celebrates and empathizes with the perspectives of *many* women, including those whose lives and experiences have been radically different from my own. Thank you all for the painstaking time and effort you took to read early drafts of my book, to think about the huddle concept through your own lens, and to give me the opportunity to listen and learn. It's not always easy to talk openly about race, class, gender, sexuality, religion, and politics, but y'all took it there and helped me recognize the limits of my own perspective. I'm still learning. And I hope I can pay forward the extreme patience and generosity you all afforded me.

And of course to CNN, my hometown network, my dream job, some of the best colleagues a gal could ever ask for: I'm sending up so much gratitude for you. And especially to my CNN show team, my *American Woman* team, my bosses, the production crews, field producers, photojournalists, and hair and makeup folks. I couldn't have pulled off writing a book and also hosting a daily live show during what seemed like an endlessly insane news cycle without your support day-to-day. You know who you are and thank you. I do want to recognize one young woman by name who has been consistently by my side these last few years and has a mighty bright future ahead of her: Randi Furman. Randall, thank you for "all of the things." Love you.

I'm a big believer in keeping a close council of wise women who will hold me accountable, make me more aware of myself, and push me to think bigger (BBGBB). And the chief woman in that council is Treena Huang. Treena, I know I came to you totally skeptical of what a "life coach" is. Several years in, I cannot imagine my journey without you. Thank you, Yoda.

To the powerful instructors of The Class, led by the indomitable Taryn Toomey: this practice has rocked me to my core. It has shown me how to drop deeper into myself on my journey in writing this book and in my daily life. Whether we're all virtual or in person, I appreciate you.

And to my closest huddle: Aki, KB, Al. I get teary just thinking of the four of us. I've never been part of a sisterhood like this before. I cherish you and cannot wait until we can finally, safely hang together again. Thanks to you and our text chain, I know, no matter what, I am never alone. And to Aki's daughter, Curren: I love you, Curren Bun. Here's to all mothers and their daughters, the next generation of huddlers.

To my husband, who I met at a holiday party at age thirty-six: James, you were worth the wait. Thank you for finding me. Thank you for moving across an ocean for me. Thank you for looking after me. You are my home. And to our sweet pug (who as I write this is curled up under my chair at age seventeen): he is one of the best decisions of my life. I was lonely and huddle-less in my second TV job in Huntington, West Virginia, when I brought this tiny pug puppy home. Pugsley, thank you for licking my tears all these years. My first and only dog, I will love you, always and forever.

To my mom: you are my original huddle. I wouldn't be the woman I am today without your endless love and support. I am so grateful to you and dad for giving me one of the greatest gifts in my life, my "baby" brother, Ryan—which also brought us his beautiful family, Wrenn, Bridger, and Hudson. Mom, what a beautiful legacy you have. And yes, Mom, we have relived that "Yellow Chair" moment several times since the original, but every single time I feel like I'm faltering in life, you give me the confidence to fly. It brings me joy to watch you really leaning into your huddle of sisters: Lycie, Anne, JJ, and Kath. I love you, ladies.

And finally to you, reading this book: thank you for spending your time with me to think bigger about what we as women can do for each other. I cannot wait to hear from you. Collectively, we have a lot of power, and we can truly be an incredible resource to one another. So here's to all the huddles you form, tend, or renew in your own life after you read these stories. You are not alone. We are in this together.

notes

Prologue

1   diversify their entire industry: Mike Isaac, "Women in Tech Band Together to Track Diversity, After Hours," *New York Times*, May 3, 2016, https://
www.nytimes.com/2016/05/04/technology/women-in-tech-band-together
-to-track-diversity-after-hours.html.

Chapter 1: The Mother of All Huddles

13   "harness the political power of diverse women and their communities
to create transformative social change": According to the Women's March
website, accessed on September 5, 2020. https://womensmarch.com/mission
-and-principles.

20   One study, the Gender Parity Index: Represent Women, "Gender Parity Index
2018 Report," 2018. https://fairvote.app.box.com/s/5tbs5jlggo01uguzjzqq5six
ac0mb3fo.

21   a first in the county's three hundred years: Michael Rellahan, "Chesco
Dems Celebrate 'Unbelievable' Victory," *Daily Local News*, November 8,
2017. https://www.dailylocal.com/news/national/chesco-dems-celebrate
-unbelievable-victory/article_8b90d162-fd3d-5682–8bb5-f7fb2af19045.html.

24   Goss's book *The Paradox of Gender Equality*: Kristin A. Goss, *The Paradox
of Gender Equality: How American Women's Groups Gained and Lost Their Public
Voice*, 2nd ed. (Ann Arbor: University of Michigan Press, 2020).

26   raising families and working full-time jobs without spousal support: By
1982, 47 percent of Black families were headed by single women, per Paula
Giddings, *In Search of Sisterhood: Delta Sigma Theta and the Challenge of the Black
Sorority Movement* (New York: Amistad, 2006), 300.

      For an overview of the criminalization of Black women in American cul-
ture, see Diana Ramey Berry and Kali Nicole Gross, *A Black Women's History of
the United States* (Boston: Beacon Press, 2020), chapter 10.

Chapter 2: The Huddle Wasn't Invented by Women in Pussyhats

29   and 7 percent are Asian: "Houston, TX," Data USA, 2018. https://datausa
.io/profile/geo/houston-tx. This 2018 article suggests that Houston still
holds the title for most diverse large city: Annie Gallay, "Sorry Jersey City,
Houston Remains the Real Most Diverse City in America," *Paper City*, May
4, 2018. https://www.papercitymag.com/culture/houston-remains-most-
diverse-city-america-jersey-city-study-flawed/.

30   fewer than a thousand women had expressed interest in running: "By
       the Numbers: EMILY's List + the 2018 Midterms," EMILY's List, September
       24, 2018. https://emilyslist.org/news/entry/by-the-numbers-emilys-list-the
       -2018-midterms.

31   and they had all *just won their races*: Actually, only seventeen of the
       nineteen had won their races. But the two who lost their bids to be on the
       Texas Court of Criminal Appeals were already sitting judges. So the out-
       come was still that nineteen Black women in Harris County were serving
       as elected judges all at the same time, which was record-setting to say the
       least.

35   220 years of experience in total: Brian Rogers, "Republican Judges Swept
       Out by Voters in Harris County Election," *Houston Chronicle*, November 10,
       2018. https://www.chron.com/news/houston-texas/houston/article/GOP
       -Free-Zone-Republican-judges-swept-out-by-13376806.php.

36   according to Thompson's website: CaShawn Thompson, accessed Sep-
       tember 8, 2020. http://cashawn.com/.

36   "the only people supporting us are other Black women": Dexter
       Thomas, "Why Everyone's Saying 'Black Girls Are Magic,'" *Los Angeles Times*,
       September 9, 2015. https://www.latimes.com/nation/nationnow/la-na-nn
       -everyones-saying-black-girls-are-magic-20150909-htmlstory.html.

39   only the second in the entire state of Texas: John Wright, "LGBT Candi-
       dates Make History in Houston, Across Texas," *Out Smart*, November 7, 2018.
       http://www.outsmartmagazine.com/2018/11/lgbtq-candidates-make-history
       -in-harris-county-across-texas/.

42   Black men in Harris County had indeed been harshly penalized for de-
       cades: According to the Prison Policy Initiative, although African Americans
       make up 12 percent of the population in Texas, they account for 32 percent
       of the incarcerated population. See: Leah Sakala, "Breaking Down Mass
       Incarceration in the 2010 Census: State-by-State Incarceration Rates by Race/
       Ethnicity," Prison Policy Initiative, May 28, 2014. https://www.prisonpolicy
       .org/reports/rates.html.

43   had more than doubled since 2014: Kerry Blakinger, "2 Harris County
       Judges Responsible for 1 in 5 Children Sent to State Juvenile Prisons," *Houston
       Chronicle*, October 22, 2018. https://www.chron.com/news/houston-texas
       /houston/article/Harris-County-judges-responsible-for-1-in-five-13322222
       .php.

48   the formidable challenges of social justice in the current day: Giddings,
       In Search of Sisterhood, 6.

48   "when they are together in their organizations": Giddings, *In Search of
       Sisterhood*, 9.

49   "Anita Hill's treatment before the U.S. Congress": Kimberly Springer,

Living for the Revolution: Black Feminist Organizations, 1968–1980 (Durham, NC: Duke University Press, 2005), 174.

52 "cronyism between private attorneys and powerful judges": Nina Satija, "Harris County Juvenile Judges and Private Attorneys Accused of Cronyism: 'Everybody Wins but the Kids,'" *Texas Tribune*, November 1, 2018. https://www.texastribune.org/2018/11/01/harris-county-texas-juvenile-judges-private-attorneys/.

Chapter 3: Girls Getting Loud in Boy-Free Zones

64 a 2020 report by the Media, Diversity, & Social Change Initiative: Stacy L. Smith, Marc Choueiti, and Katherine Pieper, "Inequality in 1,300 Popular Films: Examining Portrayals in Gender, Race/Ethnicity, LGBTQ, and Disability from 2007 to 2019," Media, Diversity and Social Change Initiative, University of Southern California, Annenberg School for Communication and Journalism, September 2020. http://assets.uscannenberg.org/docs/aii-inequality_1300_popular_films_09-08-2020.pdf.

65 enforcement later in the 1990s and 2000s: NCAA, "45 Years of Title IX: The Status of Women in Intercollegiate Athletics," June 21, 2017, 10. http://www.ncaa.org/sites/default/files/TitleIX45–295-FINAL_WEB.pdf.

65 "greater than ten times what it was when Title IX was passed": NCAA, "45 Years of Title IX," 16.

65 with 52 percent of them having played at the university level: EY Women Athletes Business Network, "Making the Connection: Women, Sports, and Leadership," 2014.

66 "which destroys the bodies of young girls": Mary Cain, "I Was the Fastest Girl in America Until I Joined Nike," *New York Times*, November 7, 2019. https://www.nytimes.com/2019/11/07/opinion/nike-running-mary-cain.html.

71 authors of the books *The Confidence Code* and *The Confidence Code for Girls*: Katty Kay and Claire Shipman, *The Confidence Code: The Science and Art of Self-Assurance—What Women Should Know* (New York: Harper Business), 2018.

    Katty Kay and Claire Shipman, *The Confidence Code for Girls: Taking Risks, Messing Up, & Becoming Your Amazingly Imperfect, Totally Powerful Self* (New York: Harper, 2018).

71 "and a bit of failure too": Katty Kay, Claire Shipman, and JillEllyn Riley, "Building Confident Girls Is All About Risk, Not Perfection," *Romper*, April 16, 2018. https://www.romper.com/p/building-confidence-in-girls-is-all-about-risk-not-perfection-8797870.

71 "don't produce as much stress hormone": Kay and Shipman, *The Confidence Code for Girls*, 133.

Chapter 4: From Scarcity to Abundance in a Man's World

87 women benefit uniquely from leaning on each other at work: The mention in the *Harvard Business Review* can be found here: Brian Uzzi, "Research: Men and Women Need Different Kinds of Networks to Succeed," *Harvard Business Review,* February 25, 2019. https://hbr.org/2019/02/research-men-and -women-need-different-kinds-of-networks-to-succeed.

And the original research study can be found here: Yang Yang, Nitesh V. Chawla, and Brian Uzzi, "A Network's Gender Composition and Communication Pattern Predict Women's Leadership Success," *Proceedings of the National Academy of Sciences,* February 5, 2019. https://www.pnas.org/content/116 /6/2033.

88 According to another study, by Catalyst: Catalyst, "Sponsoring Women to Success," 2011. https://www.catalyst.org/wp-content/uploads/2019/01 /sponsoring_women_to_success.pdf.

98 half the culinary school graduates in America are women: This statistic comes from the U.S. Bureau of Labor Statistics (reference following), but this article provides a good overview of the disparity of women in leadership in the restaurant industry: Hannah Koper, "Head Chefs Versus CEOs: An Analysis of the Women in Charge," *Graduate Journal of Food Studies* 4, no. 2 (November 11, 2017). https://doi.org/10.21428/92775833.a752c0a3.

The original data from the U.S. Bureau of Labor Statistics is here: Hilda L. Solis and Keith Hall, "Women in the Labor Force: A Data Book," December 2011. https://www.bls.gov/cps/wlf-databook-2011.pdf.

98 less than 7 percent of prominent U.S. restaurants are female owned: Per the article referenced here, "women occupy just 6.3 percent, or 10 out of 160 head chef positions at 15 prominent US restaurant groups analyzed by Bloomberg." Ryan Sutton, "Women Everywhere in Food Empires but No Head Chefs," *Bloomberg News,* March 6, 2014. http://www.bloomberg.com /news/2014-03-06/women-everywhere-in-chang-colicchio-empires-but-no -head-chefs.html.

99 where only 2.4 percent of companies elect a woman to their top position: Katherine Guerard, "Which Russell 3000 Sectors Rank Highest in Terms of Gender Diversity in Leadership Positions?" FactSet, Insight, September 27, 2018. https://insight.factset.com/which-russell-3000-sectors-rank-highest-in -terms-of-gender-diversity-in-leadership-positions.

102 both of which are male dominated: Per the sources below, as of 2017, women in the United States Armed Forces made up 16 percent of the overall active duty force and 18 percent of commissioned officers. While the numbers are better for women in national security jobs, it is still a male-dominated sector in which women have never made up more than 40 percent of senior positions at the State Department or 20 percent at the Department of Defense.

Amanda Barroso, "The Changing Profile of the U.S. Military: Smaller in Size, More Diverse, More Women in Leadership," Pew Research Center, August 6, 2020. https://www.pewresearch.org/fact-tank/2019/09/10/the -changing-profile-of-the-u-s-military/.

Heather Hurlburt and Tamara Cofman Wittes, "The Case for Gender Diversity in National Security," Brookings, July 10, 2019. https://www.brookings .edu/blog/order-from-chaos/2019/07/10/the-case-for-gender-diversity-in -national-security/.

Chapter 5: Passing the Mic

118 her message continued to be critical: Vann R. Newkirk, "How Shelby County v. Holder Broke America," *Atlantic*, July 5, 2018. https://www .theatlantic.com/politics/archive/2018/07/how-shelby-county-broke -america/564707.

123 "be reflected in the creative efforts she pursues with the brand": Alana Glass, "Simone Manuel Rewrites Athlete Activism with TYR Sport Inclusion Rider," *Forbes*, July 30, 2018. https://www.forbes.com/sites/alanaglass /2018/07/30/simone-manuel-rewrites-athlete-activism-with-tyr-sport -inclusion-rider/?sh=5925d62248b2.

125 "encourage them to be storytellers in all kinds of mediums": Reese Witherspoon, "We Have to Change the Idea That a Woman with Ambition Is Out Only for Herself," *Glamour*, September 5, 2017. https://www.glamour .com/story/reese-witherspoon-october-2017-cover-interview.

132 only 35 percent of TV writers are women: "2015 Statistics," Women and Hollywood, 2015. https://womenandhollywood.com/resources/statistics /2015-statistics/.

132 only 5 percent in nearly a decade: "The State of Diversity in Writing for Television—TV Writer Access Project Honorees," *Writers Guild of America West*, March 3, 2015. https://www.wga.org/news-events/news/press/2015 /state-of-diversity-writing-for-television-tvwap-honorees.

132 (the number of top one hundred *films* written by women is worse, at just 20 percent): Martha M. Lauzen, "The Celluloid Ceiling: Behind-the-Scenes Employment of Women on the Top 100, 250, and 500 Films of 2019," 2020. https:// womenintvfilm.sdsu.edu/wp-content/uploads/2020/01/2019_Celluloid _Ceiling_Report.pdf.

Chapter 6: From Solitary to Solidarity

145 "to let other survivors know they are not alone": Tarana Burke (@ TaranaBurke), "It made my heart swell to see women using this idea— one that we call 'empowerment through empathy'. . . to not only show the world how widespread and pervasive sexual violence is, but also to let other

survivors know they are not alone. #metoo," Twitter, October 15, 2017.
https://twitter.com/TaranaBurke/status/919704166515335174 and https://
twitter.com/TaranaBurke/status/919704393934614528.

145 "empowerment through empathy": Burke, Twitter, October 15, 2017.

145 since it was truly meant to be "about survivors": Sandra E. Garcia, "The
Women Who Created #MeToo Long Before Hashtags," *New York Times*, October 20, 2017. https://www.nytimes.com/2017/10/20/us/me-too-movement
-tarana-burke.html

148 "free from sexism, misogyny, and male-centeredness": Patrisse Khan-
Cullors and Asha Bandele, *When They Call You a Terrorist: A Black Lives Matter
Memoir* (New York: St. Martin's Griffin), 2018.

150 "greater than the sum of its parts": Leslie R. Crutchfield, *How Change
Happens: Why Some Social Movements Succeed While Others Don't* (Hoboken, NJ:
Wiley, 2018), 151.

151 "ahead of personal or organizational power": Crutchfield, *How Change
Happens*, 14.

152 couldn't find the "nationwide grassroots army": Shannon Watts, *Fight
Like a Mother: How a Grassroots Movement Took on the Gun Lobby and Why
Women Will Change the World* (New York: HarperOne, 2019), 6.

152 "to the gun lobby's bluster and posturing": Watts, *Fight Like a Mother*, 6.

159 has surpassed the number of NRA members by at least a million:
Although the NRA does not publish their membership numbers, the widely
assumed estimate of their membership is no more than five million. For reference, see: Christopher Ingraham, "Nobody Knows How Many Members the
NRA Has, but Its Tax Returns Offer Some Clues," *Washington Post*, February
26, 2018. https://www.washingtonpost.com/news/wonk/wp/2018/02/26
/nobody-knows-how-many-members-the-nra-has-but-its-tax-returns-offer
-some-clues/.

Dave Gilson, "The NRA Says It Has 5 Million Members. Its Magazines Tell
Another Story," *Mother Jones*, March 7, 2018. https://www.motherjones.com
/politics/2018/03/nra-membership-magazine-numbers-1/.

160 "grew by double digits": Karin A. Lips, "The Year of the Republican Woman,"
The Hill, November 8, 2020. https://thehill.com/opinion/campaign
/524827-the-year-of-the-republican-woman.

161 (giving her famous "How dare you!" speech): Here is an excerpt from
Thunberg's speech:

"This is all wrong. I shouldn't be up here. I should be back in school on the
other side of the ocean. Yet you all come to us young people for hope. How
dare you! You have stolen my dreams and my childhood with your empty
words. And yet I'm one of the lucky ones. People are suffering. People are
dying. Entire ecosystems are collapsing. We are in the beginning of a mass

extinction, and all you can talk about is money and fairy tales of eternal economic growth. How dare you!"

For a full transcript, see: NPR staff, "Transcript: Greta Thunberg's Speech at the U.N. Climate Action Summit," NPR, September 23, 2019. https://www .npr.org/2019/09/23/763452863/transcript-greta-thunbergs-speech-at-the-u-n -climate-action-summit.

161 two-spirit youth: Per this article, "Two Spirit people have both a male and female spirit within them and are blessed by their Creator to see life through the eyes of both genders." Tony Enos, "Eight Things You Should Know About Two Spirit People," *Indian Country Today*, March 28, 2017. https://indiancountrytoday.com/archive/8-things-you-should-know-about -two-spirit-people-294cNoIj-EGwJFOWEnbbZw.

162 "through whatever fight is yet to come": Anna Merlan, "Meet the Brave, Audacious, Astonishing Women Who Built the Standing Rock Movement," *Jezebel*, December 8, 2016. https://jezebel.com/meet-the-brave-audacious -astonishing-women-who-built-1789756669.

Chapter 7: Multiplying Respect

168 Virginia governor McAuliffe publicly called out this "hate and bigotry": Terry McAuliffe (@TerryMcAuliffe), "There's no place in Virginia for hatred & bigotry. People who've come to VA today to hurt others are not patriots, they are cowards. Go home," Twitter, August 12, 2017. https://twitter.com /TerryMcAuliffe/status/896513544006639618.

170 Clinton delivered what the *New York Times* called "a public rebuke": Mark Leibovich, "In Turmoil of '68, Clinton Found a New Voice," *New York Times*, September 5, 2007. https://www.nytimes.com/2007/09/05/us/politics /05clinton.html.

171 accused of trafficking and abusing young girls and women: The men I'm referring to here are Jeffrey Epstein, R. Kelly, and Robert Kraft.

171 "safe, fair, and dignified work for women of all kinds": "About," Time's Up Foundation, March 26, 2020. https://timesupfoundation.org/about/.

172 "There was almost a ferociousness to it, especially in the first meetings": Cara Buckley, "Powerful Hollywood Women Unveil Anti-Harassment Action Plan," *New York Times*, January 21, 2018. https://www.nytimes .com/2018/01/01/movies/times-up-hollywood-women-sexual-harassment .html.

173 had aired just a few days prior: "Hillary Clinton Interview," *Howard Stern Show*, SiriusXM, December 4, 2019.

174 "never disrespect our Country, the White House, or our Flag": Donald Trump (@realDonaldTrump), "Women's soccer player, @mPinoe, just stated that she is 'not going to the F . . . ing White House if we win.' Other than the

NBA, which now refuses to call owners, owners (please explain that I just got Criminal Justice Reform passed, Black unemployment is at the lowest level . . . in our Country's history, and the poverty index is also best number EVER), leagues and teams love coming to the White House. I am a big fan of the American Team, and Women's Soccer, but Megan should WIN first before she TALKS! Finish the job! We haven't yet . . . invited Megan or the team, but I am now inviting the TEAM, win or lose. Megan should never disrespect our Country, the White House, or our Flag, especially since so much has been done for her & the team. Be proud of the Flag that you wear. The USA is doing GREAT!" Twitter, June 26, 2019. https://twitter.com/realDonaldTrump /status/1143892326286266368.

178 "coming together not as individual players, but as one collective voice": "Competitors on Ice, Women's Hockey Players Unite Off the Ice for Change," Professional Women's Hockey Players Association, May 2, 2019. https:// pwhpa.com/for-the-game/.

181 the contagious fervor and mutual support among the various women's teams: Andrew Das, "In Fight for Equity, US Soccer Team Leads the Way," *New York Times*, March 4, 2018. https://www.nytimes.com/2018/03/04 /sports/soccer/us-womens-soccer-equality.html.

    Jim Souhan, "U.S. Women's National Soccer Team, Lynx Players Support Each Other's Fight for Excellence, Better Pay," *StarTribune*, September 4, 2019. https://www.startribune.com/u-s-women-s-national-soccer-team-lynx -players-support-each-other-s-fight-for-excellence-better-pay/559325582/.

    Stephanie Yang, "USWNT Players Support USA Women's Hockey Boycott," *SB Nation*, March 16, 2017. https://www.starsandstripesfc.com/2017/3 /16/14941718/uswnt-players-support-usa-womens-hockey-boycott.

183 "took their spot": "Hillary Clinton Interview," *Howard Stern Show*, SiriusXM, December 4, 2019.

183 "why she felt entitled to take a man's spot in her class": Emily Bazelon, "Why Ruth Bader Ginsburg Refused to Step Down," *New York Times Magazine*, September 21, 2020. https://www.nytimes.com/2020/09/21/magazine /ginsburg-successor-obama.html.

185 without any corresponding raises: Tithi Bhattacharya, "Women Are Leading the Wave of Strikes in America. Here's Why," *Guardian*, April 10, 2018. https://www.theguardian.com/commentisfree/2018/apr/10/women -teachers-strikes-america.

186 thirty-four thousand workers in West Virginia in February 2018: Jane McAlevey, "The West Virginia Teachers Strike Shows That Winning Big Requires Creating a Crisis," *Nation*, March 12, 2018. https://www.thenation .com/article/archive/the-west-virginia-teachers-strike-shows-that-winning -big-requires-creating-a-crisis/.

186 has been stripped of its "dignity and security": Bhattacharya, "Women Are Leading the Wave of Strikes in America."

191 the increasingly public dialogue about police brutality: The #SayHerName campaign was developed by Kimberlé Crenshaw. More information on the campaign can be found at https://aapf.org/sayhername.

Chapter 8: Healed by the Huddle

193 in 2018 and again in 2019: Jeffrey Gottfried, "Americans' News Fatigue Isn't Going Away—About Two-Thirds Still Feel Worn Out," Fact Tank, Pew Research Center, February 26, 2020, https://www.pewresearch.org/fact-tank/2020/02/26/almost-seven-in-ten-americans-have-news-fatigue-more-among-republicans/.

198 "anchored in a vital connection with our bodies": Bessel van der Kolk, *The Body Keeps the Score: Brain, Mind, and Body in the Healing of Trauma* (New York: Penguin Books, 2015), 274.

198 "helplessness, rage, or collapse that result from trauma": van der Kolk, *The Body Keeps the Score*, 3.

199 the healing effects of yoga on traumatized women: "After 20 weeks chronically traumatized women developed increased activation of critical brain structures involved in self-regulation: the insula and the medial prefrontal cortex," van der Kolk, *The Body Keeps the Score*, 276.

199 "a meaning beyond our individual fate": van der Kolk, *The Body Keeps the Score*, 335.

199 One in four American women have experienced severe physical violence by an intimate partner: M. C. Black et al., "The National Intimate Partner and Sexual Violence Survey (NISVS): 2010 Summary Report." Atlanta: National Center for Injury Prevention and Control, Centers for Disease Control and Prevention.

199 one in five women are raped in their lifetime: Black et al., "National Intimate Partner and Sexual Violence Survey."

200 one in nine girls under the age of eighteen experiences sexual abuse or assault at the hands of an adult: David Finkelhor et al., "The Lifetime Prevalence of Child Sexual Abuse and Sexual Assault Assessed in Late Adolescence," *Journal of Adolescent Health* 55, no. 3 (2014): 329–33. https://doi.org/10.1016/j.jadohealth.2013.12.026.

200 41 percent experience cyber sexual harassment: "The Facts Behind the #MeToo Movement," Stop Street Harassment, Reston, Virginia, February 2018. http://www.stopstreetharassment.org/wp-content/uploads/2018/01/Full-Report-2018-National-Study-on-Sexual-Harassment-and-Assault.pdf.

202 in front of a largely male Senate judiciary committee: Only five of the twenty-one-member committee were female.

203 she served as her own expert witness: Sarah Zhang, "Christine Blasey Ford Is Her Own Expert Witness," *Atlantic*, September 27, 2018. https://www .theatlantic.com/health/archive/2018/09/when-psychologist-testifies -congress/571537/.

Benjamin Wallace-Wells, "Christine Blasey Ford Is Serving as Both a Witness and an Expert," *New Yorker*, September 27, 2018. https://www.newyorker .com/news/current/christine-blasey-ford-is-serving-as-both-a-witness-and-an -expert.

203 they were being retriggered: Dakin Andone and Christina Zdanowicz, "Some Sexual Assault Survivors Were Empowered by Christine Blasey Ford's Testimony Yet Others Re-Traumatized," CNN, September 28, 2018. https:// www.cnn.com/2018/09/27/health/trigger-empowerment-trauma-blasey -ford/index.html.

208 "any other group of women from preventable chronic disease": From *Harriet's Handbook*, GirlTrek. http://d3n8a8pro7vhmx.cloudfront.net/themes /56b182c3ebad6493f0000001/attachments/original/1526320063/Harriet's _Handbook_by_GirlTrek_v1.0_RD.pdf?1526320063.

210 "other physical and emotional ailments": Resmaa Menakem, *My Grandmother's Hands: Racialized Trauma and the Pathway to Mending Our Hearts and Bodies* (Las Vegas: Central Recovery Press, 2017), 15.

211 pain, trauma, and hardship without enough support: Debbie Nathan, "What Happened to Sandra Bland?" *Nation*, April 21, 2016. https://www .thenation.com/article/archive/what-happened-to-sandra-bland/.

Chapter 9: Tend and Befriend to the End

220 "Our friends matter as much as our other attachments": Kayleen Schaefer, *Text Me When You Get Home: The Evolution and Triumph of Modern Female Friendship* (New York: Dutton, 2018), 214.

221 "We didn't do everything we could to save our friendship": Aminatou Sow and Ann Friedman, *Big Friendship: How We Keep Each Other Close* (New York: Simon & Schuster, 2020), 184.

222 "and being there for them when they aren't": Sow and Friedman, *Big Friendship*, 70.

222 "continually opt in to": Sow and Friedman, *Big Friendship*, 185.

222 "power to shape the trajectories of our lives": Lydia Denworth, *Friendship: The Evolution, Biology, and Extraordinary Power of Life's Fundamental Bond* (New York: W. W. Norton, 2020), 19.

223 immune system dysfunction, and impaired judgment: Vivek H. Murthy, *Together: The Healing Power of Human Connection in a Sometimes Lonely World* (New York: Harper Wave, 2020), 14.

223 specific diseases like cancer: "The Nurses' Health Study and Nurses'

Health Study II," Nurses' Health Study, November 2, 2020. https://www
.nurseshealthstudy.org.

223 the ways humans evolved to react in times of stress: S. E. Taylor et al.,
"Biobehavioral Responses to Stress in Females: Tend-and-Befriend, Not
Fight-or-Flight," *Psychological Review* 107, no. 3 (July 2000): 411–29.

223 tend children and befriend each other: Nancy K. Dess, "Tend and
Befriend: Women Tend to Nurture and Men to Withdraw When Life Gets
Hard," *Psychology Today*, September 1, 2000. https://www.psychologytoday
.com/us/articles/200009/tend-and-befriend.

223 "social, cultural, cognitive, and emotional factors": Dess, "Tend and
Befriend."

232 "Staying vulnerable is a risk we have to take if we want to experience
connection": Brené Brown, *The Gifts of Imperfection: Let Go of Who You Think
You're Supposed to Be and Embrace Who You Are* (Center City, MN: Hazelden
Publishing, 2010), 53.

238 "shaping the larger world we live in": Sow and Friedman, *Big Friendship*,
134.

239 allowed us to better communicate and cooperate with one another:
Brian Hare and Vanessa Woods, *Survival of the Friendliest: Understanding Our
Origins and Rediscovering Our Common Humanity* (New York: Random House,
2020), 98–99.

240 on every continent except Antarctica: Hare and Woods, *Survival of the
Friendliest*, 116.

240 "we all belong to the same group": Hare and Woods, *Survival of the
Friendliest*, 171.

240 "a roller coaster of intense contradictory emotions": Jennifer Davis,
David B. Ward, and Cheryl Storm, "The Unsilencing of Military Wives: War-
time Deployment Experiences and Citizen Responsibility," *Journal of Marital
and Family Therapy*, January 2011. https://pubmed.ncbi.nlm.nih.gov
/21198688/.

about the author

BROOKE BALDWIN is a veteran journalist and Peabody Award finalist who has anchored the 2–4 p.m. (ET) edition of *CNN Newsroom* for more than a decade. She has often been sent into the field to cover the biggest breaking stories in the US and around the world. She played a key role in anchoring coverage of the Obama and Trump administrations and has also reported on stories from Europe, Africa, Asia, and the Middle East. She joined CNN in 2008, and viewers have come to know Baldwin for her versatility, authenticity, and humanity at the news desk. As the creator and host of CNN's digital series *American Woman*, she has dedicated the latest chapter of her career to shining a light on trailblazing women in politics and culture. Baldwin graduated from the University of North Carolina at Chapel Hill in 2001 with a BA in journalism and Spanish. She lives in Manhattan with her husband, James, and their pug, Pugsley. *Huddle* is her first book.